The Art of Software Innovation

Minna Pikkarainen · Wim Codenie ·
Nick Boucart · José Antonio Heredia Alvaro
Editors

The Art of Software Innovation

Eight Practice Areas to Inspire your Business

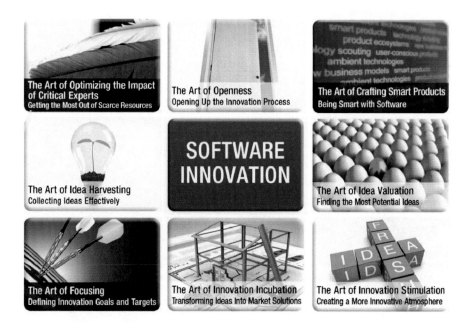

 Springer

Editors
Minna Pikkarainen
VTT Technical Research Centre
of Finland
Software Business Group
Kaitoväylä 1, Box 110
90570 Oulu
Finland
minna.pikkarainen@vtt.fi

Wim Codenie
Nick Boucart
Sirris
Software Engineering Group
A.Reyerslaan 80
1030 Brussels
Belgium
wim.codenie@sirris.be
nick.boucart@sirris.be

José Antonio Heredia Alvaro
Universitat Jaume I
Departamento de Ingeniería de
Sistemas I
Campus del Riu Sec
12080 Castelló de la Plana
Spain
heredia@esid.uji.es

ISBN 978-3-642-21048-8   e-ISBN 978-3-642-21049-5
DOI 10.1007/978-3-642-21049-5
Springer Heidelberg Dordrecht London New York

Library of Congress Control Number: 2011935532

Printed on acid-free paper

Springer is part of Springer Science+Business Media (www.springer.com)

Preface

Have you ever wondered what innovation really means to your company, and, more specifically, how software influences your innovation capacity?

At Steria, our business is to develop software as a service for other companies – software that these companies use to drive their innovation, software that is developed using the latest technologies. For our company, it is important to understand where innovation meets risk and what the innovative aspects of our customer projects are.

For a company like Steria, it is not enough to invest in the best software engineering practices to improve the productivity of our software engineers. We must also leverage the potential of all our employees in the local and global organization. It is important that we constantly use all the innovation potential of our people, share new ideas, and explore new solutions and technologies. We must not only remain competitive due to our engineering practices but also by adopting leading-edge techniques and technologies and sharing in the benefits of innovation through our customer projects.

Together with 28 partners working in the ITEI (Information Technologies supporting the Execution of Innovation Projects) project, we gained some insights that led to the first edition of this book on software innovation. This book is not the result of a theoretical approach but the synthesis of many discussions and experiments carried out involving research institutes as well as industrial partners. This synthesis is certainly not the final point however, above all because the industrial partners that contributed to this work only cover part of the very broad spectrum of companies in which innovation is driven mainly by software.

Software innovation is multifaceted and the approaches used by companies can be very different. How do you understand which aspects of software innovation may be important to your company? To facilitate this thinking process, we propose a high-level classification of 'software companies' with their specific views on software innovation. We defined eight practice areas, 'arts', and 47 activities that your company can master to drive software innovation.

As a synthesis of all the discussions, experiments, 'arts' and activities, we propose a software innovation canvas to describe the most important aspects of software innovation – a software innovation canvas that may evolve from the input of a broader range of companies that wants to contribute to the further evolution of this book.

For a different software company, some generic "'arts'" will be more relevant than the others.Some of these generic "'arts'" will be more relevant than others. For example, if you are driven by customer projects then the ideation part of innovation will play an different other role than if you develop out-of-the-box software products. This means that the "'the Art of Idea Harvesting'" may have another in importance to than the "'the Art of Focusing'" to your company.

Intrigued? In this book you will find details of what your company can do to understand, implement and sustain these "'arts'". Finally, I would like to end with some quotes from of different partners into the ITEI project that resulted in this book.

'Software innovation is radically changing the way we communicate, interact, and organise ourselves today. What is now, will be different tomorrow. The eight software innovation practice areas in this book will stimulate your creative assets to better use.'
Suvi Keinänen, Movial Creative Technologies Inc.

'Software innovation is a major concern for IT service companies like Steria whose daily business no longer only consists of delivering innovative solutions to its customers but also of helping them on their journey towards innovation.'
Pierre Paelinck, Steria

'Metso's aim is to create value continuously by improving the quality, production and environmental aspects, and the cost-efficiency of its customers' processes. Innovation plays a key role in implementing these aims.'
Antti Välimäki, Metso

'Ever-accelerating technological change has moved innovation in the software sector past mere opportunity into the heart of the business strategy. We used to be amazed that young start-ups could challenge and unseat global IT giants in just a few years. Now we measure such shifts in mere months and speculate on how the current crop will stand up to next quarters' challengers. Innovation in software is about more than planning the next product release or service methodology update. We need to embrace perpetual agile business ecosystem incubation and adaptation to increase value creation.'
Peter Stuer, Spikes

'If you are a software-intensive company about to embark on the journey towards innovation mastery, this book is definitely the best guide you will find.

This book is written by researchers and experienced practitioners who have been exploring and mapping the complex innovation landscape for years. This book brings it all together. It is an impressive collaborative effort to which I'm proud to have contributed.'
Wim Soens, Director of Innovation, Research and Development at CogniStreamer

Dr René Luyckx
CEO Steria Benelux

Acknowledgements

The critical source of information for this book was managers of software companies struggling with software innovation. Many of them are identified in the lists of authors and contributors for this book. We would like to thank all the companies that participated for sharing their software innovation experiences with us.

Without the significant contribution of the academia, this book would not exist. We would like to thank all the scientific contributors to this book.

We would especially like to thank ITEA 2 for its support and for making it possible to create this book in a European context.

The authors from Belgium would like to thank the Institute for the encouragement of Scientific Research and Innovation of Brussels (Innoviris), the Institute for the Promotion of Innovation by Science and Technology in Flanders (IWT) and the Brussels-Capital Region for the support it provided to this research and publication.

The authors from Finland would like to thank the Finnish Funding Agency for Technology and Innovation (TEKES).

The authors from Spain would like to thank the Ministerio de Industria, Turismo y Comercio (Plan Avanza).

Special thanks also go to Annukka Mäntyniemi who was one of the co-creators of the underlying research project that led to this book and Irja Kontio who put so much effort into the overall layout of this book.

INFORMATION TECHNOLOGY FOR EUROPEAN ADVANCEMENT

Contents

Editor Group

Minna Pikkarainen is a Principal Scientist in VTT Technical Research Centre of Finland. She holds a PhD about the topic of improving software development mediated with CMMI and agile practices. She has worked in numerous industrial-driven research projects and project preparations doing close industrial collaboration with large amount of organizations in Europe. Minna's work has been published in several journals and conference papers in the forums like ICSE, ICIS and Empirical Software Engineering Journal. Pikkarainen has been member of Lero, The Irish Software Engineering Research Centre between 2006-2009 and Sirris, The Collective Center for the Belgian technological industry since 2009. Recently, her work and publications have focused on research in the areas of agile development, software innovation and variability management.

Wim Codenie is programme coordinator Software Engineering at Sirris, the collective centre of the Belgian technology industry. He graduated from the Free University of Brussels in 1988 where he was involved in research on object-oriented frameworks and self reflection in object-oriented programming languages. He has a strong ICT background and currently advices companies about improving their software product development capabilities. His specific interests include product variability; agile software development and innovation management in software development. He has set up several research initiatives at the national and European level on these topics.

Nick Boucart graduated as a physician from the University of Antwerp to start a carrier as a software engineer in various companies, always working on software product development. During the 10 years he worked in software product development, Nick gained a lot of hands on experience with agile software development and software product innovation. His interest in Web 2.0, both from a technological point of view as well as from a business game changing point of view brought him to Sirris, where he now advises companies on topics like from agile software development and (community driven) innovation for software intensive product builders.

José Antonio Heredia Alvaro is Industrial Engineering PhD and Professor in the industrial systems engineering department at University Jaume I (Spain). Prof. Heredia has published numerous papers in scientific journals and has published two books on industrial management. He has more than 15 years of experience in managing research projects and directing master and doctoral thesis projects. Two spin-offs in the IT field has been created by him, after successful EU funded projects.

Contributors

Sanja Aaramaa Department of Information Processing Science, University of Oulu, P.O. Box 3000, FI-90014 Oulu, Finland, sanja.aaramaa@oulu.fi

Asta Bäck VTT Technical Research Centre of Finland, Vuorimiehentie 3, P.O. Box 1000, FI-02044, VTT Espoo, Finland, scientistasta.back@vtt.fi

Miguel Angel Bengochea Escribano Keraben, Ctra. Valencia-Barcelona, km. 44.3, ES-12520 Nules (Castellón), Spain, ma.bengochea@kerabengrupo.com

Olivier Biot Sirris, Diamant Building, Boulevard A. Reyerslaan 80, BE-1030 Brussel, Belgium, olivier.biot@sirris.be

Vladimir Blagojevic Sirris, Diamant Building, Boulevard A. Reyerslaan 80, BE-1030 Brussel, Belgium, Vladimir.Blagojevic@sirris.be

Nick Boucart Sirris, Software Engineering Group, Boulevard A. Reyerslaan 80, BE-1030 Brussel, Belgium, nick.boucart@sirris.be

Wim Codenie Sirris, Software Engineering Group, Boulevard A. Reyerslaan 80, BE-1030 Brussel, Belgium, wim.codenie@sirris.be

Jessie Dedecker Sirris, Diamant Building, Boulevard A. Reyerslaan 80, BE-1030 Brussel, Belgium, jessie.dedecker@sirris.be

Jeroen Deleu Sirris, Diamant Building, Boulevard A. Reyerslaan 80, BE-1030 Brussel, Belgium, jeroen.deleu@sirris.be

Antonio Estruch Universitat Jaume I, Avda. Sos Baynat s/n, ES-12017 Castellon, Spain, estruch@sg.uji.es

Iñaki Etxaniz Tecnalia, Parque Tecnologico, #202, ES-48170 Zamudio, Spain, inaki.etxaniz@tecnalia.com

Pepe Fuster AuraPortal, Paseo Germanias, 84. ENTLO, ES-46702 Gadia, Spain, pepe.fuster@auraportal.com

Oscar Gómez ICT Research Institute in Valencia, Ciudad Politecnica de la innovacion, UPV Building 8G Acc B, ES-46022 Valencia, Spain, ogmez@iti.es

Nicolás González-Deleito Sirris, Diamant Building, Boulevard A. Reyerslaan 80, BE-1030 Brussel, Belgium, nicolas.gonzalez@sirris.be

Ander Gorostiza Sisteplant, Edif 607 Parque Tecnológico, ES-48160 Derio, Spain, agorostiza@sisteplant.com

Vicente Luis Guaita Delgado Keraben, Ctra. Valencia-Barcelona, km. 44.3, ES-12520 Nules (Castellón), Spain, l.guaita@kerabengrupo.com

Ilkka Happonen VTT Technical Research Centre of Finland, Kaitoväylä 1, P.O. BOX 1100, FI- 90571 Oulu, Finland, Ilkka.happonen@gmail.com

Sami Härkönen Onkikuja 6, FI-90460 Oulunsalo, Finland, samih@dnainternet.net

Katja Henttonen VTT Technical Research Centre of Finland, Kaitoväylä 1, P.O. BOX 1100, FI-90571 Oulu, Finland, katja.henttonen@vtt.fi

Jose Antonio Heredia UJI, Universitat Jaume I Avda. Sos Baynat s/n, ES-12017 Castellon, Spain, heredia@esid.uji.es

Jarkko Hyysalo Department of Information Processing Science, University of Oulu, P.O. Box 3000, FI-90014 Oulu, Finland, jarkko.hyysalo@oulu.fi

Paula Jalo Inno-W Oy, Niityranta 1 B 3, FI-00930 Helsinki, Finland, paula.jalo@inno-w.com

Mikko Järvilehto University of Oulu, Pentti Kaiteran katu 1, P.O. Box 8000, FI-90014 Oulu, Finland, mikko.jarvilehto@oulu.fi

Jukka Kääriäinen VTT Technical Research Centre of Finland, Kaitoväylä 1, P.O. BOX 1100, FI- 90571 Oulu, Finland, jukka.kaariainen@vtt.fi

Kalle Karinen Movial, Porkkalankatu 20A, FI-00180 Helsinki, Finland, kalle.karinen@movial.com

Suvi Keinänen Movial, Porkkalankatu 20A, FI-00180 Helsinki, Finland, suvi. keinanen@movial.com

Markus Kelanti Department of Information Processing Science, University of Oulu, P.O. Box 3000, FI-90014 Oulu, Finland, markus.kelanti@oulu.fi

Tuomo Kinnunen University of Oulu, Pentti Kaiteran katu 1, P.O. Box 4610, FI-90014 Oulu, Finland, tuomo.kinnunen@oulu.fi

Timo Koivumäki VTT Technical Research Centre of Finland, Kaitoväylä 1, P.O. BOX 1100, FI- 90571 Oulu, Finland, timo.koivumaki@vtt.fi

Irja Kontio VTT Technical Research Centre of Finland, Kaitoväylä 1, P.O. BOX 1100, FI- 90571 Oulu, Finland, irja.kontio@vtt.fi

Kaisa Koskela VTT Technical Research Centre of Finland, Kaitoväylä 1, P.O. BOX 1100, FI- 90571 Oulu, Finland, kaisa.koskela@vtt.fi

Pasi Kuvaja Department of Information Processing Science, University of Oulu, P.O. Box 3000, FI-90014 Oulu, Finland, pasi.kuvaja@oulu.fi

Pico Lantini Sirris, Diamant Building, Boulevard A. Reyerslaan 80, BE-1030 Brussel, Belgium, pico.lantini@sirris.be

Jari Lehto Nokia Siemens Networks, P.O. Box 1, FI-02022, Nokia Siemens Networks, Espoo, Finland, jari.lehto@nsn.com

René Luyckx Steria Benelux, Vorstlaan 36, BE-1170 Brussels, Belgium, rene. luyckx@steria.be

Markku Mäntysaari HiQ, Vaisalantie 6, FI-02130 Espoo, Finland, markku. mantysaari@hiq.fi

Petri Morko University of Oulu, Pentti Kaiteran katu 1, P.O. Box 8000, FI-90014 Oulu, Finland, petri.morko@oulu.fi

Pirjo Näkki VTT Technical Research Centre of Finland, Vuorimiehentie 3, P.O. Box 1000, FI-02044 VTT Espoo, Finland, pirjo.nakki@vtt.fi

Tuomas Nousiainen HiQ, Vaisalantie 6, FI-02130 Espoo, Finland, tuomas. nousiainen@hiq.fi

Leire Orue-Echevarria Arrieta Tecnalia, Edificio 202 Parque Tecnológico de Bizkaia, ES-48170 Zamudio, Spain, leire.orueechevarria@tecnalia.com

Nilay Oza VTT Technical Research Centre of Finland, Vuorimiehentie 3, P.O. Box 1000, FI-02044 VTT Espoo, Finland, nilay.oza@vtt.fi

Pierre Paelinck Steria, Vorstlaan 36, BE-1170 Brussels, Belgium, pierre. paelinck@steria.be

Henry Palonen Inno-W Oy, Niityranta 1 B 3, FI-00930 Helsinki, Finland, henry. palonen@inno-w.fi

Minna Pikkarainen VTT Technical Research Centre of Finland, Software Business Group, Kaitoväylä 1, P.O. BOX 1100, FI- 90571 Oulu, Finland, minna. pikkarainen@vtt.fi

Nyrki Rantonen HiQ, Vaisalantie 6, FI-02130 Espoo, Finland, nyrki.rantonen@ hiq.fi

Eduardo Riol Answare, C/ Tablas de Daimiel, 2, portal 2, 1°B, ES-28925 Alcorcón (Madrid), Spain, eriol@answare-tech.com

Urko Rueda UPV-Pros, DSIC- Camino de Vera s/n, ES-46022 Valencia, Spain, urueda@pros.upv.es

Juan Sánchez Díaz UPV-Pros, DSIC- Camino de Vera s/n, ES-46022 Valencia, Spain, jsanchez@dsic.upv.es

Santiago de los Santos EyD, C/San Vicente Mártir 22, ES-46002 Valencia, Spain, sdelossantos@estrategiaydireccion.com

Jouni Similä University of Oulu, Pentti Kaiteran katu 1, P.O. Box 8000, FI-90014 Oulu, Finland, jouni.simila@oulu.fi

Wim Soens 38Indie Group, Engelse Wandeling 2 K18, BE-8500 Kortrijk, Belgium, wim.soens@cognistreamer.com

Raul Soriano UPV-Pros, DSIC- Camino de Vera s/n, ES-46022 Valencia, Spain, rsoriano@pros.upv.es

Peter Stuer Spikes, Posthofbrug 10A, BE-2600 Berchem, Belgium, peter.stuer@ spikes.be

Nebojsa Tausan Department of Information Processing Science, University of Oulu, P.O. Box 3000, FIN-90014 Oulu, Finland, nebojsa.tausa@oulu.fi

Tom Tourwe Sirris, Diamant Building, Boulevard A. Reyerslaan 80, BE-1030 Brussel, Belgium, tom.tourwe@sirris.be

Antti Välimäki Metso, Metso Automation Oy, Lentokentänkatu 11, FI-33101 Tampere, Finland, Antti.Valimaki@metso.com

Peter Verhasselt Sirris, Diamant Building, Boulevard A. Reyerslaan 80, BE-1030 Brussel, Belgium, peter.verhasselt@sirris.be

Stefaan Vermael Sirris, Diamant Building, Boulevard A. Reyerslaan 80, BE-1030 Brussel, Belgium, stefaan.vermael@sirris.be

Chapter 1
Introduction

Wim Codenie, Minna Pikkarainen, Nick Boucart, and Jeroen Deleu

Imagine that you are the CEO of a software company creating a software-based product. You have been in business for quite some time, and – where many others have failed – you have managed to bring a product to market that is liked by its customers.

Of course, you had your share of difficulties. There were times when serious quality problems threatened the future of the company. There were the many sleepless nights caused by budgets running out of control and even occasions when you were left at the mercy of the development team to have a new release out before the next fair.

Today, after surviving these engineering and delivery problems, a new breed of problems emerges on the horizon. In the last couple of years, it has become more difficult to excite your customers with new product features. Suddenly, new companies are competing in your home market and with very different, even better, solutions than yours. On top of this, there is a tsunami of new technologies that you have no clue how to use to your advantage.

If you are not a little worried by this new breed of problems, you should be. Historically, your focus has mostly been on improving and increasing the productivity of the software engineering process. Chances are high that this took so much of your energy that little room for innovation remained. Delivering the product always came first.

A decade ago, you may have got away with this, but you no longer can. Today, you are competing in an environment that does not tolerate you treating innovation as a secondary issue.

This book will help you with this.

M. Pikkarainen et al. (eds.), *The Art of Software Innovation*,
DOI 10.1007/978-3-642-21049-5_1, © Springer-Verlag Berlin Heidelberg 2011

1.1   Innovation in Software Engineering

The above scenario is just an illustration, and we could have started with other scenarios of software start-up companies, software service companies or large and small software companies. The conclusion would have been the same. Innovation is key to survival for most software companies.

At first sight, writing a book about innovation in software development seems an odd thing to do. Why do we need a book about this when there are countless good software engineering books and innovation books available? To answer this, we have to dig into the historical context of the software engineering domain itself.

Delivering software products on time, within budget and with an acceptable quality has always been a considerable challenge for most software companies. In this historical context, software companies have specialized in what can be called '*the art of software engineering*'. They have mastered the process of producing *software assets* such as code and requirement documents. Tapping from a rich toolbox of solutions (agile development, testing automation, requirements managements, architectural styles...), many of them became quite good at engineering (Agile Alliance 2011; SWEBOK 2004).

Today they are faced with a new generation of challenges that can be classified as '*the art of software innovation*'. How can I (as a company) innovate and create value with software?

The field of *innovation management* – the discipline that focuses on the systematic processes that organizations use to develop new and improved products, services and business processes – has made significant progress independently of the software engineering community. An extensive state of the art exists in this field, including ideation tools, brainstorming techniques, stage-gate processes, portfolio management, product lifecycle management, etc. (ISPIM 2011).

During the turbulent era of '*the art of software engineering*', most software companies were blind to what happened outside the software field. The software discipline was still so young and the engineering challenges so difficult that most of the energy went into solving software engineering and architectural problems. Little room remained to keep in touch with what happened outside the software field.

SWEBOK, the software engineering body of knowledge (SWEBOK 2004), illustrates this dominance of engineering very well. This comprehensive overview is considered a standard with respect to software engineering. It is remarkable to observe that, at least at the time of writing this book, it rarely mentions innovation or creativity.

The software field has little tradition in structurally supporting creativity during the development of software-intensive products (Tharp 2007). Studies have shown that innovations in software are rarely planned and are often the consequence of risky behaviour (Desouza and Awazu 2005; Shneiderman 2007).

1.2 Blending Innovation Management and Software Engineering

Forced by changes in their environment, software companies are becoming increasingly curious about what is going on in other fields and, in particular, in the domain of *innovation management*. The software development community is (sometimes even reluctantly) expressing the need to blend practices of innovation management with those of software engineering.

It is this 'blending' that is the subject of this book.

Blending these two worlds is not straightforward. It involves more than reading a good book on software engineering and one on innovation management and then applying the two theories in isolation.

Three reasons can be identified why this blending is complex.

First, software plays different roles in the innovation process. Software can be used to support innovation processes while, at the same time, being an instrument for innovation in all kinds of products. We elaborate this in Sect. 1.5.

Second, software has some unique characteristics that interfere with the way current state-of-the-art innovation management can be adopted in the domain of software development. This implies that innovation with software is somewhat different to innovation in non-software domains. We elaborate this in Sect. 1.6. Third, increased technology and market conformation force companies to leave their comfort zone of incremental innovation. We elaborate this in Sect. 1.7.

Fourth, Software companies come in different flavors, and innovation can have fundamentally different interpretations in the context of these companies. We elaborate this in Sect. 1.8.

1.3 Rationale of This Book

The book you are holding is the result of a long process that involved many contributors. Its origin can be traced back to a workshop in 2007 in Düsseldorf, Germany, where a team of software professionals from industry and the research community started a debate on innovation in software development.

The results of this workshop were confusing. The heated discussions, the disagreements and the different opinions showed that the topic is important, but still many challenges remained that were not going to be solved in a single workshop.

We needed to address this on a bigger scale.

That is why after the Düsseldorf meeting, a European project (ITEI 2007) was launched under the umbrella of the ITEA2 Programme (ITEA 2006). Its goal was to improve understanding of the way software companies innovate. It ended early in 2011 and included field studies in software companies from Belgium, Finland and Spain. Although the participating companies were very different in nature, it was remarkable to observe the convergence to a set of common patterns in the domain of innovation with software. It is this insight that made us write this book.

By now, you may wonder what we want to achieve with this book.

First of all, it is written with an industrial target audience in mind. Perhaps, its most important goal is to challenge companies by offering them a frame to become more innovation-driven, rather than engineering-driven.

The book is organized around what we call eight fundamental practice areas for innovation with software. Each practice area contains a number of *activities* that can help companies to master that practice area. It also contains industrial experience reports that illustrate the applicability of these practice areas in software companies.

Some practice areas may be highly relevant to your company, others less so. The practice areas are illustrated with practical experience reports from industry. The book is organized in such a way that you can select and read only those practice areas that are relevant to your company. Examples are provided of the application of the practice areas in companies.

The software engineering community has created (and adopted) several development processes to deliver software. Some popular examples include the waterfall model, agile development (Agile Alliance 2011), lean development (LEAN 2011) and Kanban (KANBAN 2011). The last three, in particular, have gained popularity in the last decade, not only because they attempt to speed up delivery and increase flexibility but also because they offer a better foundation on which to increase the innovation capabilities of software companies (Nilay and Abrahamsson 2009).

We wrote this book with the assumption that there is no such thing as a universal software engineering process or innovation process. Some things work well for a company, others do not.

We want to stress that the aim of this book is not to impose another process on you. The practice areas should not be interpreted as a process but rather as a set of activities that you can tune towards your existing software development processes.

1.4 Structure of This Book

The core of the book is to present a collection of practice areas. We opted for a simple structure that is illustrated in Fig. 1.1.

The book consists of three parts. Part 1 contains the introduction, and motivates the practice areas. Part 2 introduces the practice areas. They are written in such a way that they can be read independently. Part 3 provide industrial experience reports that illustrate how the practice areas can be used in practice. The book ends with a conclusion and remarks.

1.5 Software and Innovation

There's a peculiar intertwinement between software and innovation. Software plays three very different roles towards software. The three roles are discussed below.

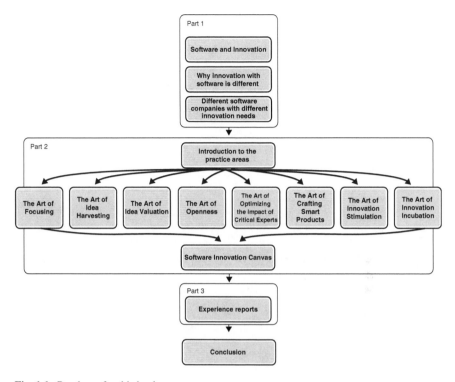

Fig. 1.1 Roadmap for this book

1.5.1 Software as an Instrument for Innovation in Products and Services

The world is increasingly evolving from a knowledge-based economy into an economy based on creativity and innovation. An example illustrating this fact is that today, up to 70% of the turnover of companies is generated by products (or product features) that did not exist 5 years ago (Weyrich 2005).

Companies in the aviation, automobile, pharmacy and telecommunications sectors consider innovation absolutely necessary to achieve their strategic objectives. In itself, this is nothing new. What is new is that software technology is playing an increasing role in realizing this innovation.

> Quote (ITEA 2009): 'In Automotive, Software Intensive Systems will account for 90% of all future innovations in cars.'

Extensive studies and publications confirm the importance of software as an innovation instrument (Lippoldt and Stryszowski 2009). It does not only apply to the IT sector but to a wide range of industrial and consumer-oriented sectors. In all sectors (transport, health, chemistry, construction . . .), software is finding its way into all kinds of products, and hence it is steadily ascending in the value chain of companies.

Software is no longer purely a supportive technology hidden and invisible to customers but plays an essential role and purpose that is at the heart of the value creation process. As a consequence, even companies that have not traditionally applied software in their products are considering software for their product innovations (ITEA 2009).

To innovate successfully with software, companies must:

- Understand the *product innovations* they want to realize with software in their products or services (e.g., what features will we offer?)
- Master the *processes* to realize these product innovations (e.g., how will we realize the product innovations?)
- In some cases deploy *new business models* to bring these product innovations to market.

The book you hold focuses on this dominant role of software towards innovation as well as the three above-mentioned dimensions.

The two other roles of software towards innovation are described below. They are not necessarily restricted to software companies but can apply to any company that creates products and services.

1.5.2 Software as an Enabler of Innovation Processes

The arrival of software on the scene has created a new market: *the market of software tools to support innovation.*

In the 1990s, entrepreneurs spotted this opportunity and founded companies that developed software tools to support different parts of the innovation process. Up until that time, the available innovation theories were mainly spread in the world through books and by consultants with slide shows.

Software had a disruptive effect on this market. Suddenly, it became possible to create all kinds of supportive tools for the various innovation theories that were out there. Today, this market of software innovation services has matured and several players are active in it. Examples include software tools for ideation (Indiegroup 2011), software tools for creativity support (Creax 2011) and software tools for innovation contests (Fellowforce 2011).

Companies active in the market are by definition software companies (they make a software product). Their customers include companies that create non-software products, software and companies.

An exhaustive overview of this particular role of software towards innovation is provided by Diener and Piller (2010).

1.5.3 Software as an Enabler for Business Model Innovation

The advances in information and communication technology have driven recent interest in business model innovation (Casadesus-Masanell and Ricart 2007).

ICT technology has pulled down the traditional geographical borders, and natural regional limitations are no longer the first constraint to doing business. If you started a new business 100 years ago, your first customers would have been located near you. You would have grown your business by acquiring market shares in adjacent regions. This constraint no longer holds. Thanks to software, it is easy to set up an e-commerce platform and find your first customers on the other side of the globe.

The impact of software goes beyond traditional web-shops and e-businesses however. Software has become an essential ingredient to enable the new sophisticated business models that made companies like Amazon and Google successful.

Several good books are available that illustrate the power of software for business model enablement (Osterwalder and Pigneur 2010; Anderson 2006).

As with the previous role, this role of software applies to software companies as well as non-software companies.

1.6 Why Innovation in Software Is Different

The activities of software development have different characteristics compared with 'traditional' non-software product development. These differences are an important factor in devising effective ways of blending innovation management techniques and software engineering techniques.

1.6.1 Software Is Malleable

Unlike other products, software products are often delivered in increments, usually called releases. Future versions of the product are created starting from earlier versions. This perceived malleability and perceived ease of change are responsible for a continuous stream of innovations that becomes alive in the slipstream of software products. Software companies often collect large numbers of ideas originating from company management, developers, customers and user networks. Choosing between the different innovation options for the next release is therefore a headache for the product managers in these companies (Fig. 1.2).

Innovation in software is typically a continuous process rather than a discrete process. Although stage gates can definitely be identified (e.g., release points), innovations tend to emerge at any time during the software development process (e.g., customers changing their minds about requirements, unclear requirements . . .)

1.6.2 Software Is 'Intangible'

Software cannot be held in the hand and it is not subject to physical wear and tear. Consequently, many existing innovation techniques that rely on the physical nature of products cannot readily be applied to software.

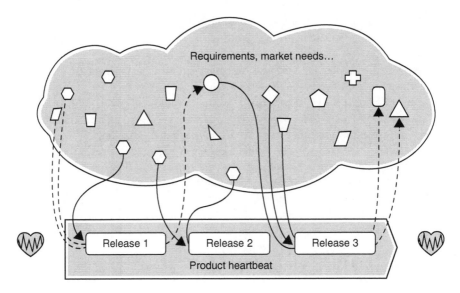

Fig. 1.2 The software product heartbeat

For example, TRIZ (Altshuller 1984) an established methodology that is often applied in traditional product development to help in the generation of innovative ideas is barely known in the software world for this reason (Mann 2005).

In software, other innovation characteristics than physical and tangible attributes seem important to innovation. An example of such a characteristic is *ecosystems thinking*: How can innovation make the product part of an ecosystem of networked products?

1.6.3   The Threshold to Enter the Software Market Is Low

Alternatively, as the successful player Google™ once demonstrated: 'you only need a computer and a garage to build a thriving software company.'

Not only is the upfront investment low (a computer, some [free] engineering tools, a garage), but the cost of production and distribution (e.g., an Internet download) is also extremely low compared with other industries.

The consequence is that in the software industry, new emerging players compete successfully against well-established players, thereby creating specific dynamics towards innovation. The established players need to speed up their innovation to keep up with these new players and their sometimes innovative new business models. The emerging players, on the other hand, must swiftly master software innovation skills, as it is only their innovativeness and creativity that can differentiate them from established players.

1.6.4 The Role Users Play in Software Development

For many products (including non-software products), user feedback is crucial, and adapting/developing products based on user input is often a recipe for success.

One such technique for user feedback is the lead user concept (von Hippel 1986).

In software, the role of the users can go beyond the role of feedback providers. They can be motivated and stimulated to become co-creators. They can help you to develop your product. The thriving open source community illustrates the opportunities that can be created by tapping into this huge crowd of co-creators. With respect to user co-creation, the software community has created results that are way ahead of other (non-software) sectors.

1.6.5 The Huge Impact of Expert/Critical Resources in Software Innovation

It is remarkable that new developments in software products can be traced back to the contribution of a few individuals (Greenspun 2002).

The productivity of a critical expert resource in software innovation is on average ten times higher than the impact of an average software engineer, while in traditional non-software engineering, this ratio is about 2–3 to 1 (Brooks 1995; McConnell 2011).

Even though these critical experts are scarce and their time very limited, companies should be aware that being able to involve these resources in the right way at the right time can boost software innovation by maximizing their impact on the innovation.

1.7 Leaving the Comfort Zone of Feature Development

Ask a random software product company what innovation means for it, and the reply is likely to be '*Adding new features to our product!*'

Software companies exhibit a form of territorial behaviour. Many are affected by *featuritis*: the constant urge to keep adding new functionalities to their products and cover more functionality domains with their product portfolio (i.e., incremental innovation).

An intriguing question is whether this strategy is still sustainable in today's context. Is *growing the software product* the best strategy for growing the software company? Is there a future for these feature-rich 'monumental' products or should software companies instead stick to well-chosen 'point' solutions that excel in performing a particular task?

It is our belief that software companies that have a desire to grow will somehow have to leave their comfort zone of *incremental innovation*, and might have to look for more radical innovations.

1.7.1   Increased Technology Confrontation

Software companies are confronted with a plethora of new technological possibilities that can offer new innovation options for their products or services. This *technology confrontation* is huge, and deciding in which technologies to invest to keep the product portfolio up to date causes many CTOs sleepless nights.

For small enterprises in particular, it is very challenging to allocate expert resources to perform the necessary technology scouting activities to ensure future competitiveness.

> An example is the emerging domain of cloud computing. It can offer established software companies new ways to bring their products to market and to generate revenue (e.g., pay per use). Turning an existing software product into a cloud-enabled offering is not just an incremental development, however, but involves acquisition of new technologies.

International research and market studies confirm that software companies are in a phase of *technology digestion* (Bartels 2009). They predict that companies able to orient themselves in these days of technology saturation can still expect significant growth, e.g., by realizing a completely new value proposition in their existing markets based on new technologies

1.7.2   Increased Market Confrontation

Apart from technology confrontation, software companies also experience market confrontation. They are either attacked in their home markets by new players offering new innovative solutions or they are themselves entering new emerging markets with their solutions. In both scenarios, software companies have to leave their comfort zone (Kim 2005).

> Example: Builders of CRM applications (Customer Relationship Management) offer software products to manage customer networks. They are facing increasing competition from LinkedIn™, a social network for connecting professionals.
> Example: Amazon™ invested a large amount in technical infrastructure to support its business model. It realized that it acquired unique competence with respect to cloud computing and created a separate business unit to bring these cloud solutions to a (for it) completely new market.

1.7.3   The Software Jungle: Threat or Opportunity?

The exploding software (technology) jungle is not necessarily a threat for software companies, although most software companies perceive it as one. In fact, it can be turned into an opportunity using the massive number of available software products out there as a lever.

Instead of becoming depressed by the endless stream of innovations in the ICT jungle, you can look at the positive side: '*Can we come up with new value propositions by a clever combination of available products, data sources, services or technologies?'*

Many examples can be found. For example, mashing up your product with Google™ maps, creating a data analysis or sentiment analysis service on top of the Twitter ™ ecosystem ... These opportunities are often hidden or may require disruptive approaches to exploit them (e.g., involving new business models or the acquisition of unfamiliar technologies). Some companies may even opt to become a source for other product builders by opening parts of their products or data sources through APIs or Mashups.

1.7.4   The Battle for User Attention

Software technology is omnipresent in the daily professional, industrial and private environments. The consequence of this successful adoption is that the number of software devices used by a single person has increased exponentially.

The attention bandwidth of users has not increased however! People have limited absorption capacity to manage all the software devices with which they are confronted. A typical user understands only a fraction of the functionality offered by the software products. Users have reached an emotional and cognitive saturation point with respect to the software devices they have to use in their environment. They are no longer interested in having more features but in fewer features and in features that help them to increase their bandwidth or demand less attention to use (Rutkowski and Saunders 2010).

This has a consequence for software companies. The strategy of the early days to feed customers with a constant stream of new product functionalities does not necessary hold anymore. Differentiation from competitors is no longer only achieved on the level of the features you offer but also on the level of attracting the user's attention. You are not only competing in your traditional home market, you are also competing with the other products your customer uses!

A study by Bartels (2009) revealed that many software companies are considering making their products more intelligent (also called smart products) so they can better anticipate the intention of the user and provide more proactive behaviour towards users. The ability to assess opportunities for *smart products* in the company context, using the appropriate business model and taking into account the specific engineering aspects, is a complex challenge for software companies.

1.7.5   Leaving the Comfort Zone

For software companies, sustainable innovations and growth are increasingly realized by leaving the traditional comfort zone of incremental innovation. This introduces a new form of uncertainty in software companies that is not necessarily

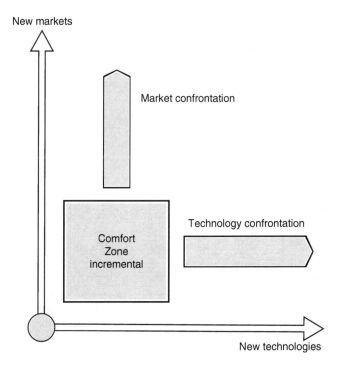

Fig. 1.3 Leaving the comfort zone

linked to engineering problems but is related to the acquisition of new technologies, entrance into new markets or application domains, and repositioning in the software jungle (Fig. 1.3).

1.8 Different Software Companies Have Different Innovation Needs

Software companies come in many flavours, and innovation can have fundamentally different interpretations in the contexts of these companies (Pikkarainen et al. 2010).

The sample group of companies on which this book is based involved SMEs and large companies: companies from different application domains and embedded system builders as well as pure software builders.

The studied companies use different strategies for the development of their software products (so-called *software development strategies*). We observed that three popular development strategies imply different innovation needs and challenges.

The three strategies can be classified according to the ratio of *domain engineering* and *application engineering* they need. Domain engineering encompasses all activities related to the development of software assets that are reusable across a set of customers. Application engineering encompasses all activities related to the development of one specific software product for a single customer. A profound overview of the different strategies can be found in Codenie et al. (2010).

For this book, three common software development strategies have been selected (see Fig. 1.4). They are representative of a large group of software companies.

- In the *project-based development* strategy, the products are developed on a contract basis. The software products are developed on demand by an individual customer and the aim is to provide a tailor-made solution for that customer. This strategy exists almost exclusively in application engineering activities.
- In the *out-of-the-box product development* strategy, the software company builds products that are offered to a large group of customers without individual customization. The assumption is that customers will be prepared to sacrifice features in favour of lower cost and product stability. This strategy exists almost exclusively in domain engineering activities.
- In the *customized product development* strategy, the software company develops a semi-finished product (or framework) that is adapted and customized to suit the specific needs of individual customers. This strategy is a combination of the two strategies above.

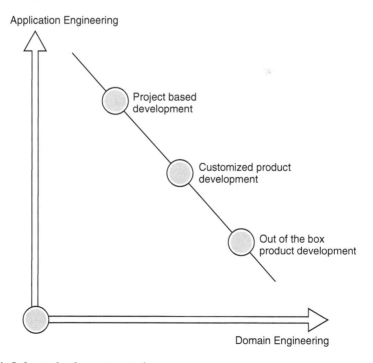

Fig. 1.4 Software development strategies

Software builders do not necessarily restrict themselves to just one of the above product development strategies. Companies that offer a rich product portfolio can apply a different software product development strategy to each product in the portfolio. Companies may also be in a transition phase from one product development strategy to another (Codenie et al. 2010).

The product development strategies represent typical ways companies use to develop and deploy products to the market. Each development strategy has different innovation needs and typically comes with different innovation approaches.

In the following sections, the innovation needs and differences of the three development strategies are explored.

1.8.1 *Innovation in Project Based Development*

Project-based development companies often focus their innovation activities on customer requests. They rely heavily on their customers to produce product ideas. In project-based companies, the ideation process is usually relatively simple because it is mainly driven by the direct need of customers.

Therefore, if producing product ideas is not the main driver for innovation, what does innovation mean to these companies? Basically, two major drivers can be identified.

A first driver is process improvement. Project-based development companies work on a contract basis and therefore need to deliver on time, within budget and with the agreed quality. Every deviation from one of these three will lead to immediate losses for the company. Project companies are therefore usually very interested in all kinds of process innovations that will help them better manage their projects.

A second driver is scalability of the offering. For these companies, there is a linear relationship between the number of projects they can handle simultaneously and the number of employees. If they want to generate more revenue, they have to hire more people (Fig. 1.5). For many companies, this is a hindrance to growth. Project companies are therefore usually very interested in all kinds of innovations that will help them to carry out more projects without having to grow their workforce in the same proportion.

The two drivers result in the following typical innovation needs for project software companies:

- Introducing more sharing between projects. In some cases, these companies have created a large pool of customer-based software and technological solutions based on past projects. They look for ways to create and manage solutions across the project portfolio.
- A key challenge of project-based development is the allocation of resources. They look for ways to involve their experts in several projects at the same time.
- Some projects can be risky and explorative. They look for ways to communicate that risk to customers and to deal with it better. How can experimental developments that are usually 'disguised' as regular customer projects be better organized?

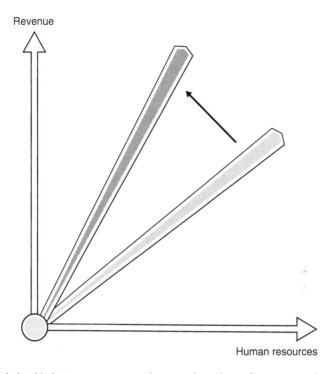

Fig. 1.5 Relationship between resources and revenue in project software companies

- Project-based development organizations are often relatively closed. This is because they innovate in the context of strict customer contracts. In these cases, open source communities and libraries can be used as a development strategy to involve third parties to develop software solutions beyond the contract limits. Many project-based companies are looking for optimal ways to exploit open source communities.
- Building a higher level service model. To increase profit margins, project companies aim to provide more complete solutions to customers. They do not only want to be the contractor but also desire to become a strategic partner and offer services higher up in the value chain of their customers. This also involves helping customers with their innovation activities. Project companies are therefore interested in ideas on how to establish long-term relationships with their customers to enhance knowledge transfer and launch collaborative innovation activities.

1.8.2 Innovation in Out of the Box Development

Out-of-the-box product companies focus their innovation activities at product level. For them, innovation is all about scoping the product. This can be either scoping the products at 'macroscopic' level when defining the product vision or 'microscopic' level when deciding which features to implement from a large pool of potential requirements (Tourwe et al. 2009a, b).

In out-of-the-box development, the valuation process is more complex than in project-based development. Companies have to manage different sets of criteria to rate the different product options (e.g., market-driven requirements, return on investment, complexity, resources, etc.). They can also tap into a variety of sources to harvest new product ideas. The sources include internal and external stakeholders, such as sales, support, development teams, customers, users, competitors products, market intelligence . . . A particular challenge of out-of-the-box companies is the battle for user attention, as described in Sect. 2.8. They are looking for ways to introduce more intelligence into their products to deal with this.

The above observations result in the following typical innovation needs for out-of-the-box product companies:

- *A workable idea management process.* Out-of-the-box product companies are looking for ways to install a workable innovation funnel to improve and measure the return on investment (ROI) of product innovations. In particular, they are interested in: (1) ways to harvest all the ideas available inside and outside the organization and (2) ways to evaluate these ideas in an efficient way.
- *Business model innovation.* Out-of-the-box product builders are interested in ideas for new business models to bring their products to the market.
- *Exploring the option of smart products.* Out-of-the-box product builders are interested in the opportunities that smart products can bring to their specific context.
- *Finding the right degree of openness.* Although open innovation is increasingly used as a strategy in out-of-the-box companies to improve the quality of innovations, great care needs to be taken on how much they actually share and not share. They are interested in a better understanding of the benefits (e.g., new ideas) and risks of sharing (e.g., giving to competitors).
- *Involving customers in innovation.* Many out-of-the-box product companies are considering new ways to involve their customers and users in parts of the innovation and product definition process.
- *Better use of available innovation sources.* Out-of-the-box product companies do not follow a customer intimacy strategy. Their products are aimed at mass markets, and the starting point is that customers can install, use and maintain the product themselves without the need for further customization. Due to the lack of direct contact with customers, there is a need to obtain knowledge and information through market research, partners and customers to steer the innovation activities. Out-of-the-box product companies are interested in ideas to help them find more sources to steer their innovation activities.

1.8.3 Innovation in Customized Product Development

In customized product development, the innovation activities are a combination of the innovation activities of the two previous development models. The valuation of ideas is often complex in these organizations because the specific needs of the customer have to be fulfilled, while, at the same time, the common product or platform has to be evolved. Not surprisingly, this can cause conflicting situations if the company decides not to implement a customer request because it does not serve the needs of several customers in the market.

Most of the innovation needs of the two previous development models also apply to customized product development. Some additional specific needs:

- *Deriving product features from individual customer features.* Customized product development companies have direct channels to their key customers. This can be both a blessing and a curse. A blessing because they can reuse development for one customer for another customer. A curse because many companies are tempted to consider the product as the union of all these individual customer features, i.e., each time they develop something they add it to the base product. In the end, this strategy leads to an overly complex product. Customized product development companies are interested in ideas on how to decide what to put in and what not to put in the product.
- *Scaling up the customization service through third parties.* The dual nature of the development work in customized development requires focus both on developing own products and responding to customer needs. Customized product development companies are interested in new ways to outsource parts of the customization work to third parties.

References

Agile Alliance (2011) Agile Alliance. www.agilealliance.org. Accessed Mar 2011

Altshuller G (1984) Creativity as an exact science. Gordon & Breach, New York

Anderson C (2006) The long tail: why the future of business is selling less of more. Hyperion, New York

Bartels A (2009) Smart computing drives the new era of IT growth. Forrester Research

Brooks F (1995) The mythical man-month: essays on software engineering, anniversary edition. Addison-Wesley Professional

Casadesus-Masanell R, Ricart J (2007) Competing Through Business. IESE Business School Working Paper No. 713

Codenie W, González-Deleito N, Deleu J, Blagojevic V, Kuvaja P, Similä J (2010) Managing flexibility and variability: a road to competitive advantage. In: Kang KC, Sugumaran V, Park S (eds) Applied software product line engineering. Taylor and Francis, pp 269–313

Creax (2011) www.creax.com. Accessed Mar 2011

Desouza KC, Awazu Y (2005) Managing radical software engineers: between order and chaos. In: Proceedings of the 2005 workshop on human and social factors of software engineering, St. Louis, 16 May 2005. HSSE '05, ACM, New York, pp 1–5

Diener K, Piller F (2010) The market for open innovation: increasing the efficiency and effectiveness of the innovation process, RWTH-TIM Group

Fellowforce (2011) www.fellowforce.com Accessed Mar 2011

Greenspun, P (2002) Managing software engineers. philip.greenspun.com/ancient-history/managing-software-engineers. Accessed Mar 2011

Indiegroup (2011) Cognistreamer. www.cognistreamer.com. Accessed Mar 2011

ISPIM (2011) Professional innovation management. www.ispim.org. Accessed Mar 2011

ITEA (2006) Information technology for European advancement. www.itea2.org. Accessed Mar 2011

ITEA (2009) Roadmap for software-intensive systems and services, 3rd edn. www.itea2.org/itea2_roadmap_3. Accessed Mar 2011

ITEI (2007) Information technologies supporting the execution of innovation projects. www.itei-itea2.org. Accessed Mar 2011

KANBAN (2011) Kanban. en.wikipedia.org/wiki/Kanban. Accessed Mar 2011

Kim WC (2005) Blue ocean strategy: how to create uncontested market space and make competition irrelevant, 1st edn. Harvard Business Press, Boston

LEAN (2011) Lean development. en.wikipedia.org/wiki/Lean_software_development. Accessed Mar 2011

Lippoldt D, Stryszowski P (2009) Innovation in the software sector. OECD Publishing, Paris

Mann D (2005) TRIZ for software. http://www.triz-journal.com/archives/2004/10/04.pdf. Accessed Mar 2011

McConnell S (2011) Origins of 10X – how valid is the underlying research? forums.construx.com/blogs/stevemcc/archive/2011/01/09/origins-of-10x-how-valid-is-the-underlying-research.aspx. Accessed Mar 2011

Nilay O, Abrahamsson P (2009) building blocks of agile innovation. BookSurge Publishing, North Charleston

Osterwalder A, Pigneur Y (2010) Business model generation. Wiley, Hoboken, NJ

Pikkarainen M, Boucart N, Alvaro JAH, Kuvaja P, Codenie W, Biot O, Koivumäki T (2010) Impacts of product development strategy on innovation activities in software intensive corporations. In: The proceedings of the XXI ISPIM conference 2010 Bilbao, Spain, 6–9 June 2010. Wiley

Rutkowski A, Saunders C (2010) Growing pains with information overload. Computer 43(6):94–96

Shneiderman B (2007) Creativity support tools: accelerating discovery and innovation. Commun ACM 50(12):20–32

SWEBOK (2004) Guide to the software engineering body of knowledge. www.swebok.org. Accessed Mar 2011

Tharp A (2007) Innovating: the importance of right brain skills for computer science graduates. SIGCSE Bull 39(3):126–130

Tourwe T, Codenie W, Boucart N (2009a) Bringing software innovations to market in release-driven organizations, building blocks of agile innovation, Charleston

Tourwe T, Codenie W, Boucart N, Blagojevic V (2009b) Demystifying release definition: from requirements prioritization to collaborative value quantification. In: 15th international working conference on requirements engineering: foundation for software quality, Amsterdam, The Netherlands

von Hippel E (1986) Lead users: a source of novel product concepts. Manag Sci 32(7):791–806. http://www.jstor.org/stable/2631761. Accessed Mar 2011

Weyrich C (2005) Siemens' R&D: tuned in to today's megatrends. In: Siemens pictures of the future. w1.siemens.com/innovation/en/publikationen/publications_pof/pof_fall_2005/corporate_technology/interview_with_claus_weyrich.htm. Accessed Mar 2011

Chapter 2
The Practice Areas

The remainder of this book describes the practice areasand their usage experiences in industry. The practice areas provide software companies with structure to use to organize innovation. The practice areas are not written from an engineering perspective. They are orthogonal to the typical software engineering disciplines such as requirements management, architecture, testing . . .

The practice areas were distilled by observing how software companies innovate. Practice areas fulfil the following criteria:

- *Relevance*: They represent a common pattern that occurs in several software companies.
- *Innovation-related*: They represent a challenge or opportunities related to innovation, not just engineering.
- *Transferable*: They allow the identification of a set of key activities that can be mastered by companies and be communicated.

Based on the above criteria, eight practice areas have been identified. An overview is provided in Fig. 2.1.

In the remaining section, the practice areas are introduced briefly and motivated. At the end of this chapter, the structure of the practice areas is introduced.

2.1 The Practice Areas at a Glance

2.1.1 The Art of Focusing

The problem of your software company may not be a low volume of ideas. It is probable that many team members and customers produce plenty of ideas in your organization. Generating, collecting and processing these ideas can consume a large amount of energy.

M. Pikkarainen et al. (eds.), *The Art of Software Innovation*,
DOI 10.1007/978-3-642-21049-5_2, © Springer-Verlag Berlin Heidelberg 2011

Fig. 2.1 Eight practice areas for software innovation

> The perceived malleability of software (Sect. 1.6.1) and the large innovation potential put many software companies in a situation in which there are too many ideas to pursue.

Your company may have specific innovation targets it wants to achieve. These targets are most probably not explicit and are difficult to communicate. Suppose you could steer your available creative resource in such a way that it produced ideas within the scope of these targets.

> Software companies that are able to funnel the ideation process in a specified, well-defined direction have a competitive advantage over more reactive companies that shoot in all directions. Knowing what to pursue – but most of all what not pursue – is a necessary skill that software companies need to master.

This practice area is about defining (measurable) innovation targets and goals, thereby allowing funnelling of ideas in well-defined and intended directions.

2.1.2 The Art of Idea Harvesting

How do you collect ideas for your next software release? Where do your ideas originate? Who identifies and follows up ideas? Where do you store ideas and input for your product?

Several software companies were a little embarrassed when we asked them these questions. Answers included: *'We don't really do now, there is no time'*, *'We are not managing this explicitly'*, *'It's Alain you should talk to, he does all of it'*.

Our field studies revealed that, if present at all, most software companies have a rather ad-hoc idea harvesting process, hence the motivation for this practice area. Software companies need to consider carefully how they will harvest ideas. Ideas can originate from various sources inside and outside the company. An infrastructure will need to be put in place to store ideas systematically so they are not lost.

This practice area is about installing the mechanisms for achieving efficient and effective idea harvesting in software companies.

2.1.3 The Art of Idea Valuation

If you are a product manager in a software company, you will like this practice area and recognize the dilemma. Imagine that you are faced with a number of requests and you have to select the most valuable one. Which one do you choose? The technical refactoring proposed by two developers who can speed up future developments or the new feature proposed by a sales representative for the German market?

Once captured, the software company needs to understand the value of ideas. Attributing value to ideas is a challenging endeavour. Value can be expressed in many different ways, and value frames tend to vary greatly between different companies. Even internally in the company, different stakeholders will have different interpretations of value. We observed that this can lead to great confusion in software companies, hence the motivation for this practice area.

This practice area is about installing uniform and consistent value frame models for: (1) reasoning on the value of ideas between stakeholders, (2) making ideas 'comparable' and (3) finding the best ideas.

2.1.4 The Art of Openness

On several occasions, we confronted CEOs of software companies with the question: 'Are you doing anything with open source software'? The answer was often no. Later, during interviews with the development team, it became apparent that they actually were doing much with open source communities (even contributing), but that the management was not aware of this.

In software companies, doing everything yourself is becoming an illusion. On the other hand, companies need to acknowledge about how much they actually do and do not share. Being open can take many forms. Companies can create open products (e.g., by using open source), have open development processes (e.g., open innovation) or have an open business model (e.g., business models based on open innovation). An organization should be aware of its degree of openness (or closeness) with respect to these different dimensions.

This practice area is about defining an openness strategy for the companies. It is about finding the optimal level of openness at each level, i.e., product, process, organization and business models.

2.1.5 The Art of Optimizing the Impact of Critical Experts

Some people can have a huge impact on software innovation within your company. Somehow, their productivity seems higher and their insights are invaluable when it comes to steering your innovations. Having access to these experts at the right time, even if it is only for a short time, can change the way you innovate.

Unfortunately, most of these people have busy schedules. When you come to think of it, some of them, e.g., lead users, are not even on your pay list.

This practice area is about how you can create an environment in which the Impact of critical experts for your innovation can be increased and optimized. This practice area deals with understanding your innovation bottlenecks, installing means to deal with these bottlenecks and ultimately installing communities around your innovation bottlenecks.

2.1.6 The Art of Crafting Smart Products

If you feel threatened by the abundance of software technologies out there or if other players are invading your home markets with innovative solutions, this practice area will interest you.

It will show how to exploit the ICT jungle and how to turn this threat into innovation opportunities: Making your product more user conscious, environment conscious and ecosystem conscious.

This practice area is about being smart with software. It is all about creating products that use information about themselves, the environment in which they operates, or other products in their environment, with the goal to offer new differentiating functionalities.

2.1.7 The Art of Innovation Stimulation

As software is increasing in the value chain, you may want to give higher priority to innovation, but how do you stimulate innovation in a software company when every release is a rat race to meet the next deadline?

> In software engineering innovation, it often boils down to problem solving and fire fighting. There is no real innovation culture in many software organizations. Rather there is an attitude of high productivity and working towards deadlines.

Giving time and resources to innovation is a necessity, and this practice area explains how you can get the most out of that investment, and why these activities are needed. Stimulating innovation is so much more than brainstorming.

This practice area is about fostering the right culture to enable innovation. It is all about encouraging internal and external people to participate in the innovation process.

2.1.8 The Art of Innovation Incubation

You have identified a nice and promising new opportunity to explore, but it involves entering a completely new market and mastering new technologies. How will you manage the risks and how will you turn these ideas into real products *or radical innovations*?

> As more software companies are leaving the comfort zone of incremental innovation, the need for dedicated incubation support is increasing. Incubation is the process of transforming more disruptive ideas into market solutions. Software companies may be very good at producing ideas but weak in their realization. Innovation incubation can take many forms; it can range from incremental innovations in the form of new product innovations to launching spin-out companies.

This practice area is about creating an incubation infrastructure for transforming disruptive ideas into market solutions so that the software company can move out of its innovation comfort zone in a safer way.

2.2 Structure of the Practice Areas

The eight practice areas are written by different authors and can be read independently. Each of the practice areas is structured in five main sections. A short description of each of these sections is given below.

- *Description and scope*
- *Main activities*
- *Links to other practice areas*
- *Questions*
- *References*

2.2.1 Description and Scope

This section describes the overall purpose and scope of the given practice area. It describes why this practice area is important to software companies and explains the typical challenges to tackle. Where applicable, it presents the way different types of companies interpret the given practice area. Examples are provided to illustrate the importance of the practice area.

2.2.2 Main Activities

This section highlights a set of core activities a company should perform in order to master the given practice area. The way a particular company interprets these activities depends greatly on the specific context in which the company operates. These activities provide a strong basis on which to start implementing the practice area.

For each practice area, a drawing similar to the one in Fig. 2.2 is provided. It is taken from the *Art of Focusing* (Sect. 2.3) as an example.

As shown in the figure, the activities are clustered around three categories:

- Activities that allow a company to **understand** the given art
- Activities that allow a company to **address** the art
- Activities that allow a company to **sustain** the art

Activities in the ***Understanding the Art*** category are required to start or boot-strap the practice area (*'Where do you start'?*). Activities in this cluster often have to do with gaining an insight into what the practice area means in the context of the organization. They explore the practice area. In *the Art of Focusing* practice area, for instance, the activity of *Preparing the Innovation Canvas* involves preparation work for activities in the other categories.

Activities in the **Addressing the Art** category describe activities that allow the company to implement practical measures and processes for a given practice area. In the case of *the Art of Focusing,* the activity of *Discovering Innovation Targets* describes an activity a company should perform in that practice area.

Activities in the ***Sustaining the Art*** category of activities need to sustain the practice area (*'How do you keep it alive in your company'?*). In the above example of the *Art of Focusing,* the activity of *Innovation Target Portfolio Management* suggests that the company is actively managing its innovation goals on a continuous basis.

In some cases, the interpretation of the practice area is different depending on the software development strategy (see Sect. 1.8) that a company uses. If this is the case, the differences are included in the description of the practice area. In the case that an activity is only relevant to a particular development strategy, it is indicated in the scheme. In Fig. 2.2, for example, the activity Point Solution Thinking is only relevant to out-of-the-box development (label OB) and custom development (label CD). It is not relevant to project-based development because the label (PB) is not mentioned. If no labels are assigned to an activity, it is applicable to all development strategies.

2.2.3 Links to Other Practice Areas

Each practice area describes the links to the other practice areas. These links are also drawn in the scheme (see Fig. 2.2 for an example).

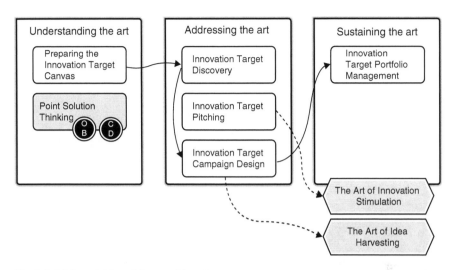

Fig. 2.2 Main activities of the art of focusing

In the example, a link is depicted between the Art of Focusing and two other practice areas: the Art of Idea Harvesting and the Art of Innovation Stimulation. The link is shown at the level of the activities.

2.2.4   Questions

Each practice area is concluded with a series of challenging questions. They help you to reflect on the practice area in your context.

2.3   The Art of Focusing

Nick Boucart, Wim Codenie, Nicolás González-Deleito, and Peter Verhasselt

2.3.1   Description and Scope

For software product builders, a lack of ideas is usually not the problem. On the contrary: it is the abundance of ideas 'floating around' in the company that causes most headaches. Many software builders, especially the out-of-the-box and customized product builders, have bug databases or issue trackers filled with *ideas* for improving the product. The items in such issue tracking systems range from simple bug reports and feature requests to ideas for new products or processes. The real challenge for a company in this situation is to create a concrete focus for its innovations, thereby limiting the number of ideas that can really make a difference to the company. In other words: they need to define their *innovation targets* and decide how to reach them. This is what the *Art of Focusing* is all about.

2.3.1.1 Trying to Focus Today

Good ideas are valuable and a terrible thing to waste. That is why many companies we studied try to collect all the ideas that are available in the company. Most companies realize that randomly launching ideas, hoping that somebody will pick them up, is not the way to go and try to implement a comprehensive process to focus on innovation. The use of a suggestion box, whatever its form, is the most obvious approach.

In software companies, the suggestion box usually takes the form of a centrally-accessible idea database, which is the springboard for the company's innovation efforts. Any database should facilitate the search and submission of ideas. These 'virtual suggestion boxes' come in all kinds of formats and shapes, including Excel files, issue tracking systems (Serrano and Ciordia 2005) and dedicated idea management tools (Diener and Piller 2010), to name a few. Some companies even open these systems up to their customers.

2.3.1.2 Idea Databases – The Cons Outweigh the Pros

The suggestion box may well be a universal concept, yet it is seldom used successfully in software companies. In most cases, employees are so enthusiastic to share their ideas that the database fills up much too quickly, even more so if, for example, the management encourages its use by offering incentives to employees who come up with ideas that are later implemented.

The abundance of ideas quickly poses challenges, however, as the database will contain suggestions in different areas, and at varying levels of maturity and detail. It is very hard and time-consuming to compare and assess this eclectic collection of ideas, making it very difficult to manage the idea database. As a consequence, the processing of suggestions takes a very long time, which disappoints and demotivates employees. Ultimately, the idea box initiatives fail because of their initial success.

2.3.1.3 Innovation Targets: An Instrument for Focusing

In order to avoid this abundance of ideas, software-intensive companies must find a way to channel the creativity of the stakeholders in a direction that is beneficial to their business and in line with the strategy of the company. They need to define clear *innovation targets,* thus setting tangible and measurable goals for the company with respect to innovation. These targets define the boundaries within which stakeholders can be creative and for which ideas are solicited.

Surprising as it may seem, this stricter approach actually encourages creativity, as well-defined innovation targets force stakeholders to focus on clear goals. Consequently, their suggestions will be more concrete and of a higher quality. As the ideas put forward are much better aligned with the company goals, their impact is likely to be bigger. In turn, this will result in more effective results. This is illustrated by both (Fellowforce 2011) and (Innocentive 2011) that use the concept of "challenge" to funnel ideation.

Innovation targets can be very diverse and will depend to a great extent on the type of company. Companies can define innovation targets at product level, process level or business level, and for the short or long term.

Defining the right targets for innovation solves the problem inherent to idea databases: consequently, the suggestions will be focused, more concrete and applicable within the company's longer term strategy. This will result in an easier and less time-consuming idea harvesting and valuation process, and significantly improve the company's efficiency.

Why is focusing so difficult for software builders?

To best illustrate why focusing is so hard for many software builders, let us consider two examples.

Example 1. *Out of the Box Inc.* the organization of Out of the Box Inc. consists of many stakeholders, all potentially busy generating and processing ideas and innovations:

- **Vision and Strategy**: Managers who develop the corporate vision and make the strategic decisions that drive the business.
- **Product Management**: Focus mostly on managing the product portfolio. Here the corporate vision is translated into tangible products and services.
- **Sales**: The link to the 'outside'. The sales and marketing teams take the software products to customers, negotiate deals and often capture requests for new product features.
- **Development**: Deals with all software engineering activities, including requirements engineering, implementation and testing, as well as support.

Why does *Out of the Box Inc* needs to define innovation targets?

- **Scattered Ideation**: Stakeholders often generate ideas stemming from their own context and perspective. Therefore, many ideas differ in nature in accordance with the stakeholder that initiated them. Ideas are therefore difficult to compare. Is an idea for a technical refactoring better than a suggestion made by a customer and reported by a sales person? This differentiation of ideas makes it difficult to create a consistent and coherent overall focus.
- **Assumption-Driven Ideation**: Activities and people in part of the organization are not always as aligned as they should be. This gives rise to 'assumption-driven ideation'. Sales people assume that a certain idea is trivial to implement, while developers assume that their new product idea will eventually be a killer feature,

without really knowing what customers actually want. Focusing proves challenging because only very few people, if any, get to see the big picture.

- **Highly Dynamic Context**: The domain of software engineering is inherently a very dynamic environment where changes in markets and technologies often require a company to shift its focus.
- **Vision not Properly Translated into Usable Guidelines**: Even though the company's main value drivers are often well understood by management, in reality they do not provide a developer or product manager with sufficient guidance. Sometimes, employees spend more time arguing about how and why given features are in line with the overall company value drivers than coming up with new product features.
- **Overwhelming Feature Streams**: Most software products contain a large number of features, and, as illustrated above, plenty of ideas for even more features float around in the organization. Out of the Box Inc. is often tempted to just do it all, thereby creating a very feature-rich product frequently watering down the clear focus on the purpose of the software the company once had.

Example 2. The Project Company. In the Project Company, the dominant activities are fundamentally different from those of Out of the Box Inc. The prevailing activities can be divided into two categories:

- **Project-Related Activities**: As most, if not all, software at the Project Company is developed within the scope of well-defined customer projects, each of the projects forms a stream of activities in itself. In addition, each project is already highly targeted at the customer's individual requirements and at ensuring an optimum software delivery process to the customer. In many of the projects run by the Project Company, methodologies like Scrum ensure that the teams are focused on delivering.
- **Cross-Project Activities**: These are initiatives deployed by the company across projects. They can include the development of frameworks to speed up the project work, initiatives to stimulate knowledge sharing and transfer between projects, etc.

Why is it so difficult for the Project Company to focus?

- **Unavailability of Resources**: The great majority of the company's resources are allocated to individual projects. Yet, company-wide innovation – like speeding up the execution of projects, developing different kinds of services, creating a shared infrastructure – cannot be achieved within the scope of a single project. Furthermore, as staff are often assessed on the results of their projects, activities that contribute to common, non-project-specific goals are not prioritized and therefore performed in-between project tasks.
- **Timing**: Simply bringing people together to work on cross-project initiatives proves difficult: what is the incentive for them? If the Project Company is unable to answer this question properly and clearly, and cannot demonstrate the objective of the exercise, it will have a hard time convincing its people to go the extra mile.

- **Framework Development**: Many organizations, like the Project Company, focus on developing frameworks and infrastructures that can become common building blocks to be used in all projects, and as such they aim to create leverage between projects. Even though these structures may help channel the focus initially, they are often a source of distraction. The innovation needs of the individual projects will typically conflict with them, and much time and energy will be lost arguing about the correct approach.

2.3.1.4   Examples of Innovation Targets

To conclude this section, a number of example innovation targets are presented as an illustration. It is clear that innovation targets are company-specific, yet some commonalities can be observed across companies, especially between companies operating within similar product development models.

Example 1: Innovation targets for out-of-the-box product software builders. It should not come as a big surprise that many out-of-the-box product builders define product-related innovation targets, although some process-related targets are also seen:

- Collect ten ideas to adapt our offering so we can enter this new market and have a reach a market share of 10%.
- Collect five ways to solicit early feedback from users for our new upcoming product release.
- Find five ideas to develop new revenue streams with our products and services that earn us at least ten thousand euro per month.
- Identify four data resources we could exploit.
- Make three proposals to break down our complex legacy product and derive a suite of point solutions out of it.

Example 2: Innovation targets for project-based software builders One of the big challenges project-based companies face with respect to achieving growth is that their way of operating is very resource hungry. In fact, if they want to do twice as many customer projects, they need to hire twice as many people. Many project-based companies define innovation targets around this challenge, although project companies also often tend to define process-related innovation targets:

- Identify four 'things' we can share across projects, such that the execution of the projects is speeded up by 20%, allowing us to do 20% more with the same resources.
- Identify two areas of expertise that we could 'productize' as new solutions, rather than just deploy the expertise in our projects.
- Collect ideas to improve the accuracy of our estimates by 15%.

Note that innovation targets are not phrased as questions. They follow a grammatical structure that starts with a verb and is followed by a quantifiable goal or result.

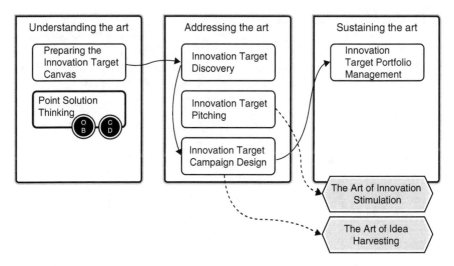

Fig. 2.3 Main activities of the art of focusing

2.3.2   The Art of Focusing – Main Activities

Although the basic principles of innovation focus are universal, the recipe for success is different from one software company to the next (Dehoff and Neely 2004). Describing a number of template innovation targets is therefore impossible. In this chapter, we elaborate on the main activities companies must deploy in order to identify the targets that best suit them and master the Art of Focusing (Fig. 2.3).

2.3.2.1   Preparing the Innovation Target Canvas

In order to identify effective innovation targets, a company needs to understand the environment in which it is operating (i.e. the innovation target canvas). It needs to understand its own position in the value chain, its value propositions, the activities it deploys for delivering this value proposition, etc. (Kim 2005; Osterwalder and Pigneur 2010). Other types of information, ranging from market demand and trends, technological trends, own products and technologies, etc. can be part of this 'innovation target canvas'. If a company fails to compose such a canvas, it will fail to spot effective innovation targets.

Some useful questions when building an innovation target canvas:
  What products and services is the company actually selling?
  What kind of assets does the company hold?
  What does the company's business model look like?
  What are the main elements?
  These questions are especially important for bigger, more mature companies with many legacy products and services:

How can we leverage resources in new ways?
Trends analysis: which trends in our industry can we harness?
What are the anticipated customer needs?

2.3.2.2 Point Solution Thinking

Many companies try to make their products as generic as possible in order to appeal to a larger audience. Examples are CRM and ERP systems, collaboration platforms, database software, etc. This makes it very difficult to define and state their exact value proposition. The scope of the company is then so broad that it becomes almost impossible to define a reasonable number of innovation targets that fully grasp the company's innovation ambitions.

In order to counter this problem, many software companies are converging their offering towards *point solutions*, i.e., solutions that solve one particular problem without considering related issues. In doing so, they try to make their value proposition much more tangible and specific and focus on how the company differentiates itself from the competition.

Companies that apply point solution thinking will find that they become better at deriving concrete value propositions from their ideas. This will help them put constraints on ideas, and as such even stimulate creativity.

Defining innovation targets will indeed be easier for companies that have these point solutions, but of course building point solutions is not an option for every companies. For example, this activity applies less for project companies.

2.3.2.3 Innovation Target Discovery

Innovation target discovery can be described as translating potential value propositions into concrete and measurable goals, respecting the company's specifics. The company will use its innovation target canvas as input to do this. Innovation targets thus create a context in which stakeholders can be creative. The challenges the company is facing constitute another source for innovation target discovery. These challenges may relate to engineering, but they may well be organizational or linked to marketing. The discovery of innovation targets is a creative process in itself and should therefore be treated as such.

2.3.2.4 Innovation Target Pitching

Once an innovation target is defined, it needs to be communicated to the stakeholders. As it is crucial to convince stakeholders of the importance of these targets, the innovation targets really have to be pitched and sold to them.

Arguing clearly and passionately in favour of an innovation target and making a case as to why you should start thinking in this or that direction is a prerequisite for stimulating the creativity of your stakeholders, given the fact that many stakeholders will interpret an innovation target from their perspective, it is necessary to adapt the pitch for the innovation target to the different audiences. Failing to pitch a given innovation target will almost always result in a misunderstanding of the target, thereby leaving too much room for interpretation by different stakeholders, resulting in a loss of focus.

2.3.2.5 Innovation Target Campaign Design

Once a company has identified a certain target, it should start thinking about the best way to address the given target. The way it is addressed depends greatly on the individual targets: some innovation targets can be addressed during short intensive brainstorms behind whiteboards, while other innovation targets may require big sustained campaigns supported by online platforms reaching hundreds of people.

An example from industry can be found in (Fraser 2005).

2.3.2.6 Innovation Target Portfolio Management

Innovation target discovery is not an exact science with only one possible result. Just as a software builder's environment may contain a wide variety of ideas, so that company can set a broad range of potential innovation targets. That is why, depending on their size and structure, and the number of on-going initiatives, companies usually have a number of innovation targets running in parallel. Note that this is true for many companies, although these targets are often not made explicit. This gives all employees the opportunity to participate in a campaign, as otherwise, many people would be left out when the innovation target is purely technical.

Managing the portfolio of innovation targets is an art form in its own right. The company needs to determine when to launch which innovation target and decide which innovation targets are no longer valid. At the same time, an understanding of how well stakeholders respond to innovation targets should be developed. Can they handle more targets without losing focus? Determining and understanding the level of engagement of your stakeholders is crucial, as launching many innovation targets at once may overwhelm them and cause distortion in the focus, resulting in scattered contributions and too little progress. On the other hand, if too few innovation targets are launched, companies risk not using all the available innovation potential.

2.3.3 Relations with Other Practice Areas

The Art of Focusing provides input to the Art of Idea Harvesting through innovation targets.

Innovation targets can be used to stimulate innovation within the company. Through well-defined challenges you can promote the creativity of your people.

Innovation targets put forward measures for success, depending on the individual targets, and as such deal with the Art of Idea Valuation.

For each innovation target that is put forward, it is necessary to assess how open to be in addressing the target. Which stakeholders do we invite? External, internal or both? As such, the practice area of focusing interacts with the Art of Openness practice area.

2.3.4 Questions

In order to start thinking about the Art of Focusing, you could ask yourself the following questions:

- What is your focus with respect to innovation? Are your initiatives well aligned or quite scattered?
- How do you identify your innovation targets?
- What are your innovation targets? Do you explicitly define on what you should innovate?
- How do you measure your innovation targets? Do you define metrics and KPI's for your innovation targets?
- Who defines your innovation targets?
- How do you follow up trends in your domain? How do you keep up with evolutions in technology? How do you communicate all this within your organization?
- How and when do you evaluate your innovation targets?
- How does time affect your innovation targets?
- How do you ensure that everyone who should know about the targets actually does?
- How do you motivate people to engage with your targets?

2.4 The Art of Idea Harvesting

Wim Soens

2.4.1 Description and Scope

Idea harvesting is quite straightforward as a concept. It is about capturing and storing ideas as they emerge from different sources across and beyond the organization (i.e., ideation) and subsequently shaping them into high-value concepts (i.e., concept definition) ready for further exploration.

As simple as it may seem, the practice of idea harvesting is not trivial. Yet, when it comes down to end-user involvement in idea harvesting – also known as crowdsourcing – software companies have an enormous advantage over other industries. Today's online technology offers software builders the unique opportunity to continuously monitor and observe the way end-users use their software, in addition to conventional techniques of online polling and questioning end-users, which have already been adopted by other industries. The tracking, logging and interpretation of real-time behavioural data provide a huge source of inspiration for new software features and even entirely new business models. The main advantage of this approach is that it is a non-intrusive technique that remains hidden to the end-user compared with other techniques, which require active user participation.

In order to exploit this possibility fully to their advantage, software companies need to set up **an efficient process to capture, organize, shape and execute diverse ideas flowing in from different sources**. Today, many software companies use their bug or issue tracking system for this, with ideas taking the form of feature requests. This approach is suboptimal for a number of reasons. First, the real purpose of issue tracking systems is to support engineering activities. Hence, they are located in the New Product Development (NPD) phase of the innovation process, which comes after the Front End phase in which the real ideation should be happening. Second, issue-tracking systems are by default closed and process-centric applications that do not correspond to the (semi-) open and people-centric nature of collaborative idea management tools.

In this practice area, we do not put much focus on idea generation and creativity techniques, as this topic is addressed in the Art of Innovation Stimulation practice area. The real issue here is how to trigger the idea generation process and then – after the ideas have been generated – how to capture and further process the ideas. Later in this chapter, we cover the different activities related to idea harvesting (the *hows*) in detail, but first we start by explaining the challenges at hand (the *whys*).

The Art of Idea Harvesting focuses on addressing three specific problem domains:

Balancing the quantity and quality of ideas
Eliminating screening bottlenecks
Minimizing assessment risks (Fig. 2.4)

2.4.1.1   Balancing the Quantity and Quality of Ideas

In order to increase the value, number and success probability of ideas and concepts entering the development process, software companies have to evolve from a closed innovation process controlled by a centralized and collocated research team towards a more open, collaborative way of innovating (see Sect. 2.6).

The opening up of the ideation stage of the innovation process to larger groups has proven to have a strong positive effect on the number of harvested ideas (Valacich et al. 1992). The downside of open ideation or crowdsourcing, however,

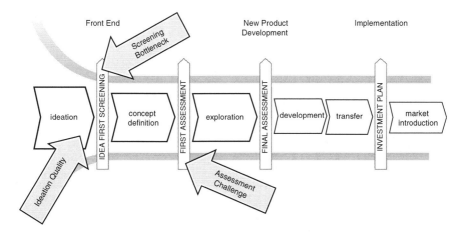

Fig. 2.4 Common problems related to the art of idea harvesting

is that the quality of the idea portfolio – expressed as the ratio of radical ideas (i.e., ideas touching a solution or problem areas that are new to the company and still have to be explored) versus incremental ideas (i.e., ideas that stay well within a company's trusted solution and market domains) – does actually deteriorate. Of course, it could be argued that the quality ratio does not really matter because the probability of ending up with more radical ideas does increase with quantity – albeit not proportionately (Reinig and Briggs 2008). The consequence, however, is that the huge number of ideas that has to be harvested for that purpose may cause a screening bottleneck downstream, which should be avoided in order to drive a constant flow of ideas towards implementation in the software development process. Hence, in order to maintain a good balance between quantity and quality, it is crucial to give **strategic guidance and focus** to an innovation community. The harvesting of ideas should therefore not be restricted to capturing unsolicited ideas. It is also good practice to solicit ideas actively through targeted innovation campaigns (see Sect. 2.3).

2.4.1.2 Eliminating Screening Bottlenecks

Crowdsourced ideation often introduces a strong first-screening problem because of the large number of unstructured ideas that is injected into the innovation funnel. The scarcity of review resources (see Sect. 2.7), the sequential nature of the screening process and the high uncertainty of determining the success probability of ideas and concepts causes a bottleneck at the front end, which in turn threatens to stall the complete innovation process. Once people start to feel that their ideas remain 'undealt with', they will eventually stop sharing them. We will come back to the motivational aspects of idea generation in more detail later, but it must be clear that a good process backbone is needed to build and sustain a strong innovation culture.

There are several approaches to improving screening efficiency, but most companies tackle this problem by implementing a **professional idea management software tool** (an option that is generally preferred over the more expensive alternative of increasing screening resources and frequency). The market of idea and innovation management tools is growing exponentially, and many solutions are available today, from very simple and low cost solutions to very advanced and expensive ones. They all offer some kind of Web 2.0 aggregation technology to identify, track, filter, rank and analyse ideas in order to improve screening efficiency. Most tools use a simple collaborative filtering algorithm based on explicit voting. More advanced tools use aggregators that predict the future success of ideas with complex algorithms that combine explicit peer-review data (voting and scoring) with implicit community behavioural data such as page views, ratings, social bookmarks and tags.

2.4.1.3   Minimizing Assessment Risks

Opening up the front end of innovation and successfully addressing the above-mentioned challenges eventually results in rich and valuable ideas or concepts being produced. The final challenge is then to choose which ideas or concepts to invest in for further development (see Sect. 2.5). This is a difficult decision due to the high uncertainty in the early development stage. On the other hand, there is little room for error, as the cost of failure increases exponentially from this point onward.

The basic approach to minimizing assessment risks is to evaluate the idea or concept from as many different and diverse angles as possible. Here too, software technology can bring an answer. Collaborative innovation management systems tackle this assessment challenge by tapping into the collective intelligence of large innovation networks using **group decision support systems (GDSS)**. The clear benefits of using a GDSS (over more traditional assessment techniques) are more precise communication and cross-pollination (members are empowered to build on the ideas of others), leading to a more objective evaluation of ideas.

2.4.2   The Art of Idea Harvesting – Main Activities

There are several ways to organize and structure idea harvesting, depending on the specific innovation strategy (e.g., incremental vs radical, tech push vs market pull . . .) and the goals that need to be achieved, but any process will usually consists of five major activities (Fig. 2.5):

- Triggering Ideas
- Capturing Ideas
- Organizing Ideas
- Shaping Ideas
- Idea Portfolio Management

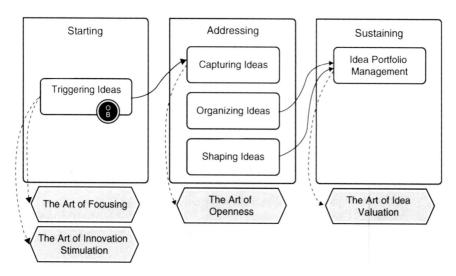

Fig. 2.5 Main activities of the art of idea harvesting

2.4.2.1   Triggering Ideas

There are two basic approaches to triggering ideas. The first is to call for ideas through targeted innovation challenges or idea campaigns (i.e., solicited ideation). This practice is covered extensively in another chapter (see Sect. 2.3).

The second approach is to create an innovative culture that stimulates people to share their ideas spontaneously (i.e., unsolicited ideation). Stimulating creativity by fostering the right innovation culture is a practice area in itself (see Sect. 2.9) dedicated to creating an inspiring environment to encourage internal and external people to generate and share ideas. In order to turn ideation into a continuous and self-sustaining process, however, the stimulation of spontaneous ideation should also be strongly embedded into the idea harvesting process, mainly by providing effective **inspiration** and **feedback** channels.

Triggering ideas *for out-of-the-box software companies.* The activity of triggering ideas is of special concern to software companies offering out-of-the-box solutions to the market because their relationship with the end-user is more distant and indirect than that of custom software developers. The latter have a very close and direct relationship with their customers, which in most cases are also the end-users. Close interaction with the customer/end-user is a natural part of a custom development project, creating many opportunities for both parties to share knowledge and ideas in a very spontaneous way.

For most out-of-the-box software companies, the direct customers are retail partners, not end-users. More importantly, neither retail partners nor end-users initiate (let alone finance) the software development project, which is solely the responsibility of the software developer. In order to trigger ideas from end-users, out-of-the-box software companies have to invest in dedicated communication channels to inform the end-user community about the project and provide a transparent platform on which to share and discuss ideas.

Inspiration

Inspiration can come from many different sources but probably first from other people's ideas. The provision of a transparent **repository in which to browse and search for all ideas** will trigger many new ideas. Repositories as such tend to fill up with a huge number of very diverse ideas over time, and it is necessary to provide additional tools such as recommender systems or social bookmarking to help users find ideas that may inspire them. Most idea management systems let users vote and tag other ideas and then use these votes and tags to suggest other links they may find interesting. High-end tools use advanced recommendation algorithms or correlation engines to achieve cross-fertilization of ideas.

As well as ideas, other types of content such as papers, blog posts, news articles, etc. can inspire users and trigger new ideas. When setting up an environment for capturing and sharing ideas, it is therefore good practice to allow users to also **publish and share experience and knowledge** in all possible formats

Feedback

It is very important that idea owners are able to follow up the status and progress of the ideas that they (and others) have submitted. **Efficient and transparent feedback** channels are therefore a key requirement of any idea harvesting system. Feedback can be partially automated and communicated through e-mail notifications or dashboard messages that are generated based on user activity data. Peers or superiors should also give feedback about ideas or other contributions in a personal way during informal and even formal conversations.

2.4.2.2   Capturing Ideas

The main concern here is to capture all ideas. In order to master the activity of capturing ideas, there are four important aspects to look into: **openness, accessibility, ubiquity** and **diversity.**

Openness

Idea management software tools have become widely accepted in most industries because of their effectiveness at harvesting ideas. The level of openness of such systems varies greatly from one company to another (see Sect. 2.6).

When companies start to adopt idea management tools they usually opt for a closed system in which access is only granted to internal employees, i.e., **closed ideation**.

More experienced companies will gradually open up their ideation system to selected external partners such as university labs, knowledge centres or key suppliers, i.e., **semi-open ideation**.

The use of true Ideagoras – places on the Internet where large numbers of people and/or businesses gather to share ideas – is growing in importance, and an increasing number of companies have already successfully adopted this strategy, i.e., **open ideation**.

Ideagoras fall into three broad categories:

- **True-Market Ideagoras**
  Intermediary brokers organizing ideation campaigns for their clients set up this type of Ideagora. Contributors (or problem solvers) are usually attracted and incentivized with cash rewards or prizes. Well-known market Ideagoras are innocentive.com, yet2.com and ninesigma.com.
- **Competition-Based Ideagoras**
  A competition-based Ideagora generally works on one specific problem or challenge launched by one promoting company. The competition is usually open to anyone, offering a chance to win prize money for solving a problem. A well-known example in the software industry is the US video rental company Netflix's competition to improve its recommendation algorithm, offering a $1 million prize to the winner.
- **B2C Ideagoras**
  This type of corporate Ideagora engages customers to bring in ideas on ways to improve a company's product or service. They are typically hosted by big companies with strong brands. B2C Ideagoras tend to generate incremental ideas that are generally not rewarded financially. Two very popular examples are mystarbucksidea.com and Dell's IdeaStorm.

Accessibility

It should be extremely simple and straightforward to submit and share ideas. It should not take more than a few seconds for anybody to submit an idea; otherwise people will not bother. Idea forms should be very basic: an idea title and a short description should be all that is needed to capture and register an idea. Remember that this is the only and most important thing at this stage. It is not a problem that the idea will not be fully fleshed out. Many companies make the mistake of forcing users to fill in complex idea forms with many mandatory fields. This will discourage idea submitters and many ideas will never make it to the submit button. There will be enough time later to complete the ideas (see Sect. 2.4.2.4).

Ubiquity

Ideas can emerge during many activities and in different places: discussions with people in meeting rooms, producing reports behind a desk, interacting with others at the coffee machine, handling requests from customers on the phone, reading reports on the train ...

Capturing ideas where and when they occur is key to successful idea harvesting. Idea management systems should therefore be ubiquitous, i.e., accessible anywhere, at any time and through any media, e.g., smartphones, LANs, the Internet, messaging software and e-mail clients. In the specific case of software or software-intensive products, ubiquity can also be achieved by integrating online idea publishing functionality into the software itself. As already mentioned in the introduction to this practice area, this is a unique opportunity for software companies and it is currently not being exploited fully.

Diversity

On a personal level, diversity triggers alternative ways of thinking and behaving. Hence, people who live in intersections of social worlds (i.e., people on the 'edge' of organizations) tend to have better ideas than people with a higher network constraint (Burt 2003).

The identification and management of idea sources for maximum diversity is therefore crucial to harvesting quality ideas. Diversity means involvement of people from multiple disciplines in the ideation process, internal sources (marketing, sales and software engineers) as well as external sources (research partners, suppliers, customers and end-users).

With applications such as Facebook and Twitter, software technology has become deeply social. As such, it has become a key enabler to exploit effectively the diversity of large user communities. Through social software, end-users can become an integral part of the innovation and development ecosystem. As a consequence, products – especially software products – are becoming dynamic in the sense that they are not merely consumed or used as they are but are customized, redesigned or even re-engineered to fit the specific requirements of individual users or user groups (von Hippel 2005). Social media are an important source for innovation. Observing and listening to these channels in order to capture new ideas must become a best practice in every company (Fig. 2.6).

2.4.2.3 Organizing Ideas

This activity consists of filtering, merging, ranking and/or clustering all captured ideas in order to prepare them for further processing. Depending on the innovation strategy and the expected outcomes, however, the organization (and processing) of ideas has to be managed in different ways.

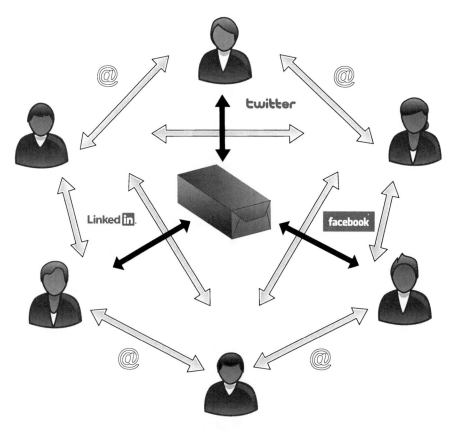

Fig. 2.6 Networked innovation

There are four types of innovation, which are visualised in the graphics below (core growth, market pull, technology push and basic research), though in fact only Classes I, II and III are relevant domains for applying idea-harvesting techniques. Basic research (Class IV) innovation falls outside the scope of this practice area because it is a highly knowledge-centric domain. As such, ideas cannot really exist in this space of unknown unknowns because in order to be explicit they must be linked to at least one known problem or solution domain. Hence, there is less need for a true idea harvesting system here. A collaborative knowledge management system is a much better option (Fig. 2.7).

Organizing Class I Ideas

For core growth ideas (incremental or Class I innovation), a sequential process-driven approach is most common. The basic concept is to separate the good ideas from the bad ones based on simple quantitative criteria such as cost/benefit ratio,

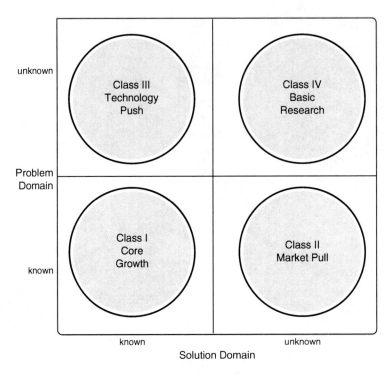

Fig. 2.7 Four types of innovation

technical feasibility and development cost. Less than 20% of all ideas usually survive this initial screening, with other ideas being 'killed' or archived.

Here, the main challenge is to design a process that can screen **large numbers of ideas**. This problem is usually tackled by tapping into the collective intelligence of an innovation network through community voting, based on the popular theory from Surowiecki (2004a) (Wisdom of Crowds) that the aggregation of information within a community can lead to better decisions – better than could have been made by any single member of the group. In practice, screening algorithms based on explicit voting prove to be effective in solving screening bottlenecks, but the quality of the filtering may still be questioned. (Are we sure we did not 'kill' good ideas?)

In order to improve screening quality, more advanced innovation platforms try to predict the future success of ideas with collaborative ranking algorithms that combine explicit voting with implicit community behaviour data such as page views, ratings, bookmarks and tags. Provided these algorithms have used the correct association rules, i.e., the relation between the value of an idea and a certain activity (e.g., bookmarking), this approach has proven effective. The key issue, however, is that association rules differ from one community to another due to the variation in behavioural patterns, and they are influenced by cultural, social and other differences. Community behaviour also tends to change over time within the same community. As a consequence, the fine-tuning of these algorithms (usually by trial and error) is a complex, time-consuming and never-ending effort.

In order to solve the problem described above, a new generation of algorithms is emerging. These adaptive (or self-tuning) collaborative ranking algorithms use data mining to extract association rules from activity facts in relation to the success rate of ideas. In other words, the algorithms seek relations between the collaborative behaviour of an online innovation community and the value of the ideas and concepts it generates in order to predict the value of new ideas based on these behavioural patterns.

Organizing Class II & III Ideas

For radical innovation (or Class II and III innovation), a sequential process will not do because ideas need to develop organically before being subjected to a quantitative assessment. Pushing ideas through a quantitative assessment would simply kill most of the so-called 'out-of-the-box' ideas, which are exactly the type of ideas that are needed for this kind of innovation. Instead, the organization of ideas should focus on finding and clustering those ideas that carry a germ of a strong innovative concept and need to be developed further during incubation. Hence, instead of a process-centric approach, a people- (or network-) centric approach is more appropriate. In Class II and III innovation, an emergent and people-centric collaborative model is therefore better than the Class I sequential and process-focused stage gate model.

The core architecture of such 'collaborative systems' is built around creation spaces in which communities can address innovation opportunities and challenges, generate and share ideas and insights and shape them into strong concepts with strategic value for the company.

In order to facilitate the process of filtering and clustering ideas, these systems apply the concept of '**Collaborative filtering**'. Collaborative filtering is part of a bigger concept called 'harnessing collective intelligence' (coined by), which refers to using advanced social science algorithms to identify, track, filter, rank and analyse social media content. It also includes applying semantic technology to track discussions on specific topics and analysing the share of voice and tonal sentiment.

Collaborative Filtering. The term collaborative filtering was first used by David Goldberg at Xerox PARC in 1992 in a paper called 'Using collaborative filtering to weave an information tapestry'. He designed a system called Tapestry that allowed people to annotate documents as either interesting or uninteresting and he used this information to filter documents for other people.

There are now hundreds of web sites that employ some kind of collaborative filtering algorithm for movies, music, books, dating, shopping, other web sites, podcasts, articles and even jokes.

Examples of 'Harnessing Collective Intelligence':

- PageRank algorithm (Google)
- 'Interestingness' algorithm (Flickr)
- 'People who bought this also bought...' feature (Amazon)
- 'Similar artist radio' algorithm (Last.fm)
- Reputation system (eBay)
- AdSense (Google)

2.4.2.4 Shaping Ideas

As idea submission has to be made extremely easy (see Sect. 2.4.2.2), it is very likely that the initial idea description will not be much more than a captive title and a short abstract. To allow for a detailed review and reduce the assessment risk, however, a full idea description that addresses all review criteria is needed. This is why an additional shaping activity is needed.

Shaping Class I Ideas

With regard to organizing ideas, the activity of shaping ideas is handled differently for incremental (Class I) ideas vs radical (Class II and III) ideas. The shaping of incremental ideas usually takes one or two iterations with the idea generator itself in order to 'fill in the gaps' and prepare the idea for review, for which the assessment criteria are quantitative and very well defined. Shaping consists of documenting the idea (e.g., with drawings) or building up a good case against the evaluation criteria (e.g., what the costs and the benefits are, whether it is technically feasible, etc.).

Shaping Class II & III Ideas

Shaping radical ideas – in order to turn them into concepts – takes more time, is more complex and needs the engagement of several people besides the idea generator. In most cases, radical concepts are the result of combining and building on several other ideas over time. These kinds of emergent processes are quite 'fuzzy' and organic, and not yet fully understood by social scientists, let alone applied by process designers. The current state-of-the art in this domain is still at an experimental stage, and no real standards or best practices have been defined yet. Innovative, collaborative software companies are already implementing socio-cognitive features in collaborative innovation software, however, in order to lever-age the social dynamics of communities, for instance, by integrating social science technology to connect people and knowledge in order to trigger 'serendipitous' events.

2.4.2.5 Idea Portfolio Management

Idea Portfolio Management is about creating and maintaining a well-balanced portfolio of ideas based on a number of different criteria such as the strategic innovation domain, innovation class, development time, investment, risk, etc. The main goal of idea portfolio management is to secure continuous output of ideas addressing short-term business improvements (doing things better) as well as long-term business opportunities (doing things differently).

Strategic Innovation Domains

The top-level 'strategic' differentiators of ideas are their innovation domains, which can be categorised into four main domains and ten sub-domains according to the model by Doblin (see Table 2.1).

Innovation is not just about improving product performance, although it is still the domain in which most companies 'fight their battles'. Too few companies realise that there are many innovation opportunities besides the product performance domain. There are huge opportunities for innovations in the **business model** domain, especially for software companies. Dell, for instance, became very successful in the finance category domain by making the customers pay for their PCs before assembly and shipment. Another well-known example in this domain is software companies that changed their payment model from charging flat licence

Table 2.1 Ten types of innovation

Innovation category	Innovation type	Description
Finance	Business model	How you make money
	Network and alliances	How you join forces with other companies for mutual benefit
Process	Enabling process	How you support the company's core processes and workers
	Core processes	How you create and add value to your offerings
Offerings	Product performance	How you design your core offerings
	Product system	How you link and/or provide a platform for multiple products
	Service	How you provide value to customers and consumers beyond and around your products
Delivery	Channel	How you get your offerings to the market
	Brand	How you communicate your offerings
	Customer experience	How your customers feel when they interact with your company and its offerings

Ten types of innovation is a trade mark of Doblin, (http://www.doblin.com/AboutInno/innotypes. html)

fees to offering free basic functionality with paid special services. Yet another example, this time in the **product system** domain, is bundling several software applications into a single 'suite'.

Innovation Portfolio

Inside each of the ten strategic innovation domains, all four classes of innovation that were described earlier apply. This results in a 3D space that can be used to map all ideas, research projects, development projects and products or services in the innovation pipeline (Fig. 2.8).

In order to obtain a well-balanced innovation portfolio, ideas should be harvested in all four main innovation categories (i.e., finance, process, offerings and delivery) and innovation classes I, II and III (i.e., core growth, market pull and technology push). A good balance does not mean that there has to be an equal

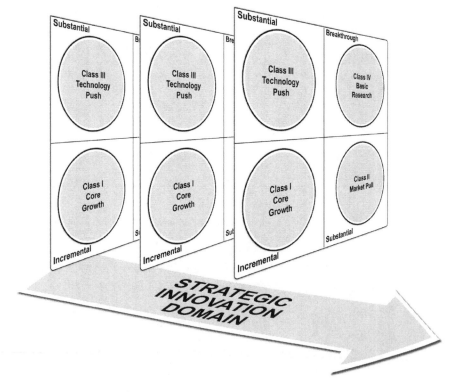

Fig. 2.8 Innovation portfolio

distribution of ideas across all innovation categories and classes. This should not be an objective as it is practically unachievable. There will always be more Class I ideas than Class II and Class III ideas (which are harder to obtain), and most of them will be situated in the product performance domain (because this domain is directly related to your offering). It is important, however, not to neglect the other domains and to take the appropriate steps to harvest a substantial proportion of non-Class I product performance ideas. Targeting specific ideation campaigns in the other domains can do the trick (see Sect. 2.3).

2.4.3 Relations with Other Practice Areas

Art of Openness

- Balancing the quantity and quality of ideas:opening up ideation to larger groups in order to increase the value, amount and success probability of ideas and concepts entering the development process
- Capturing Ideas:the three levels of openness: closed ideation, semi-open ideation (selected partnerships) and open ideation (true Ideagoras)

Art of Focusing

- Balancing the quantity and quality of ideas:it is crucial to give strategic guidance and focus to an innovation community through innovation targets.
- Triggering ideas:one of the basic approaches to triggering ideas is to call for ideas through innovation challenges or idea campaigns (i.e., solicited ideation)
- Idea Portfolio Management:focused ideation campaigns to push an innovation community outside its comfort zone in order to harvest radical ideas (Classes II and III)

Art of Optimizing the Impact of Critical Resources

- Eliminating screening bottlenecks:the scarcity of review resources – among other problems – can cause a bottleneck in the front-end ideation process.

Art of Idea Valuation

- Minimizing assessment risks:dealing with the high uncertainty at the front end to choose the right ideas or concepts for further development

Art of Innovation Stimulation

- Triggering Ideas:another approach to triggering ideas is to create an innovative culture that stimulates people to share their ideas spontaneously (i.e., unsolicited ideation)

2.4.4 Questions/Checklist

- How can you find a good balance between the quantity and quality of ideas?
- How can you avoid or eliminate screening bottlenecks?
- How can you minimize the risks of idea assessment?
- How should you provide effective inspiration and feedback channels in order to stimulate spontaneous ideation?
- How can you create open, accessible, ubiquitous and diverse harvesting systems in order to capture ideas efficiently?
- How can you filter, merge, rank and/or cluster all captured ideas in order to prepare them for further processing?
- How can you organize and process ideas based on your specific innovation strategy and the expected outcomes?
- How can you shape different types of ideas?
- What are the top-level 'strategic' differentiators of ideas?
- How can you distribute the ideas in the innovation portfolio across the different innovation categories and innovation classes?

2.5 The Art of Idea Valuation

Wim Codenie, Nick Boucart, and Tom Tourwé

2.5.1 Description and Scope

Consider the following scenario. You are a product manager in an out-of-the-box software company and have to decide which features to include in the upcoming release of your flagship product. You have carefully assessed all the requests in your issue tracking system and considered all the estimates provided by the developers.

There is only room for one more request. It is up to you to choose. Two options are available: request number 89 and request number 543. Request 89 is a feature that is highly attractive to the Brazilian market. Request 543 is technical refactoring in the data access layer, resulting in a moderate performance gain, better overall reliability and easier maintenance.

Which one will you choose? Which of these two requests is most valuable?

The scenario above demonstrates that for out-of-the-box software companies, the Art of Idea Valuation is all about mastering *release definition*, the process of determining the content of the next product release by selecting the most valuable requirements from a large pool of ideas (Tourwe et al. 2009a).

Now consider a second scenario in which you are the CEO of a project-based software company.

One morning, two of your lead architects enthusiastically pay you a visit and pitch an exciting new idea to you to introduce a framework that could be leveraged in most, if not all, the company's customer projects.

The architects argue that such a framework would dramatically speed up development, increase the productivity of the developers, create a standardized way of working and reduce the chances of reinventing the wheel. Looks nice doesn't it!

You lean back in your chair; sigh silently and think: once again two guys struck by framework fever. This proposal is at least the sixth 'framework proposal' you received this year. You received one for a user interface framework and three for data persistency frameworks. Only a week ago, two people suggested a security framework that would bring us nothing but benefits.

All these proposals are attempts to share and reuse knowledge between projects, and although all these proposals were made with the best intentions, calculating the return on investment of such initiatives seems very hard.

The scenario above demonstrates that for many software companies that use a project-based development strategy, the Art of Idea Valuation has much to do with understanding the return on investment of cross-project initiatives. In individual customer projects, the value of what is delivered is usually clear; for project companies, it is the customer that dictates which innovations are most valuable. The release definition problem is less relevant to these companies.

An overview of the way software companies value ideas can be found in Tourwe et al. (2009b). We briefly describe three common strategies on the way companies handle this.

2.5.1.1 Idea Valuation by an Enlightened Product Manager

Many organizations, especially software companies producing out-of-the-box software, appoint a gatekeeper, in the form of the product manager, to resolve the valuation challenge. The product manager guards and structures the potential requirements and selects the best ones. In order to do so, the product manager studies the market and competitors and listens to customers, users and prospects in the hope of spotting the most interesting opportunities. All this information should give the product manager enough insight to choose the most valuable requirements, leaving less valuable ones for later.

Managing all this quickly becomes a complex task for the product manager. In fact, the product manager needs to combine different pieces of information to determine the value of a potential requirement (e.g., business value, technical risk, cost, etc.). In many cases, this information is scattered across different people within the organization, incomplete and even tainted by personal opinion. In practice, the task of valuing ideas is simply too complex and overwhelming for any single person.

2.5.1.2 Idea Valuation by Voting

Another technique for valuation used by software companies is voting. Participants are presented with a list of requirements and ideas and are asked to cast a vote on those requirements they like most. This can be in the form of simple yes/no voting, or voting with a number of a particular scale (e.g., one to five). The requirements that receive most votes are considered most valuable.

Due to their simplicity and ease of use, voting systems seem attractive. Unfortunately, they are not without problems: in order for a stakeholder to cast an informed vote, he/she needs to understand all the aspects not only of the given requirement but also of all others. In fact, it is only then that a person can truly understand when to vote yes and when to vote no.

Understanding the advantages and disadvantages of each and every request is time-consuming for stakeholders and requires them to be very knowledgeable about all the value aspects. Hence, for many software companies, voting does not completely meet their needs when it comes to valuation.

2.5.1.3 Idea Valuation by a Requirements Prioritization Algorithm

As voting is clearly simple and simplistic at the same time, people have looked for ways to overcome its disadvantages while retaining its advantages. This has given rise to research into automated requirements prioritization through algorithms (Lehtola 2006). These algorithms capture the value of a requirement in a single number, computed by means of a formula that combines the values of relevant criteria in a clever way. Based on this number, the list of requirements is sorted.

Although the concept itself is quite clear and promising, it is hard to apply in practice. You may wonder whether it is possible to identify one generally applicable formula to be used by different organizations in different domains:

- What **criteria** should such a formula take into account? Most probably a combination of predefined criteria, such a cost, effort and risk, and user-defined criteria such as product stability or attractiveness to a given market. Some criteria may be more important than others, and a formula should also take this into account.
- Which **scales** would such a formula use to express a value for each given criteria? Criteria such as cost and effort can be expressed in absolute terms (money or estimated time) while others, such as attractiveness to a given market, are much more difficult to express as numbers.
- How should the **uncertainty of estimates** for the given values be dealt with? As the different values can only be estimated, and estimates depend heavily on the experience and knowledge of the stakeholders providing them, the outcome of the requirements prioritization algorithm may differ depending on the stakeholder using it.

Although requirement prioritization algorithms can have their merits, solely relying on them to address the Art of Idea Valuation is not enough.

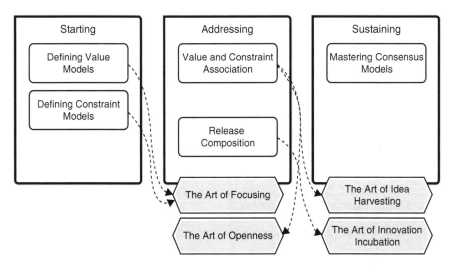

Fig. 2.9 Main activities of the art of idea valuation

2.5.2   The Art of Idea Valuation – Main Activities

The picture below describes the different activities a software company should implement in order to master the Art of Idea Valuation (Fig. 2.9).

2.5.2.1   Defining Value Models

When asked, different stakeholders in a software company will give different definitions of value.

Developers will look at 'value' from a technical angle such as increasing maintainability of the product, increasing performance or decreasing complexity.

Sales and marketing departments will often interpret 'value' in terms of market share or simply revenue. For the management 'value' will be elements that help to realize the company mission (e.g., achieving product excellence).

Somehow the software company needs to bring together these different interpretations of 'value' into a *value model*, a terminology that stakeholders can use to reason and communicate about value. The ultimate goal of such a value model is to make it possible to compare different ideas and requests in the context of this value model.

A value model describes a set of value elements (called factors in Kim 2005). These are characteristics that are important in some way to a company and are usually linked to a particular way of realizing a competitive advantage.

Some examples are given below. Value elements can be driven by different objectives of the company:

- Quality-driven value elements (e.g., inspired by the ISO 9126 Software Quality Standard)

  - Performance of the product
  - Usability of the product
  - Maintainability
  - ...

- Delivery-driven value elements

  - Trainability on the product (ease of training new users to use the product)
  - Ease of deploying new versions
  - ...

- Market-driven value elements

  - Attractiveness to the German market
  - Compliance with safety regulations in a market
  - ...

After having a clear value model, there is a need to establish an appropriate measure for that value. For quantitative definitions of value, these measurements can be quite easy to determine, e.g., if value is defined in terms of net present value, financial measures should be used. If the definition of value includes qualitative factors, a plethora of different measurements is available:

- Interval scoring (e.g., measuring the improvement in user experience on a scale of 1–10)
- The Kano model of customer satisfaction (Kano et al. 1984) introduces three possible values: *basic, linear* and *exciter*.
- The MoSCoW Method (Clegg and Barker 2004) proposes four values: *must, should, could* and *won't have*.
- Strategy Canvasses (Kim 2005) visually present the value elements of the model and score them from 'low' to 'high', compared with the rest of the industry.

Many out-of-the-box software product builders have quite a complex value model, taking into account the many interpretations of value that are used in the company by different stakeholders.

As mentioned before, developers will look at value from a technical perspective while the sales and marketing department typically assesses value from a more financial and new business perspective. The biggest challenge with respect to defining the value models is solving the tension between these various interpretations of value. How do you make them comparable and how do you translate value from one interpretation to another?

Ideally, there is one value model for the whole company, but this is not always realistic.

A company we met during a survey struggled with its release definition process. It had a strong development team that pushed technical features and a strong sales team that pushed market features. It never managed to make it all comparable and had many disputes trying to sort out what was most valuable. The company solved this problem in a pragmatic way. Instead of defining one overall value model to be used by all stakeholders, different models for different stakeholders were introduced. It allocated a 'budget' to each release for each group of stakeholders. The company typically allocated 20% of the total release effort to requests nominated by developers, 60% to sales and marketing and 20% to the support team. Within each release slot, each stakeholder group defined its own value model and filled up its slot according to that value model.

Note that for project-based software companies, the situation is different. Within a given project, it is the customer of the project that dictates what is most valuable. The software company has to follow the value frame imposed by the customer. For *cross-project initiatives,* on the other hand, the value model often boils down to determining the return on investment of a certain shared activity.

2.5.2.2 Defining Constraint Models

Understanding the value of an idea is important but not enough. Software companies also need to understand the implications of realizing a certain idea. For many companies, this means that they like to understand the risks and costs associated with the idea as well as possible implications when the innovation may fail. Other properties often seen in constraint models are timing (can the innovation be delivered on time) and resources needed to implement the idea.

Fortunately, in the field of software engineering, many techniques are available for effort estimation. A good overview can be found in McConnell (2006).

2.5.2.3 Value and Constraint Association

Value and constraint association is the activity of estimating value and cost with concrete ideas. It consists of applying the value and constraint models to the individual ideas and rating them with possible values.

- *Example*: This idea for new functionality contributes to our goal to enter the German market (= value element). It will provide us with two new customers in Germany next year (= the value).
- *Example*: This refactoring of our code contributes to the look and feel of the product (=value element). It will ensure that all future new screens we develop will have the same format (= the value).

Software companies need to define *who* to involve in associating value with a given request, *when* this value association needs to be made, *how* it is going to be made and *what* method is going to be used.

Associating value is not a straightforward activity:

- As the real value of a request is only known after it has been realized, value attribution relies on **estimates and guesses**. As a consequence, the software company has to deal with the uncertainty associated with these values and constraints.
- Typically, **a large number of requests** need to be valued, which means that whatever approach is used, it needs to be scalable and efficient.
- **Many different stakeholders** may need to be involved in the value association activity. The value and constraint models will indicate what information is needed and hence which stakeholders to involve. Software companies may involve customers in the valuation activities to obtain valuation information directly from the market (Blank 2005a).

Several different techniques are used by software companies, ranging from relying on the wisdom of crowds by aggregating the opinions of many individual stakeholders (Surowiecki 2004b) using stakeholder weighting (Tsiporkova et al. 2006) to give domain experts' opinions more weight, to applying lean principles such as *deciding as late as possible* (Poppendieck and Poppendieck 2004) so that decisions are taken when more information is available and uncertainty is reduced.

Value association strategies based on the wisdom of crowds are promising (Tourwe et al. 2009a). They try to involve all stakeholders by allowing them to express their opinions on the value of an idea. Stakeholders can use their own vocabulary when expressing the value of a requirement by using free-form 'tags' (e.g. 'innovative', 'sellable', 'quality-improving' ...). Inspired by the work on folksonomies, this can allow a company-specific definition of a value model to grow in a bottom-up way.

Example: The art of Idea Valuation at Nokia Siemens Networkd (NSN), by Tuomo Kinnunen. NSN has a business case practice for idea valuation. Business cases combine three aspects of idea valuation: *market assessment, technical study* and *financial analysis*. The market assessment checks whether an idea matches with a real need, identifies the size of the potential market, and analyses payback and pricing possibilities. The technical study investigates technical feasibility of an idea and assesses work efforts of different technical alternatives. The financial analysis utilizes a market assessment to predict added revenues by an idea. In addition, the technical study is used to estimate costs caused by bringing an idea to market. The financial analysis is culminated into an estimation of payback level and cash flow.

Business cases are used to support decision-making. For this purpose all the business case aspects are compared to strategy and risks. Technical and market risks are viewed against expected reward and strategic objectives. The aim of the business case practice is that only potentially valuable ideas for the company will go into further development.

2.5.2.4 Release Composition

Release compositions are all about taking decisions.

It is within this activity that a software company decides which requests to include and which ones not to include in the upcoming release. In order to make decisions effectively about releases, it is important to state the goals explicitly that the company wants to achieve with the upcoming release, preferably indicating the goals in a measurable way.

Examples of such goals could be: increase the performance of the product by 20%, make the product compliant with regulations in a new target market or increase the market share by 5% in the Latin-American region. Goals can be defined top-down or bottom-up. In a top-down approach, release goals are defined based on a product roadmap or strategic analysis. In a bottom-up approach, the release goal is derived from the request database itself: requests that are repeatedly asked for by customers or requests that originated from big customers may be taken as release goals in such a scenario.

Once the goal of a release is put forward, it is necessary to start populating the release, i.e., decide which requests fit best with this goal, while at the same time fulfilling the constraints, such as timing and budget. Different guidelines for populating a release exist and a full overview is provided in (Tourwe et al. 2009a, b; Karlsson 2006; Lehtola 2006). Some techniques include:

- **Clustering in importance groups**: These approaches divide the requirements into a small number of different importance groups. Methods include Kano (Kano et al. 1984), the MoSCoW Method (Clegg and Barker 2004) and the Planning Game (Beck and Fowler 2001). Cohn (2005) suggests selecting low-cost, high-value requests first, then high-cost, high-value, then low-value, low-cost, etc.
- **Consensus-based approaches**: These are specifically geared towards reaching consensus among a group of stakeholders. An example is the Delphi method (Rowe and Wright 1999).
- **Multi-criteria ranking**: Automatic ranking of the requirements based on the value of multiple relevant criteria and a specific formula that combines these values into a single value (Release Planner 2011).
- **Pair-wise comparison**: Approaches that rely on mutually comparing all requirements and identifying the most valuable one for each comparison. An example is the '20/20 vision' innovation game (Hohmann 2006).
- **Voting systems**: Approaches that involve different stakeholders and ask each one to express his/her preference in some way or another. Examples include the 'Buy a Feature' innovation game (Hohmann 2006).
- **Financial approaches**: Approaches based on financial measures, such as the Internal Rate of Return, Net Present Value or business cases.

The number of requirements available for the next product increment influences the trade-off between a lightweight, coarse-grained approach and a fine-grained, more heavyweight approach. The latter approach can be used when few requirements are available and an in-depth analysis of each and every requirement is feasible. This makes the choice for a particular set of requirements to be included in the next release very well motivated and rational. These approaches do not scale well when the number of potential requirements is high, however, as specifying the value of thousands of requirements in detail is too time-consuming. In such cases, coarse-grained approaches can be applied.

2.5.2.5 Mastering Consensus Models

Inevitably, conflicts will arise when different stakeholders are involved in request valuation. To have a sustainable valuation process, it is important to identify the reasons for such disagreement and take the appropriate measures to reach consensus.

The reasons for disagreement on the value of a particular idea can be manifold: the idea may not be sufficiently clear to all stakeholders. The idea may have a high degree of uncertainty.

Different methods exist to identify such disagreements (e.g., planning poker, various information radiations such as internal stakeholder disagreements and stakeholder satisfaction) (Regnell et al. 2001; etc.).

Planning poker for instance offers a way of reaching consensus. It offers a workshop-based approach in which stakeholders move towards a consensus by stating their opinions and learning from one another. Other ways of reaching consensus include stakeholder weighting, which takes into account the importance of stakeholders, and the multi-step ranking algorithm presented in Tsiporkova et al. (2006).

Some companies use the enlightened product manager approach and reach consensus by definition, as only one stakeholder decides. Other companies are looking for ways to remove the bottleneck of this approach and realize that a model for reaching consensus is a necessity.

Key ingredients for mastering consensus building among stakeholders:

- **Motivating value models and constraint models**: Stakeholders need to understand why the company focuses on certain value elements and not on others. For example, a company desiring to enter a new market may value *speed to market* above *feature richness*, because the company wants to enjoy the first mover's advantage. Without this rationale clearly communicated, it may be hard for certain stakeholders to understand why features that are essential in their opinion are not valued highly.
- **Motivating value and constraint estimates**: Claiming that an idea has a certain value is one thing. Capturing the rationale behind this claim is more difficult, especially when no obvious consensus is reached. Stakeholders should be able to communicate clearly and motivate their reasoning behind their value estimates. In line with the example above, stakeholders will have to motivate why a certain feature is essential despite the fact that it costs a considerable amount of time to implement.
- **Motivating release compositions**: Clear reasoning should be given why a certain release contains the given set of features and why another (maybe equally valued feature) is left out. This motivation starts by clearly motivating the goal of the release. Again, in the spirit of the above example, the release goal could be to have a minimal product available for the new target market ready to ship in 4 months from now.

- **Allow the controversial requirements to emerge**: There is usually consensus on the value of most ideas. For some ideas, however, the valuation by different stakeholders can be polarized. It is important that these ideas emerge, as they may be interesting to explore.

2.5.3   Relationships with Other Practice Areas

The Art of Focusing is related to other practice areas in the following way:

- **Art of Focusing**:Within the Art of Focusing, the company sets forward the concrete innovation goals, thereby (partially) indicating what kind of values the company is looking for. This gives guidance to the value and constraint models as well as the release composition activity.
- **Art of Openness**:A company will have to decide which stakeholders to include in the value association activity. It may opt to include stakeholders that are not part of its own organization (e.g., customers, suppliers, etc.).
- **Art of Idea Harvesting**:The link to idea harvesting is obvious; without ideas and requests, there is no real need for valuation.
- **Art of Innovation Incubation**:Ideas that are considered worth pursuing are candidates for incubation.

2.5.4   Questions

- How do you evaluate and rate (feature) requests? Do you follow any specific process (workflow)?
- Which criteria do you consider important for evaluating features?
- How do you compare different ideas?
- Who evaluates (feature) ideas?
- What do you do when people do not agree on idea valuations?
- How do you define the focus for a release?
- How do you select features to include in a release?
- Do you trace decisions to motivate why a feature is (not) selected?
- What are the typical disagreements with valuation?
- What happens when stakeholders do not understand certain features?

2.6 The Art of Openness

Timo Koivumäki, Kaisa Koskela, and Pirjo Näkki

2.6.1 Description and Scope of the Art of Openness

The Art of Openness practice area deals with finding the best ways for different types of software companies to use the opportunities of external resources – enhancing the company's competitiveness by using external knowledge in the innovation process and creating new revenue streams through exploitation of external channels.

Increasing dynamics in the business environment, such as the rapid pace of technological development, intensified competition through market globalization, evolution of customer needs and new technology-enabled value creation possibilities, have challenged software-intensive organizations to work more openly also in terms of innovation. The nature of the software industry, and the ICT industry as a whole, has confronted radical chances, and the scarce resources inside companies are therefore not enough to maintain their competitiveness in the dynamic market. In order to be successful, software companies need to discover ways to use the innovative potential in the ICT environment by opening the boundaries of their value creation processes. In fact, a company's ability to absorb external knowledge has become one of the main drivers of competitiveness (Spithovena et al. 2009). Equally important is learning to maximize the value of in-house ideas that are not suitable for the company by taking them to the market through external channels (Chesbrough 2004).

The Art of Openness is closely related to the concept of open innovation introduced by Henry Chesbrough (2004). Although the concept has become widely used, the software viewpoint is largely neglected in the general open innovation discussion (Pikkarainen et al. 2009). Open source communities have been used as a source of innovation in software development, but there are also many other possibilities for practising openness that emerge due to the special nature of software. Openness becomes easier as software products and services can be shared at virtually no cost once they have been produced. Different versions of the software can thus be distributed to customers and other stakeholders for testing and obtaining improvement ideas already before the product launch – if a fixed launch is needed at all. More and more software products are used online, where continuous updating and improving of the software is possible. Many software companies also provide public feedback and idea channels to involve users in the continuous innovation process. User innovations occur, especially when the software is used, when users find new practices and purposes for it. Online collaboration tools can also be used for customer and/or user involvement during the software development phase. New ideas can come up when increments of the product can be available to the stakeholders all the time.

The Art of Openness can take many forms and should in itself not be the purpose. Very few companies can be described purely as open or closed. Instead, openness should be seen as a continuum that ranges from more closed approaches to more open ones (Paasi et al. 2010). A company needs to find the strategy most suited to its situation – the type of software product and the characteristics of the markets. Openness is a strategic decision in the company and is supported by high-level management, though the actual practices can vary from case to case.

2.6.1.1 Outside-in and Inside-Out Approaches in the Art of Openness

Basically, the Art of Openness can be practised in companies using two different approaches, namely the outside-in and the inside-out approach, or by combining the two (Gassmann and Enkel 2004). The outside-in approach refers to the internal use of external knowledge through which companies can integrate, for example, external stakeholders into the process of exploring and co-creating new innovations. Dell IdeaStorm[1] is a good example of using innovative ideas that reside within users. Dell IdeaStorm is a web site launched in 2007 on which users can post development ideas related to Dell products. Another successful example of using the outside-in openness approach is the SAPiens community established by SAP in 2007. SAPiens is a community platform for students and academics within the scope of the SAP University Alliances Programme.[2] Using or licensing external software components in a company's products is another example of the outside-in approach.

The inside-out approach deals with the external exploitation of internal knowledge. The key benefit is that through activities such as licensing and commercializing ideas in different industries, companies can gain faster access to the market than through internal development. This way, companies can also increase their revenues through a wider customer base. Companies relying on open source software in their commercial products are good examples of successful inside-out openness strategies. For example, Sugar CRM[3] offers its basic customer relationship management solution as free and open source software, but the more advanced professional version is sold at an annual fee. MySQL[4] is another example of a company that provides the open source code free, but additionally sells training, certification, consulting and support services. These companies use the external developer community in the development of their offerings and receive revenue from the supplementary services.

A combined approach, in which outside-in and inside-out approaches are incorporated in order to benefit from external knowledge and new opportunities of idea commercialization, can be carried out in, for example, strategic cooperation

[1]http://www.ideastorm.com/.

[2]http://www.sdn.sap.com/irj/scn.

[3]http://www.sugarcrm.com.

[4]http://www.mysql.com.

partnerships or networks/alliances. In a strategic partnership, the focus is not on bringing resources over the company borders (inside or outside) but on innovating together. Co-creation challenges the whole business model of the company, as the owner of the ideas and products can no longer be strictly defined, and a win-win situation is more difficult to achieve, although it would be highly beneficial to all parties (Prahalad and Ramaswamy 2004).

2.6.1.2 Approaching the Art of Openness at Three Different Levels

The Art of Openness can be considered at three different levels: product, process and business/strategic level.

Openness at product level revolves around the topic of opening up the product in different ways. For project-based and out-of-the-box software companies, this could mean, for example, using open source software as part of the product or contributing to open source communities and that way gaining recognition that can lead to profit-making orders in the future. Online services can be opened to third parties at the application programming interface (API) level so that other services can interact with them or even create new services combining your product with those of others (so-called mash-ups). A speciality of the software domain is that, when working on customized software product development, you do not need to create the customizations from scratch but can use pieces of other parties' software (via Open APIs or open source) freely as part of your own offering, which saves your resources. The customization can even be left to the customer itself, if your software is made to be modifiable.

Openness at the process level deals with opening up company processes to external influences/resources. Process-wise, a software company can apply the Art of Openness in different phases of the process and by using different external resources. The resources can include new technology, ideas or other input from different stakeholders. An out-of-the-box software company, for example, can use its large end-user base and co-create with the users in several phases of its innovation process, e.g., idea generation and testing prototypes or including the users as active participants throughout the new product development. For software companies involved in project-based development, a close relationship with the customer is natural. Customized product development companies can cooperate with third parties to create standards for new APIs or create other technical enablers for software customization.

The business/strategic level recipe for software business has been to constantly create new innovative out-of-the-box products that can be sold to the masses at a virtually non-existent marginal cost. Due to the increasing pace of new emerging technologies and the speed of change in the business environment in the software domain, this has become a challenging path to follow. To tackle the challenges of finding a new competitive edge, companies are turning to more and more customized offerings, preferably mass-customized in the sense that users can customize their products themselves. Openness is one of the key enablers of this shift because close producer-client interaction is one of the key sources of value co-creation.

2.6.2   The Art of Openness – Main Activities

2.6.2.1   Specifying an Openness Strategy

The openness strategy specification deals with evaluating the company's existing business model, vision and strategy and then deciding on the appropriate openness strategy. The strategic decision on the degree of openness includes analysing the value of the Art of Openness, i.e., the way openness affects the company's value creation, the timing of openness (when/how long in the product cycle to be open) and the type of openness suitable for the company (Fig. 2.10).

The value of the Art of Openness to the company depends heavily on the underlying business model. Chesbrough (2006a) states that the business model has two essential functions: (1) it creates value within the value chain and (2) it captures a share of the value for the focal firm in the chain. Sometimes, the company's existing business model can present constraints on the use of open innovation. For example, if a company is committed to a closed product ecosystem, such as Apple, a relatively closed approach to product innovation may be the rational choice. Apple has succeeded in reaping the benefits of openness on the application side of the ecosystem, however, i.e., the App Store. As Chesbrough (2006a) points out, redefining the existing business model towards openness could create significant benefits for the company in terms of both cost savings (leveraging external resources) and additional revenue (spin-offs and licensing fees).

R&D management issues may also present challenges when applying openness to the company's innovation and engineering processes. Greenstein (1996) points

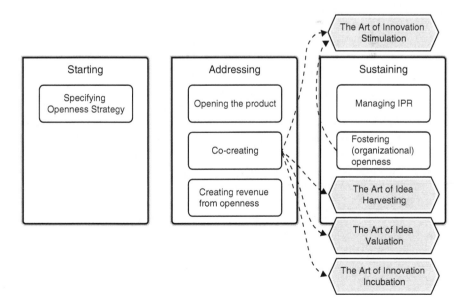

Fig. 2.10 The art of openness, relation to other practice areas

out that openness increases coordination costs because it requires the cooperation of multiple actors (e.g., suppliers, complementors). Almirall and Casadesus-Masanell (2010) argue that the degree of openness that is suitable depends on the complexity of the product under development. They state that very complex and very simple products are unlikely to benefit from openness. Simple products have little to gain from the more complex process, and complex products may be hampered by increased complexity and communication challenges between partners. In their view, the products that are best suited to open innovation are those of medium complexity for which the benefits of open innovation outweigh the negative effects. Boudreau (2006) found that in the case of complex systems, closed innovation is more successful in the early phases of the innovation process. Later when the complexity is reduced, however, different kinds of, for example, co-creation approaches are more successful.

2.6.2.2 Opening the Product

This activity encourages software companies to adopt a new kind of perspective when thinking about their products. Could opening up the product or parts of it provide novel opportunities for your firm? In some cases, the whole product can also be open, as in the case of pure open source products. What would be the benefits of, e.g., transforming a proprietary software product into an open development and integration platform and allowing your customers to make their own modifications to it as SAP did (Farhoomand 2007)? These decisions are related to the type and degree of openness of the product and are closely linked to the company's business model.

A software product can be opened up in several different ways. One strategy is to make software products that feature a high degree of 'connectivity' to other products. This can be achieved, e.g., with open standards that companies create together to ensure that different products are interoperable. With regard to open standards, a company can even decide to try to create a new standard in the market.

Software companies can also consider making the product accessible through an open API. This approach can only be applied to parts of the product, e.g., for certain data sets that are not crucial to the company. By enabling different software to interact with each other, companies can also find new synergies and revenue-creation opportunities. Another approach to open APIs is to make the product as a mash-up that uses and combines information from several sources in order to create new value.

Open source software also creates many unique opportunities for software companies. The company can create the product entirely through open source or turn an existing product into an open source community. For example, the development of the software development environment Eclipse first started as an internal IBM project, but later on, the software was published as open source and a foundation was created to further the development of the software. Using software from open source communities can be a viable option to buying or building decisions. Open source communities can also be used as a channel for releasing software that no longer creates value in-house.

Ecosystem thinking should be considered in the activity of opening the product: in an open environment, products and services cannot be considered separately but as parts of the bigger product ecosystem. Products by different players can be combined if the combination yields more value than the individual components.

2.6.2.3 Co-creating

Here, openness at process level is called co-creation. It means interactive value creation with customers, users, partners and other stakeholders starting from the early phase of the innovation process (Prahalad and Ramaswamy 2004; Piller and Ihl 2009). Software companies can involve customers and other partners in direct collaboration during the ideation and software development phases. Customer involvement is essential, especially in the project-based software business. Customers' ideas and needs must be heard, and they can be involved in development processes, e.g., using workshops in which developers and customers meet.

In addition to customers, the actual end-users of the software product offer huge innovation potential. They are the experts of the use situation and can therefore provide valuable insight into the way the software product could be developed. In the context of B2C software products, users can even be involved in the daily practice of software development via the Internet. New versions of the software can be opened for, e.g., a group of beta testers who provide feedback and improvement ideas for the developers. Users, as well as other software builders, can also participate in the actual software development either by modifying the original software, developing add-on components or integrating different components as mash-ups.

Co-creation activities can integrate the whole value network – not only customers and users but also suppliers and other software product builders, with whom an alliance can be created to target new markets. In the case of customized software products, other stakeholders can also participate in the customization, either in collaboration with the company or on their own if the company provides a toolset for customizing the software based on own needs.

Co-creation activities can be divided into closed and open co-creation. Closed co-creation involves known partners with established business relationships. The objectives of closed collaboration are twofold. First, closed co-creation networks can be used to increase intra-network knowledge and collaborative learning. Second, these closed networks can be used to achieve direct commercial gains. When the necessary level of trust between partners has been gained, the contractual agreements can be rather informal to ensure the innovativeness of projects. When dealing with open co-creation networks with unknown participants, it is essential to make sure that vital IP and tacit knowledge are protected with the proper level of agreements. Hence, the level of contractual protection preferred in co-creation networks will be higher the more unknown the network participants.

2.6.2.4   Creating Revenue from Openness

Openness at the strategic and business level is addressed in the activity of creating revenue from openness. The prerequisite for creating revenue from applying openness to software innovation is the reformulation of business models to adapt the openness perspective. As one of the key purposes of a business model is to identify how the company can capture its share of value creation, the inclusion of the openness perspective can help companies define new ways to create and extract value, e.g., through creating new open product ecosystems. An example of active new ecosystem creation is the FlexiDis project coordinated by Phillips Electronics in which the goal is to create flexible displays that can be bent, rolled up or even attached to clothing. Such flexible displays will create a plethora of new markets ranging from supermarket displays to e-readers.[5]

One of the main drivers of increasing openness is the possibility of gaining revenue streams from innovations that are discarded during the innovation process and are not used in the core offering of the company. Software companies are constantly making go and no-go decisions on their innovation and development projects. When targeting stable known markets, these decisions can be made with fairly complete information and, hence, the percentage of false project terminations (and the number of lost revenue opportunities) is marginal.

Due to the increasing speed of change in the business environment of the software domain, stable markets are becoming scarce and companies are being forced to venture into new uncharted markets. This means that companies are forced to make go-no-go decisions under increasing amounts of uncertainty: How will technological development change the markets? How will our customers' needs evolve? What other potential markets exist for our inventions? This change in markets creates a challenge for companies: increased uncertainty leads to an increase in lost revenue potential due to less accurate decision-making.

Chesbrough (2003b) introduces the metaphor of playing poker to describe the management of innovation when facing uncertain markets. According to the poker metaphor, when faced with information uncertainty, companies need to find a way to reduce the probability of lost revenues due to false termination decisions. One way to tackle this challenge is to adjust the innovation strategies and business models to embrace openness.

Openness strategies in innovation exploitation, i.e., the inside-out strategies, are means for companies to manage the increased market uncertainty. These strategies include licensing or selling innovations that are not used in the company's own products and establishing spin-off companies to commercialize the discarded innovations. The use of open source as a means to reach new markets can also create new revenue streams. At the end of the practice area, the case of Mahiti Infotech highlights the opportunities of open source. Sugar CRM and MySQL,

---

[5]More information at http://cordis.europa.eu/fetch?CALLER=PROJ_ICT&ACTION=D&CAT= PROJ&RCN=72069.

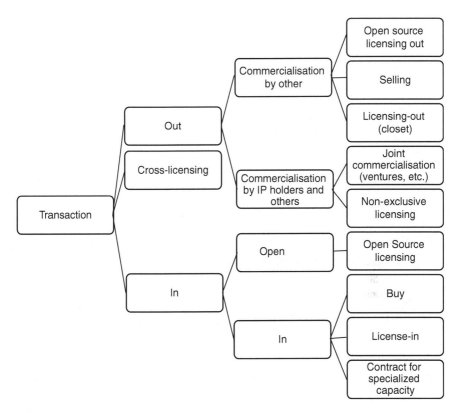

Fig. 2.11 Types of transaction relationships (Paasi et al. 2010)

discussed earlier, are good examples of this type of inside-out strategy. Due to these in- and outflows of ideas and knowledge and possible different licensing schemes, IP management plays a crucial role in the implementation of the defined strategies (de Jong et al. 2008; Chesbrough 2003a, 2006a) (Fig. 2.11).

2.6.2.5 Managing Intellectual Property (IPR)

Intellectual property rights (IPR) are an obvious aspect affected by openness. In IPR management, two different practices can be recognized: external sourcing of innovation (protecting IPR when collaborating openly) and external commercialization of innovation (selling and buying IPR).

With regard to external sourcing of innovation, IPR and ownership of the products must be considered carefully before starting open collaboration. Among the organizations, contracts should clearly state the roles and rights for the outcome of the collaboration. When involving consumers and users in the innovation process, their rights for the innovation must also be expressed. The ownership of all the results of user-driven, open innovation typically belongs to the company, but users must also gain some benefits. In Internet-based crowdsourcing, in particular, users know that their contribution is voluntarily and for them it is enough to obtain better products instead of a share of the revenue.

There are different strategies and approaches for managing IPR in an open innovation context. IPR can be purchased and sold either directly between partner organizations or by using intermediaries. New innovations may also lead to the establishment of spin-off companies.

The awareness of issues related to IPR and its management should be communicated between all the layers of the company from management to product development. In software companies, the developers need to be aware of the consequences of, e.g., using open source components in the firms' products or sharing company-sensitive information in open source communities.

2.6.2.6   Fostering (Organizational) Openness

As the foundation of all innovation is ideas and knowledge that reside inside the people involved in the innovation process, fostering corporate culture that nurtures openness practices within the company is crucial to increasing the possibilities for companies to benefit from the Art of Openness. In other words, companies should avoid the 'not invented here' syndrome by all means if they want their openness activities to succeed.

In making their R&D efforts suitable for applying openness, companies need to focus on both team and individual level motivation and working practices. Hence, this activity is closely linked to the Art of Innovation Stimulation. Ancona et al. (2002) showed that teams that are externally focused, adaptive and see positive results across a wide variety of functions and industries would be most successful. They state that successful teams emphasize outreach to stakeholders inside and outside the company boundaries and that this entrepreneurial focus will help them to adapt easily to a changing environment.

In addition to the organization of teamwork, motivation can be regarded as a key enabler of the Art of Openness in practice. According to de Jong et al. (2008), individual and team level innovativeness can be motivated by investing in employees' ideas and initiatives, creating autonomous teams with dedicated innovation budgets or stimulating employees' external work contracts in order to enhance opportunity exploration.

In an open innovation context, different partner organizations constitute a business ecosystem. Coordination and management are needed at the inter-organizational level in addition to each organization's own processes. An essential task is to identify different stakeholders in the innovation ecosystem and define their roles (e.g., customers, users, competitors, subcontractors) and the importance to their own organization. Once the network exists, trust must be built among the participants.

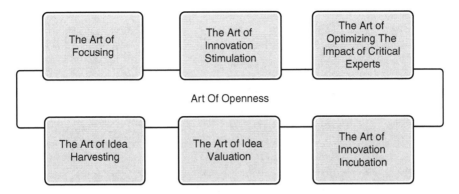

Fig. 2.12 Relations of the art of openness to the other practice areas

2.6.3   Relations with Other Practice Areas

The Art of Openness practice area can be considered as a context for other practice areas. The decisions made about the type and timing of openness affect all of the other software innovation practice areas (Fig. 2.12).

The relationship between the Art of Openness and the Art of Focusing is twofold: first, the innovation goals and targets set in the Art of Focusing affect the decisions related to openness. Second, inputs (e.g., information, technologies) obtained by opening up innovation activities may have an impact on innovation goals.

The Art of Openness has a major impact on the kind of innovation stimulation activities that should be applied. Inputs obtained by openness may act as innovation stimulation inside the company. It is also important to foster such an innovation culture in which openness is encouraged.

With regard to the Art of Optimizing the Impact of Critical Experts, it should be remembered that by applying openness, companies are not only restricted to the resources inside the firm. Instead, depending on the type/degree of openness, they have the opportunity to access almost unlimited resources outside the company. If a company relies on external resources, they can also become critical.

It is necessary to be able to measure and evaluate the effects of the chosen openness strategy on products, processes and business in order to adjust the decisions. Thus, the Art of Improving Innovation is also very important from perspective of the Art of Openness.

The strategic decisions of the Art of Openness impact on idea harvesting, depending on the degree and type of chosen openness strategy. For example, it is important to plan, how the ideas are harvested and from whom. It should also be noted that the company could act as a source of ideas for others.

Furthermore, depending on the decisions made on the Art of Openness, it is important to determine, how the external ideas are evaluated and by whom, what kind of ideas can be shared or published and what will remain confidential.

With regard to the Art of Innovation Incubation, the type and timing of the Art of Openness offers new possibilities, for example, external resources can be brought into the incubation process. It is important, however, to determine which external people are involved in the incubation phase and how.

2.6.4   Questions

- What could drive you to make your organization more open?
- How could your product/organization benefit from external innovations? What kind of risks are there with respect to openness for your product/organization?
- Which forms of openness are relevant to your product/organization?
- At what stages or phases of your innovation process would openness be applied?
- To what extent do you involve different stakeholders in your innovation process? Could you involve them more?
- Do you know the end-users of your product? How could you use their innovation potential? What kind of value would they gain from co-creation?
- How could your company use social media and online communities to obtain external ideas?
- How do you make your product open?
- What is the role of open source in your business?
- Which stages or phases of you innovation process could be opened?
- What is the timescale of openness (continuous or in certain phases)?
- Which stakeholders and roles are needed (e.g., customers, users, competitors, subcontractors)? What is the importance of each stakeholder in each phase of the innovation process? Which innovation tools can be used?
- Which other resources are needed?

2.7   The Art of Optimizing the Impact of Critical Experts

Nick Boucart, Vladimir Blagojevic, Olivier Biot, Wim Codenie, Peter Stuer, and Jeroen Deleu

2.7.1   Description and Scope

Imagine that you are the CEO of a software company. Your company has successfully brought a software product and accompanying services to the market. You faced some fierce competition, but in the end, you managed to establish your position in the market. You did not sit still to enjoy your victories; instead, you observed the market, the competition and the technology landscape. You realized that you need to stay on the bleeding edge. You have therefore identified a clear focus for your innovations and put forward some challenging innovation targets that your company needs to address (see Sect. 2.3).

You ask yourself: What are the critical resources that our software company needs in order to achieve our ambitious goals? Which activities are critical and who do we need to partner? Ultimately, who are the critical **experts** when it comes to realizing our innovation goals?

You quickly realize that answering these questions is far from trivial but that providing an adequate answer to them is crucial to success. You understand that new developments in software products can largely be traced back to the contributions of just a few (Greenspun 2002; Brooks 1995). You know that the difference in productivity and impact of innovation between an expert and an average software engineer can be as great as ten to one[6] (an extensive discussion on the origins of the $10\times$ productivity differences can be found in McConnel 2011).

At the same time, you know that these experts are scarce. The OECD has already reported that the acquisition of skilled human capital is seen as a key challenge in the software sector (Stryszowski 2009). Even if you could identify exactly the kind of experts you need to address your innovation targets successfully, you may have a hard time accessing them. Some of these resources will not be working for you. You may think of some *earlyvangelists* (Blank 2005b) or lead users (von Hippel 1986) who could help shape your new products and services, but you really wonder how to reach them and how to engage with them. Nevertheless, these people are critical experts to your innovation targets: they possess knowledge and experience that will be key to the success of your innovations.

You understand that your company should cherish experts who are critical to the success of your innovation targets and create an environment in which these experts can have their biggest impact. The *Art of Optimizing the Impact of Critical Experts* is all about creating such an environment in a software company.

Critical experts may be internal (software architects, software engineers, product managers, etc.) or external to the organization (customers, domain experts, etc.).

Which people can make the difference between a successful and a failed innovation in software development? The answer depends very much on the context in which a particular software company operates.

2.7.1.1   Critical Experts at the Technical Level

Technical experts have deep knowledge and experience of technical matters. In a typical software organization, experts can be identified in a wide range of areas. Senior software architects, software developers, testers ... can all become critical experts at one point, depending on the needs of the project and the history of the

---

[6]In traditional engineering environments, the difference in productivity between an expert and an average engineer is two-three to one.

product. In today's complex software environment, many engineers are seen as critical, as few people have a complete overview of the situation.

2.7.1.2 Critical Experts at the Product Level

Product experts translate the market demands into tangible products and product functionalities. Their job is to define the product vision, translate that vision into a product roadmap and define the individual software releases that implement this product roadmap. Product managers will engage with many stakeholders, including sales, marketing, development, support and customers.

2.7.1.3 Critical Experts at the Business Level

Business-oriented experts are a third category of critical innovation experts. They include project, sales and marketing managers and CEOs. These executives are able to generate and pursue new business opportunities and may also be able to rethink the current business approach and innovate at the level of the company's business model.

Three examples of companies and their critical innovation experts are presented below.

Example 1: A start-up company that wants to bring new software to the market. Consider a start-up company. The innovation target of this new venture is to build a solid business around solving a pressing customer problem identified by the founders of the company. They envision a software solution as the answer to this problem. They realize that there is still a long way to go from idea to viable business however. They have identified the critical experts as:

- An entrepreneur that is strong in **customer development**. According to Steve Blank (2005b), customer development is about testing the founder's hypothesis on what constitutes a product/market fit with the minimum feature set, thereby answering the questions: Does this product/service, as specified, solve a problem or a need that customers have? Is our solution compelling enough that customers will want to buy or use it today? You know you have achieved a product/market fit when you start receiving orders (Blank 2011).
- A committed and flexible **software developer.** In order to attain a product/market fit, prototypes may have to be built to test hypotheses. The start-up will need to have access to a committed software developer who can build these prototypes fast and without the need for formal specifications. Ideally, he/she can 'hack' together a prototype overnight, just in time for a crucial demo to a promising prospect.

Example 2: An established software company with a legacy out-of-the-box product. The company in this second example has been active in the market for several years. It launched its flagship software product 6 years ago and has evolved it ever since. Today, it is shipping release 4.2. Under pressure from customer requests, its once simple product has evolved into a complex one overloaded with features. The company has decided to rethink its product fundamentally for its upcoming 5.0 release, whereby the product will be broken down into a suite of dedicated solutions targeting specific market niches.

They identified the most critical experts as:

- A strong **product manager.** The product manager's task is to define the upcoming release. He/she has defined four targeted applications to be derived from the big monolithic product that is sold now. The product manager is constantly battling the urge to make the software more complex for the end-users. In parallel, he/she is preparing the existing customer base by explaining the new product vision and soliciting feedback. He/she works closely with the **sales** and **support** teams so that these teams are ready when the new version launches.
- An enlightened **software development manager.** The role of the software development manager is to guide the whole team through this tough transition. It is clear that release 5.0 is not just another release with some new features and re-factorings. The developers will have to reinvent the product, unlearning old assumptions and thinking patterns, and it will all need to happen under serious time pressure. The development manager will have to coach the team not to give up on good habits (the focus on quality, the collaboration in tightly knit Scrum teams) while shielding the team from the pressure inflicted by product management.
- **Senior software architects.** Only a few people in the company qualify as senior software architects. These architects joined the development team early on in the development of the product. They were responsible for selecting the architecture, the technologies used, the design, etc. In this new endeavour, the senior software architects await a difficult task. They need to 'forget' the product's legacy architecture and rethink the product in terms of the new product vision. Some of them see this as an excellent opportunity to phase out some of the older technologies used in favour of state-of-the-art open source alternatives. Others will have a hard time letting go of the old, familiar product architecture and design. Notwithstanding these difficulties, the company needs to rely on the team of senior architects to redesign the product in a future-proof way and count on the architects to translate their years of experience into a new product vision.

Example 3: A project-based software company with a strong ambition to grow. This third example presents a company that builds custom software. The company delivers all its software through customer projects. The company is very successful and has optimized the way it deals with these projects by deploying dedicated teams located at customer sites.

To realize its ambition to grow, the company cannot simply accept more projects. In fact, in its current business model, it can only generate more revenue by executing more projects, for which more staff are needed. This does not scale very well, especially when talent is scarce.

An alternative growth strategy is to develop new services and/or products of higher value. To realize this, the following experts are critical:

- **Product visionaries** in a service company: these are people with a strong vision of creating new, high-value offerings. They can see beyond the operational day-to-day project work and engage the organization to realize new offerings. They usually have a tough job arguing their case to the management to obtain enough resources to realize the vision. The management will have to balance an immediate return from ongoing customer projects and investing in new, more risky ventures. If such product visionaries are not endorsed by management, there is little chance that the company will allow experts to be allocated to high-risk, new service development instead of being deployed at customers' sites where they generate revenue by the hour.
- **Domain experts** working at the customer's premises: the project company deploys a large number of people at customers' sites. Its best experts are often the ones who are most wanted by the customers. These are exactly the type of experts who can prove very valuable when the company intends to develop new services. Their domain knowledge in itself is invaluable and their knowledge of the customers and their needs is indispensible.

2.7.2 The Art of Optimizing the Impact of Critical Experts – Main Activities

Five activities across three phases must be mastered in the Art of Optimizing Critical Experts (see Fig. 2.13). Each activity is described in detail in the remainder of this section.

2.7.2.1 Innovation Bottleneck Identification

Once a software company has defined its innovation targets (see Sect. 2.3), it needs to understand what kind of activities, resources and partners are key to realizing the targets (Osterwalder 2010). Some of these activities are straightforward to implement, while others may pose real innovation bottlenecks.

Some examples of innovation bottlenecks are presented below:

- **Lack of customer insights when targeting a new market.** A company aiming to serve a new market should ideally have strong knowledge of that market. Are there differences in legislation with respect to the home market? Do customers in the target market use the same vocabulary as customers in our existing markets? Do customers in our new target market understand technology like our current customer? Not having a deep knowledge about the new target market could seriously endanger the success of the endeavour.

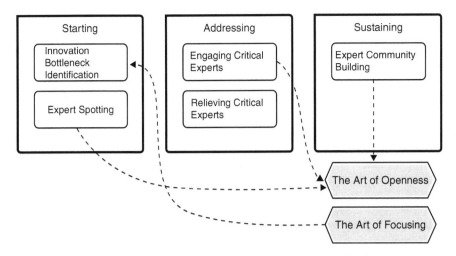

Fig. 2.13 Activities of the art of optimizing the impact of critical experts

- **Lack of software technology expertise in non-software companies.** An increasing number of non-software companies identify opportunities to enhance their current offerings with the support of ICT and software. Many of these companies are experts in their own domains but lack knowledge of ICT and software technologies. Four types of knowledge need to be acquired. First, these companies have to establish a technology scouting program to understand the complex software technology landscape (Rohrbeck 2010). Second, they have to be able to understand the opportunities of a particular technology in their context. Third, they have to master the specificities of the selected technologies. Finally, they have to acquire the necessary skills to manage software and ICT development projects. Without access to such critical experts, a company in this situation will have little chance of success.

2.7.2.2   Expert Spotting

Through expert spotting, companies are better able to understand who to look for when specific expertise is needed. Expert spotting is often a consequence of identifying innovation bottlenecks: once a company explicitly identifies certain innovation bottlenecks, it can start looking for people to address these bottlenecks, either inside the organization or outside it.

Different strategies are used by companies to spot experts. An in-depth overview of the expert seeking problem and a number of solutions is given in Yimam-Seid and Kobsa (2003). The authors state two reasons for seeking experts: the need for *information* and the need for *expertise*. Often both needs meet in one expert search quest. The former requires users to formulate their needs in terms of information, which typically boils down to translating the request in a search query on an information retrieval system. In the latter case the needs are more complex to state, since the expert's skill levels often play an important role.

Traditionally, knowledge intensive organizations have been investing in creating and maintaining **expert databases**. These systems burden management and experts to encode and update their skills by hand. It is observed that these skills are often stated in a very generic way and are infrequently updated, while expert search operations tend to use very fine grained qualitative criteria (e.g., expressing the level of acquaintance with applying a certain technology in a very specific context under special restrictions). The scope of these systems is often the organization's staff, which obviously disregards experts external to the organization.

Knowledge intensive organizations create more knowledge today than they will ever be able to document explicitly. Creating and maintaining an exhaustive and up-to-date corporate knowledge encyclopedia in the spirit of the French eighteenth century encyclopedists is an illusion. These **knowledge repositories** are however an important source of tangible and digitally accessible and transferrable know-how. In this context, the need for an expert often boils down to accessing undocumented knowledge, efficiently identifying relevant expertise, re-formulation of a problem into more directed search statements, or in interpretation of knowledge in a particular context.

Example Web 2.0 realizations of such knowledge repositories are IBM's Wiki Central (IBM Wiki Central), a corporate wiki open to any participant, and IBM's internal Blog Central blogging platform. Both platforms have tens of thousands of members today (Lewis 2008).

Identifying experts via knowledge management systems means searching for 'know-who' instead of 'know-how'. By smartly combining Web 2.0 technologies with semantic technologies such as text mining and ontologies and social metrics, a host of **expert search solutions** have been proposed. An example is the Technorati blog search service (Technorati) which uses tagging and social metrics such as reference counts for determining a blog author's authority for a given search query. A similar approach is presented in Dooley et al. (2002) where the authors propose a solution for accessing knowledge that is outside your own area of expertise.

Some companies encourage team members to 'broadcast' their whereabouts. In another words, the experts announce to the rest of the organization what they are working on, which lessons have been learned, etc. At a later stage, this can be used by other people in the organization to track the missing pieces of information or, at least, to locate the expert who may have a solution to a given issue. Scrum (Scrum) is an example of a process that promotes this broadcasting, as all team members have to communicate what they have been working on during daily stand-up meetings.

Another strategy is the use of innovation tournaments or innovation boot camps to spot experts. During boot camps, a team tests its new venture idea or validates the validity of an existing venture from fellow entrepreneurs. The team is simulated to assemble an entrepreneurial venture. An example of such a method is Innocoop, which is described in one of the case studies in this book (see Sect. 3.13).

Finally, an interesting technique for expert spotting was suggested by Sarma et al. (2009). This paper described Tesseract, a tool that mines data from software code source repositories and issue tracking databases, and tries to link experts to certain software artifacts. The tool provides an interactive visual exploratory environment that utilizes cross-linked displays to visualize the myriad relationships between artifacts, developers, bugs, and communications. Microsoft also has an initiative, Codebook, that uses social network techniques to find experts (Begel et al. 2010).

2.7.2.3 Engaging Critical Experts

Even when a company understands which people are most critical to successfully pursuing innovations, it does not mean that these people are accessible and available. They may be occupied on other projects, as is often the case in project companies. Alternatively, these critical experts may only be found outside the organization (e.g., lead users, external experts, etc.). Having access to these critical experts, if only for a very short period in time, can impact an innovation significantly. A software company therefore needs to understand how to access and, even more importantly, how to engage the critical experts in a timely fashion, carefully avoiding overloading them.

Three key questions need to be asked when setting up engagement with experts:

- **When do you need to engage the expert?** Timing is a crucial factor. It is important that experts are involved early enough, so that their contributions can make a difference. Involving a senior architect in code reviews 3 days before shipping a large release will not make a big difference. When the critical experts are not readily available, their involvement should be anticipated and prepared upfront.
- **How will you access the critical experts?** Which channels will you use to reach out to them and trigger them? This may be easy when the critical experts are part of the team, but it can be much harder when you depend on experts outside the company.
- **How will you obtain commitment from your experts?** You may know who your critical experts are, you may even know where to find them, but how are you going to ensure that they engage with your innovation challenge? How will you answer the 'what's in it for me'? question. In some cases, explicitly recognizing someone as an expert and simply asking him/her for an expert opinion is enough. In other cases, you may have to put in much more effort to obtain the proper engagement.

Consider two examples of how experts are engaged in software companies. The first example is based on the product owner in (Scrum Schwaber 2002) as a critical expert. The second example focuses on technical experts outside the company.

Example 1. Scrum recognizes the criticality of the product manager by introducing the explicit role of *product owner*. His/her role is to understand which features create most business value for the company. The product owner communicates this understanding to the team. Scrum introduced explicit access channels, timings and means to obtain commitment for the team and product owner: during the sprint planning meeting, the product owner and team sit together to discuss priorities and plan the next software increment. During the sprint review meetings, the team demonstrates the product increment to stakeholders, effectively creating an access channel to stakeholders, allowing the team to solicit feedback on its work.

Example 2. Today, technology makes it easier for software engineer to explore weak ties[7] with experts outside the organization. Software engineers can connect to online communities in which experts in specific areas are present to exchange experiences. For technical software engineering questions, engineers can turn to a community like Stackoverflow (Stackoverflow), a Q&A community entirely devoted to solving technical software engineering challenges. Platforms such as LinkedIn (LinkedIn) or more recently Quora (Quora) offer like-minded professionals the ability to create groups around certain topics. Many software-related groups can be found there. Many of these platform support some form of reputation management, whereby users gain more recognition when they success-fully engage with others.

2.7.2.4   Relieving the Experts

The pressure on the experts is high. Their knowledge and experience are often in high demand. Ideally, the software company will deploy measures to relieve the pressure off these experts, allowing them to concentrate on those tasks that abso-lutely require their expert input, while unloading less critical activities onto others. The experts can be relieved in many ways:

- **Planning the availability of critical experts**: By carefully planning and anticipating where and when experts will be needed, companies can hope to ensure the availability of those experts at the times when they are needed most. This will only work well when future expert needs can be anticipated correctly.
- **Capturing expert knowledge**: Some software companies ask experts to create documentation on the development processes, experiences, product architectures etc. The aim of this effort is to make expert knowledge available to all. Training is organized in which experts teach team members best practices, standard operating procedures, etc. Larger companies, in particular, apply this strategy, often forced by external factors such as safety or other types of

---

[7]In sociology, **interpersonal ties** are defined as information-carrying connections between people. Different kinds of interpersonal ties are identified: *strong, weak* and *absent*. The 'strength' of an interpersonal tie is a relation of the amount of time spent between people, the emotional intensity and the intimacy of their interactions (Interpersonal ties) (Granovetter 1973).

certification (e.g., ISO, CMMI). Training sessions are organized through which team members gain expert insights in domain knowledge, technical expertise, etc. These are often supported by (online) tools such as **wikis, frequently asked questions**, etc.

- **Formalization of processes**: Companies often try to formalize processes to relieve experts from being involved all the time. By using checklists, best practices, etc., which are often developed by the field experts, companies hope to leverage experience and knowledge from experts, without the need to access the experts themselves. Another example of formalization is the development of common frameworks, in which software architects develop a common architecture for use in many projects. This reduces the critical importance of software architects in individual projects.

- **Automation**: Many companies seek to automate the contributions of expert resources. Automation is one example of the formalization of processes. An example of automation is test automation: while testing experts initially spend their time defining the best possible test suite for a given software product, they often end up performing these tests over and over again, leaving little or no time for inventing new tests. By automating the performance of the tests, test execution can run automatically (or at least be attended by less experienced testers), freeing up the testing experts to create more impact with new and better tests.

- **Specific collaboration models**: In some agile software methodologies, such as eXtreme programming, the use of pair programming and pair rotation is advocated (Beck 1999). With pair programming, each developer task is taken up by two people who share a computer. Combined with pair rotation (i.e., the developer pairs split up after the completion of their tasks to form new pairs for the next task), these collaboration models aim to make all developers experts or, to put it another way, to actually ensure that there are no critical experts at all. Although this can be helpful when a company has innovation bottlenecks in the development area, these models are hard to realize when the critical experts are outside the software development team.

- **Critical resource community building**: A promising new approach is to build online communities aimed at creating redundancy around the critical experts. Project companies deploy communities of practice around specific engineering topics. Out-of-the-box software companies, on the other hand, use customer communities to solicit feedback on products and services. This is illustrated in the next activity.

2.7.2.5   Expert Community Building

In order to keep the practice area of optimizing the impact of critical experts alive and sustainable, software companies tend to build communities around their most critical experts. This way, software companies hope to create enough critical mass around the individual experts, effectively lowering their criticality.

Many **project-based software companies** deploy *communities of practice* (Wenger et al. 2002) to bring together experts in domains such as software architecture, software testing, security, service-oriented architectures, etc. Companies do this to leverage the expert's experiences beyond the project they are working on. This allows project-based companies to increase effectiveness and efficiency.

Example: Community of practice on software architecture. Steria, a large service organization, started a community of practice around software architecture. Software architects working on different customer projects were invited to join and discuss issues, best practices and experiences of different complex software architectures. The aim of the community was to ensure that experience and best practices did not become 'trapped' inside individual projects. The members of the community document and share their findings on an online platform, making their experiences accessible to a broader audience within the company. It is a trend that more and more software companies support their communities of practice with online Web 2.0-inspired tools, such as wikis, forums and Q&A platforms (McAfee 2009),

Many **out-of-the-box** and **customized product software companies** are interested in building user communities around their products or brand. The goal of such communities is to extract insights into how users perceive the company's products and services. These insights then help product management to steer further development. Companies organize focus or user groups, and many out-of-the-box software builders organize yearly conferences to bring together customers and learn from them. In this area, Web 2.0 and social media are also increasingly used by software companies to solicit more and better feedback from customers. Dell's Ideastorm (Ideastorm) is an example of one such online community.

2.7.3   Relations with Other Practice Areas

This practice area is supportive towards all the other practice areas. Two practice areas, in particular, interact with the Art of Optimizing Critical Experts:

- The **Art of Openness**. As already indicated in this chapter, some of the company's critical experts may not be found inside the company. Engaging with these critical experts should be considered carefully and needs to be aligned with the organization's stance towards openness.
- The **Art of Focusing**. Defining your critical experts with respect to innovation is hard when you do not have explicit innovation targets. It is only in the context of a specific innovation target that the innovation bottlenecks can be identified and start to be addressed. The Art of Optimizing the Impact of Critical Experts therefore has strong interaction with the Art of Focusing.

2.7.4   Questions

With respect to the Art of Optimizing the Impact of Critical Experts, company leaders should ask themselves a number of pertinent questions:

- Who in our software company are the critical experts when it comes to innovation? Are these experts technical people, people with excellent market and customer knowledge, our senior software architects? For each type of critical expert, why are they critical, what exactly makes their contributions so valuable?
- In our organization, how do we keep track of who is knowledgeable about what? What do we track with respect to knowledge and experience? Do we monitor and model technical skills, customer experience, product knowledge, etc.?
- How do we make sure critical experts are involved at the time when their impact is greatest? And, how do we do this without overloading them?
- What measures do we take to relieve our critical experts? Can we relieve them? Can we implement measures that will ensure that their impact increases without necessarily increasing the pressure and workload on them?
- How do we determine when expert advice is needed? When and how can our teams call on expert help?
- Do we have expert teams/champions/centres of excellence? Should we build some form of community around our most critical innovation experts?

2.8 The Art of Crafting Smart Products

Jessie Dedecker, Wim Codenie, Jeroen Deleu, Stefaan Vermael, and Pico Lantini

2.8.1 Description and Scope

Today, ICT technology is omnipresent in everyday environments, and it is used to support a broad spectrum of activities. It's a Smart World ICT products are ubiquitous in industrial, public and private environments. A consequence of this successful adoption is that the number of ICT products used by a single person has soared. This is the case for professional as well as private use (a qualitative representation of this evolution can be seen in Fig. 2.14).

In contrast, the attention bandwidth of users has not increased. People have a limited capacity to absorb and control the ICT products with which they come into contact. A typical user understands merely a fraction of the possibilities that these ICT products can offer. What is more, for a typical user, the abundance of ICT products in his or her environment has reached an emotional and cognitive saturation point (Rutkowski and Saunders 2010).

This gives rise to what we call *the bottleneck of the attention bandwidth*. It leads to users who are saturated and intimidated by the number of ICT applications they have to use. Users have to divide their attention between many different products, so they have less time to spend on a single product (a product can be anything from an ICT appliance to a web service).

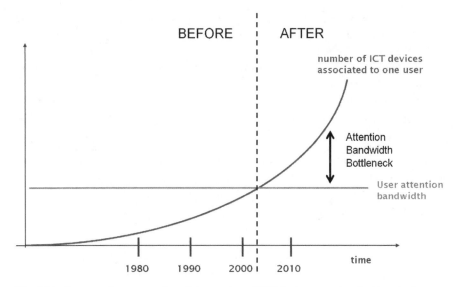

Fig. 2.14 Conceptual representation of the number of ICT devices associated with a single user

One effect of the attention bandwidth bottleneck is that users are becoming more receptive to software products that demand less attention and effort to use. This has consequences for the way in which product builders have to innovate in their product portfolio. Before the bottleneck arose, software innovation boiled down to feeding users with new functionalities to which they responded favourably. Due to the bottleneck, such a strategy is becoming outdated. The transition in user needs offers software companies a growing opportunity to revise their product innovation strategy with the aim of responding to the growing need to make their products more attention bandwidth-efficient (Norman 1998).

Another consequence is that it introduces a new dimension of competition for software companies. As there are so many software products available, it becomes increasingly difficult to stand out in this growing jungle of software products. This results in a race for customer attention. In addition to the normal competition model that governs their market, software companies now compete with many other products to receive the (limited) attention of the user.

The challenges presented above need not necessarily be perceived as a threat. On the contrary, they can present themselves as opportunities to exploit the possibilities offered by the new generation of ICT technology. We identified two families of opportunities:

- *Opportunity 1: product innovations that respond to the problems of attention bandwidth pains of users.* As argued above, the number of ICT products users have to deal with today is many times that of just a few years ago. Users are more conscious of the attention bandwidth problem and prefer products that either only require a limited amount of their attention bandwidth or increase it. An ICT product builder can differentiate its product portfolio by building products that help users to address this problem.

Question 1: *How can an ICT product builder innovate in its product portfolio to address the problem of attention bandwidth?*

- *Opportunity 2: product innovations that respond to the new level of competition between ICT products.* This type of product innovations exploits the oversupply of ICT products. This oversupply generates a rich ecosystem of building blocks. A product builder can draw on multiple open data sources, available technological infrastructures and innovative business models (Osterwalder and Pigneur 2009). Companies can innovate in their product portfolio by responding to this new reality.

Question 2: *How can ICT product builders identify and exploit the existing sources in an ICT ecosystem and combine them with their own product portfolio?*

Question 3: *How can ICT product builders reposition their product portfolio so that it can serve as a source for other players in the ICT ecosystem?* (Bartels 2009)

Both opportunities boil down to a common industrial challenge: *How do I innovate in my product portfolio to make it 'smart' or 'intelligent' with ICT?*

This brings us to our definition of a 'smart product', which is a product that uses information about *itself*, the *environment* in which it operates or other products in its environment, with the aim of differentiating it in its market.

Smart products can address the attention bandwidth bottleneck in several ways. In general, the goal is to offer products that show proactive behaviour, i.e., they rely on the knowledge inside the product, the environment or other products to predict, detect and support the user's intentions as closely as possible so that the user is relieved.

This can be done in different ways (Eggermont 2002):

- *Monitoring*: A product monitors an environment and only informs users about relevant opportunities in the environment, e.g., a surveillance system with motion detection that alerts the operator only when there is activity in the observed area. This relieves the operator from continuously having to scan the screens (hence addressing the user attention bottleneck).
- *Advising*: A product advises the users (proactively) about a particular strategy to realize an intention. Users are free to follow the advice if they wish, e.g., a car navigation system detects the user's position and offers advice on how to proceed to a location.
- *Assisting*: A product is in constant interaction with the user during the realization of the goal. For certain tasks, the product actively assists the user during the execution, e.g., Toyota™ introduced an Intelligent Parking Assist System that allows the car to steer itself into a parking space with little input from the user.
- *Intervening*: A product can intervene when a user makes a wrong decision, e.g., in a chemical plant, a software system could stop the production line when a life-threatening situation occurs.

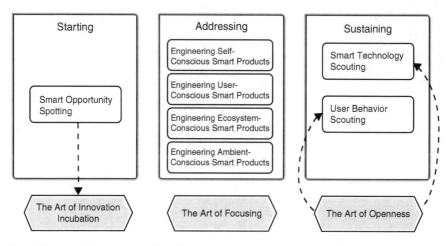

Fig. 2.15 Activities of the art of crafting smart products

2.8.2 The Art of Crafting Smart Products – Main Activities

Seven activities across three phases must be mastered in this art (see Fig. 2.15). Each activity is described in detail in the remainder of this section.

2.8.2.1 Smart Opportunity Spotting

The focus of this activity is on identifying the opportunities that a software company has for making its product smart or smarter.

Four strategies can be adopted to make products smarter with software. They are depicted in Fig. 2.16 and explained below.

- **Self-Conscious Products**: A self-conscious product is one that uses assets that are already available within it to offer new value to existing or different users. For example, Automatic Data Processing™ is a US-based company that processes payroll data. It possesses knowledge about the wages of personnel at different companies. This company aggregates these data (anonymously) in a new service called the ADP Employment Report™[8] and offers them to investors, governments and HR departments. The company has made its product more self-conscious and has created an additional revenue stream by exploiting data that it already had in its possession.
- **User-Conscious Products**: A user-conscious product is a product that is designed to be aware of its users (e.g., user preferences, goals, intentions,

---

[8]http://www.adpemploymentreport.com.

Fig. 2.16 A framework for reasoning about opportunities for making products smart

emotions, etc.). Based on this information, the product can adapt its behaviour, i.e., to offer user bandwidth-saving functionality. For example, a provider of news content (e.g., an online newspaper) can analyse a user's preference with respect to the kind of news articles he or she reads. Based on this information, it can offer a personalized news stream that contains the articles in which the user will be most interested. This relieves the user from having to search through the news items.

- **Ecosystem-Conscious Products**: An ecosystem-conscious product is one that is designed to be aware of other products and platforms that are (or can be) used together with it. Many different software ecosystems (e.g., AppExchange™, Apple App Store™, iGoogle Widgets, etc.) have become available. For example, Zoho CRM™ exploits the Google Apps for Businesses™ platform that integrates with Gmail™ so that account managers can track all emails sent from within the organization to an account. Besides such integration possibilities between these two cloud applications, the platform also acts as a marketplace for B2B products. An example is a hardware ecosystem around the ioHomeControl™ in which different businesses in home automation systems have jointly developed a standard that enables different home automation components to interoperate.
- **Ambient-Conscious Products**: An ambient-conscious product is one that uses information about the operating environment of a product to offer new value. This type of smart product exploits the wide variety of sensors that is available today. For example, a city-wide bicycle rental service could embed sensors in bicycles to gather information about the location of the bicycles. This would enable the bicycle rental service to recover bicycles that were not returned. If sensors were also added that could measure noise and other pollution, it would allow such a company to sell this information to governments. Note that the sensors do not necessarily need to be hardware sensors. The short geo-tagged

messages from a service like Twitter™ could also be used as sensors. This would require the text messages to be analysed with text algorithms.

Applying this smart product framework to a product will usually result in a substantial list of opportunities that need to be filtered to a shortlist. When filtering opportunities down to such a shortlist, it is important to know where to put the focus (see Sect. 2.3). Such filtering can be done by scoring the opportunities according to the value they would bring and the risks associated with pursuing them (see Sect. 2.5).

2.8.2.2 Engineering Self-Conscious Smart Products

Engineering of self-conscious products is the extension of a product with ICT functionalities that exploit the assets available in that product in some smart way. In order to engineer self-conscious products, it is important to ask a number of questions that can provide an insight into how to approach such opportunities.

What is the inventory of available assets to exploit?

Engineering of self-conscious products starts from an in-depth analysis of the assets that are available within the product portfolio of the company. An asset can be data-oriented (e.g., a data set stored in a product), a community (e.g., a user community using the product) or an algorithm. It is important to understand which assets are unique with respect to the competition and which assets are a commodity. This can change over time, as illustrated by digital cartography.

> Less than a decade ago, digital maps were unique and required huge investments (special trucks had to drive along all roads to chart the different roads and accompanying traffic signals). This made digital maps a unique asset. More recently however, efforts such as OpenStreetMaps[9] have used public communities to create cheap and accessible alternatives so that the digital maps themselves became a commodity. Vendors of commercial digital maps were forced to partner with application providers (e.g., the acquisition of TeleAtlas™ by TomTom™) that could provide them with a community[10] (e.g., TomTom™ enables its users to send updates about changed roads and traffic conditions, which enables them to update the digital maps much more frequently).

When drawing up the inventory of available data assets, the underlying structure of the data should also be taken into account because it can heavily influence the usability of the data for a specific purpose. Semantic technologies such as RDF, OWL and other metadata systems may provide solutions to bring the data into the necessary formats, perhaps also complemented with a partial redesign of the existing underlying data models.

> In the example of the payroll software (see Sect. 2.8.2.1), customers of ADP™ will probably use different titles for their employees. In one company, an employee may be called a 'software engineer' whereas in another company an employee performing the same

---

[9]http://www.openstreetmaps.org.

[10]Navigation Companies Crowdsource Maps, Traffic Services,http://www.wired.com/gadgetlab/2009/02/user-generated/.

tasks may be called a 'software developer'. To aggregate the information, these titles need to be matched.

Which available third-party assets can complement my assets?

In order to realize a value proposition based on the existing assets of the product, some data sets that are required to realize the value proposition will often not be in the possession of the company. Besides preparing the existing data models, it may therefore also be necessary to gather new types of information that are missing.

This information can come from third-party resources (e.g., address information can be looked up by querying the Google Maps™ API; a company called InfoChimps™ provides an API to access different kinds of data, allowing companies to share them).

Some information may at first not be readily available in the product itself but can be harnessed by redesigning parts of the existing product based on Crowdsourcing techniques. For example, Google™ optimizes search results by analysing user behaviour with respect to search results, i.e., after a search query, the user chooses to visit one or more links that the query has returned. These clicks can be considered votes by users on which results were relevant and which were not. By logging these clicks, they can be used to further optimize the results that were returned.

Finally, once all the necessary data are gathered in the required formats it may be necessary to process the data so that they are made available in the required format. This processing of information is not always straightforward from a technical point of view and may require the use of advanced AI algorithms, such as neural networks. For example, in the case of optimizing the search results by logging the clicked links, a multilayer perception network may be used to learn the ranking of a link for a given set of keywords.

How can the available assets be transformed into innovations?

A first option is to explore whether it is possible to use the available assets to offer functionality for a safe attention bandwidth for the user. The frame described in the introduction to this chapter can be used to do this:

- *Monitoring*: Can the assets be used to offer monitoring functionality?
- *Advising*: Can the assets be used to offer better advising functionality?
- *Assisting*: Can the assets be used to offer better assisting functionality?
- *Intervening*: Can the assets be used to offer intervening functionality?

A second option to explore is whether it is possible to 'package' the assets somehow as a new service in which other parties would be interested. An example is the ADP Employment Report™ service discussed above.

2.8.2.3 Engineering User-Conscious Smart Products

A user-conscious product is aware of its user and offers functionality that exploits this awareness.

A *user intention* is some kind of goal or purpose that a user wants to achieve and for which he or she will use the product (Why are users using your product?). Examples of intentions include business goals (e.g., generating a report, paying employees, increasing sales …) and personal goals (e.g., weight loss, learning to run a marathon …)

When realizing their intentions, users are influenced by different parameters. Examples include:

- *The role of a user in a collaborative workflow.* Is the user a decision-maker, an expert … Depending on the role, users will act differently.
- *Emotion.* Depending on the emotional state, users will act differently, e.g., Google offers a feature (Gmail™ Goggles) that prevents users from sending emails in a drunken state. A number of sensors have also become available in recent years to detect the emotional state of users (Conati et al. 2003; Alastair et al. 2008; Gill et al. 2009 Sebe et al. 2004).
- *Stress level.* Users under pressure will behave differently to those in a relaxed environment.

To provide advanced support for user intentions, software products should capture these parameters in order to understand the information related to a user who can influence the realization of a particular user intention (= *the user state*). For example, in a stressful situation, the support of the software product may shift from merely 'monitoring' to 'intervening'.

The crafting of user-conscious products requires insights into these two important aspects of the user: the *user intentions* and the *user state*.

The following questions need to be answered.

How will the user state and user intention be captured?

In some situations, the user intentions and user state remain the same throughout the use of the product. In this case, it can be considered during the requirements analysis phase and the design phase of the software product.

In other cases, it may be necessary to observe the user when he or she uses the product, so that the behaviour of the product can be adapted to changes in user intention and/or user state. Many options are possible:

- Attaching physical sensors to the user (e.g., to measure stress)
- Non-intrusive observation of users (e.g., with cameras)
- Observing how the product is used (e.g., by logging the actions users perform)
- Observing social software platforms in which the user is active (e.g., what can be derived from public information on Facebook™)
- Use of user profiles (e.g., asking users to provide a profile)

How will knowledge about the user state and user intention be used in product innovations?

First of all, it will be necessary to include a model of the user state and user intention in the software product (e.g., emotion model). The size and complexity of this model depends on the kind of information that needs to be captured: Which intentions are relevant for capture? Which emotions are relevant for capture? What information about the user is important with respect to the tasks that he or she is doing?

Next, this model has to be used to offer product functionalities. An example is the Volvo-On-Call-Plus™ system that detects car crashes. When a car crash occurs, it automatically sends the last known GPS location to a dispatching service and puts it in contact with the driver through a speaker system. After assessing the situation with the driver or, in the case that no one is able to respond, the dispatching service can warn the emergency services.

2.8.2.4   Engineering Ecosystem-Conscious Smart Products

Ecosystem-conscious products are aware of other products present in the user environment. They attempt to use this awareness to realize new value propositions. The result is a so-called *product ecosystem* in which each product has its own value proposition but can lever the value offered by the ecosystem to make its value proposition stronger.

Examples of ecosystems include:

- iPod™ Ecosystems: Apple has created different ecosystems around its iPod™ product. One such ecosystem is geared towards car manufacturers that enable the iPod to be controlled from the car audio system. Another ecosystem combines the iPod™ with Nike™ running shoes via a sensor in the shoes so that an iPod can select music based on the rhythm of the runner.
- Google for Businesses™ is a B2B platform that enables cloud-based business applications to interface with the different Google Business Applications. Different types of integrations can be made, such as access to Google Mail, Google Calendar, etc. The platform also acts as a marketplace.

You can either decide to participate in an existing ecosystem (such as Google for Businesses™, AppExchange™, Facebook™, etc.) or become an initiator of an ecosystem. Decision criteria include:

- The availability of assets (e.g., data, user communities, etc.) of interest to your product in other products used by your users. A product such as Google for Businesses™, which has gained a fairly large user community of SMEs, becomes interesting as a new channel to reach customers. It is also important to gain a good understanding of which products, besides yours, a user uses to perform his or her tasks. Once you have this insight, providing a smooth integration (from the perspective of usability and data) can help in addressing attention bandwidth bottlenecks.
- You have an asset to **share** with other products. Successful products may have assets that enable it to create an ecosystem around it. For example, Heroku™, a cloud-based platform provider, opened its platform to third-party component developers once it gained a critical mass of application developers. In this case, the asset was the community of application developers. In order for such an ecosystem to work, it is important to search for win-win combinations in which both the owner of the ecosystem and the participant have sufficient benefits.

- You capture information that would be better captured elsewhere. Another way of looking at it is to shift the capturing technology away from your product. Is there another product that does a better job of capturing the data that could be of benefit to your product? And, would/could you connect to it?
- You want to enter a new market. New markets have their own dynamics with which you may not be familiar, but you may have assets that are new and disruptive to this market. Finding an ecosystem that is already established in this market may offer a way to gain access to the required resources to address this market.

Three main challenges will need to be addressed.
What is the impact on the product from participating in an ecosystem?
Joining an ecosystem requires rethinking about the product in the context of the ecosystem. Below are some strategies on how the product can be rethought in the context of the ecosystem.

- **Simplification of the product**: joining an ecosystem can provide an opportunity to reduce the complexity of using a product. Users who make use of different products to work towards a goal can expect the different products in the ecosystem to cooperate towards achieving this goal. For example, consider a salesperson who needs to drive from one customer to another. The car navigation system can automatically set the destination by consulting the agenda on the salesperson's mobile phone.
- **Enhanced functionality**: joining an ecosystem can also offer opportunities to differentiate the product by offering new functionality. One such example is the iPod™-Nike™ ecosystem, which enables an enhanced running experience that is impossible to achieve without the ecosystem.

How will the product interact technically with the other products in the ecosystem?
Besides the business aspects of creating an ecosystem, there are several technical aspects that have to be taken into account. The product has to be (re)designed so that it supports the interoperability vision of the ecosystem. Choosing the right architecture and technical interoperability standards can make or break the adoption of the ecosystem. For example, in hardware systems, standards can impose certain requirements on the chip or require certifications that increase the unit costs of the product. In pure software products, these issues usually do not play such a big role. In these, the challenge is to provide support for the rich variety of software implementation frameworks and technologies.

How do you set up alliances with other product builders in the ecosystem?
To what extent will other software providers need to be involved. In some situations, the other products may already provide an API or interface that you can use to hook up your product. In other situations, an alliance will have to be set up with one or more other software companies. Another important consideration is to understand the balance of power in the ecosystem. Apple™ was/is often criticized for its unclear policies with regard to the apps it allowed in its App Store™. The result was that several Mobile Apps were rejected or even removed

from the App Store™. Policies could also change at any time so that there was great uncertainty for Mobile App developers.

2.8.2.5 Engineering Ambient-Conscious Smart Products

In this strategy, we aim to make the product aware of the ambient environment (the word *ambient* refers to the product's surrounding environment and is used inter-changeably in the text below) in which it operates. This strategy is implemented by augmenting the product with an interface to its ambient environment. Using this interface, it can make interpretations about its environment and use that knowledge in different ways.

Can you become a source of information about the surrounding environment to other parties?

In order to identify the possibilities of becoming a source, an inventory of existing activities and an understanding of the possibilities of ICT technologies with respect to collecting information about the surrounding environment (=potential ambient data-sets) are required.

For each of these, its value, uniqueness and sustainability have to be considered so that a business case can be developed.

> Example: A bicycle rental company has different (automated) rental stations posted across the city. People enter their credit card into one such station to rent a bicycle and return it to one of the many stations posted throughout the city. The company considers integrating GPS tracking devices into the bicycles so that lost bikes can be found. It could go one step further, however, by integrating other types of sensors into the bicycles. Sensors that can measure air and noise pollution could be used to gain an understanding about its evolution over time. Such information has the potential to be sold to local governments.
>
> Example: A mobile phone operator has multiple cellular network masts posted across a country. It has the ability to track the position and movements of mobile phones across the network, and by aggregating this information it can identify traffic congestions.

The examples above illustrate how existing business activities can be leveraged by fitting appropriate sensor technology to these activities. Note that the sensor technology that is used to collect the required information can be hardware sensors, as in the first example, or software algorithms such as the triangulation algorithms in the second example.

An important consideration when collecting ambient data sets is privacy. In both examples presented above, the tracking of individuals may be problematic from a privacy point of view. By aggregating the information and making it impossible to track information back to individuals, such issues can be handled.

How can the available ambient information be transformed into innovations?

The use of ambient information in applications can provide support for the attention bandwidth bottleneck problem. The examples given in Sect. 2.8.1 illustrate how ambient information can be used to support *monitoring*, *advising*, *assisting* and *intervening*.

Another option is to combine ambient information with information about user intentions.

Example: Consider an alarm clock, for example, that is made aware of the reason a user needs a wake-up call and can take advantage of this information. If a user is woken up with the aim of not being late for work, then it could consider the traffic conditions on the road to work. Based on this information, it could decide to wake the user up a little earlier (e.g., in the case of traffic congestion) or let the user wake up a little later (e.g., in the case of good traffic conditions).

2.8.2.6 Smart Technology Scouting

Several state-of-the-art technologies are available to support engineering of smart products. Examples of these technology domains include:

- Sensor technologies is a big domain that encompasses a wide range of sensors, such as positioning sensors for indoors (Hui and Wang 2006) and outdoors (Sun et al. 2005), sensors for measuring biological processes (Yang et al. 2006), sensors for detecting emotion (Conati et al. 2003; Alastair et al. 2008; Nicu et al. 2004) and software sensors (Fortuna et al. 2007).
- Ubiquitous computing (Weiser 1991; Poslad 2009), pervasive computing (Satyanarayanan 2001) and ambient intelligence (Aarts et al. 2001): these names refer to a post-desktop model of human-computer interaction in which information processing has been thoroughly integrated into everyday objects and activities. In this technology domain, we find technologies that help save attention bandwidth because the objects can process information for their users and interpret that information for them.
- The Semantic Web (Berners-Lee et al. 2001) is a collaborative effort between researchers and industry with the aim of providing a common framework that allows data to be shared and reused across application, enterprise and community boundaries. The data are accompanied by meta-information that enables automatic aggregation and reasoning. In this technology domain, we can find technologies that support sourcing of data and services by (semi-) automatically recombining data and services in a novel manner. Many different standards such as RDF, OWL, SPARQL and Microformats have been developed.
- Web 2.0 (O'Reilly 2005) is a commonly associated web application that facilitates interactive information sharing through collaboration. The technologies for creating web mash-ups are of a form in which information in services can be blended and moulded into a new web service. These technologies can be regarded as enablers for supporting sourcing of data and services in the context of the web.

For software companies to be successful at crafting smart products, the setting up of a smart technology scouting program is an important activity (Rohrbeck 2010). Actively hunting for new technologies and understanding the opportunities they offer is essential to remaining up to date and staying ahead of the competition.

Although many of these technologies have matured to the extent that it has become feasible to employ them in products, not many software companies are actually exploiting their use. This is especially true of smaller companies that cannot afford the resources.

There are so many ways in which these technologies can be used that it becomes difficult for software companies to understand their options and make choices. Some technologies are heavily promoted by the research community, while others are less well known, even though they may be very valuable options to explore. In the domain of ambient intelligence, for example, (wireless) sensors are being used to sense context information. For software companies in domains like *home automation* or *mechatronics,* there is clear innovation potential to incorporate these sensors into products. This is less obvious to software companies in the domain of banking and administrative software however. The differentiation approaches can therefore be very different dependent on the product and company context. An effective and efficient scouting program should take this into account and offer the necessary criteria to decide and steer the technology-hunting in the desired direction.

2.8.2.7 User Behaviour Scouting

Your software company will probably have installed processes to monitor its market and competitors so it can act in time when the market expresses new needs or competitors launch new innovations.

How much does your company actually know about the other (non-competitor) software products that your users are using today? And, how much do you know about the way your users use your product?

Gathering this information is important because it could provide the necessary knowledge to hook the software product up to other products or to create an enhanced user experience that results in bandwidth savings for the user.

Nagravision™, a company producing set-top boxes for digital broadcasting channels, has found that many users are actually sitting in front of their TVs with laptops, iPads, etc. While watching TV, they are interacting on social networks, looking up extra information on what is being broadcast, etc. In order to better support this combined use of so-called second and third screens with a set-top box, it has created a multi-screen consumption model. This enables the integration of cloud- and client-centric models to be combined with the TV watching experience. For example, users can obtain recommendations on what to watch, start watching a fragment on a second screen and flawlessly switch to the TV set and continue to watch it there.

Doing this on a continuous basis is important, as it will generate opportunities to make the product smarter (see Sect. 2.8.2.1).

A straightforward way to gather this information is just to ask your customer through periodical querying.

Other companies carry out brainstorming activities with their customers. One example is innovation games (Hohmann 2006). The innovation game 'Me and My

Shadow' can be used to observe the way users use a product. Another interesting innovation game in this context is 'Spider Web'. The product is placed in the middle of a spider web and customers are asked to what other products they think your product is related. These products are also put on the spider web and the relationships between these products are made explicit.

How and where is your product used?

This question explores the immediate physical space around the use of your product. Explore the possibilities this space could give you in added value by creating a collaborative system. Are there possible collaborations and connections you could make with other products in the environment?

2.8.3 Relations with Other Practice Areas

The Art of Crafting Smart Products relates to several other practice areas:

- **The Art of Openness**: opportunities that are identified in the Art of Crafting Smart Products may require the use of advanced technologies that demand in-depth understanding of the possibilities and limitations. This expertise can be built up entirely in-house or with help from outsiders. The technology scouting activity will provide an insight into choosing the right partners for sourcing the lack of expertise.
- **The Art of Innovation Incubation**: smart opportunities that are of a more disruptive nature or outside the established markets of a company may require an appropriate incubation process. For these opportunities, it is important to gain an in-depth understanding of the market needs and the adoption cycle.
- **The Art of Focusing**: after having identified multiple possibilities, it will be important to choose a focus and to keep that focus from conception to innovation.

2.8.4 Questions

In order to start thinking about the Art of Crafting Smart Products, you could ask yourself the following questions:

- What assets does your product have available in the inventory that are difficult for other parties to replicate?
- Which available third-party assets could complement my assets?
- How can the available assets be transformed into innovations?
- How can knowledge about the user state and user intention be used in product innovations?
- What other products are our users using together with our product? Is it possible to join or build an ecosystem around those products?

- Is it possible to become a source of information about the surrounding environment?
- How can the available ambient information be transformed into innovations?
- What are the technological trends? Who are the potential partners who can allow us to quickly gain the required expertise in these technologies?
- How and where is your product used?

2.9 The Art of Innovation Stimulation

Asta Bäck

2.9.1 Description and Scope

Very often in software engineering, innovation boils down to problem solving and firefighting without any real, long-term innovation culture. Instead, there is an attitude of high productivity and meeting deadlines. In the current competitive environment, companies must be involved in constantly renewing their products, services and processes. The increasing role of software in products and services, and the global business possibilities offer huge opportunities for new innovation but also make innovation imperative.

Many examples and much research show that the most successful companies are able to create new innovations continuously, not just randomly as lucky guesses. This practice area looks at what can be done in a company to stimulate innovation from a wide perspective. It does not only look at stimulating creativity at single events – such as brainstorming sessions – but at the whole company and what can be done to stimulate innovation on a continuous and systematic basis.

A software company should have continuous innovation activities to produce incremental and radical innovations. With regard to software, there are many different areas for innovation. Innovation may concern the purpose of and to whom software is offered; which standards, platforms and ecosystems the software is built on; what the business model is; how users interact with the application; what production methods are used; and solving various specific technical issues.

This chapter includes theoretical as well as practical aspects of innovation stimulation. *Creativity* and *innovation* are closely related concepts. Creativity is what is needed to get innovation started. The main activities relating to innovation stimulation are presented based on the theories behind organizational and individual creativity, and practical experiences.

The natural way to start is to analyse where the bottlenecks are to producing and sharing creative ideas and turning them into innovations. Some things, like the company climate, are slow to change, whereas other things, like learning to use a new creativity enhancement method, can be learnt quickly. For permanent, long-term improvements to the company's creativity and innovativeness, all the levels must be seen to be in order. Quick results are also needed, however, in order to raise interest and keep the motivation up for further development.

2.9.2 Main Activities

Seven activities have been identified relating to the Art of Innovation Stimulation: two to the *Starting* phase, three to the *Addressing* stage and two to the *Sustaining* stage. Figure 2.17 shows all the activities involved in the Art of Innovation Stimulation and their relationships to the rest of the arts.

2.9.2.1 Evaluate Your Organization's Creativity

The first step is to assess the current situation in order to find out what your organization's strengths and weaknesses are in relation to creativeness and innovativeness. This way you can target the development work to tackle the issues that have the highest impact potential but, before measuring, it is crucial to know what creativity and innovativeness are and how they can be assessed.

In this book, we define *creativity* as the ability to produce new ideas and solutions, and innovativeness as the ability to produce new innovations. An innovation starts as a creative idea. Much work is then needed to turn the idea into a real, profit-making product or service. Creativity is also needed along the way from idea to innovation to solve all the issues that are faced during the innovation process.

Based on this definition, *innovativeness* can be measured by looking at high-level performance measures such as the number of new products and services that the company is able to bring to the market on a yearly basis and the revenue generated from them. These kinds of measures can also be used to give concrete targets to innovation stimulation, but they are slow and do not help to identify where the weak spots are. The company should therefore develop additional measures that shed light on issues dealing with creativity – the potential to come up with new ideas.

Seminal research relating to creativity in organizations was published in the nineties. Ekvall (1996) introduced the metaphor of climate to describe the organizational conditions affecting creativity, and Amabile (1997) the componential theory of individual and organizational creativity.

Ekvall's theory (1996) identified nine climate dimensions. These climate dimensions have been shown to discriminate between the best and the worst environments and between the most and the least creative teams. The dimensions are involvement, freedom, trust, idea time, playfulness, conflict, idea support, debate and risk taking (Isaksen and Ekvall 2010).

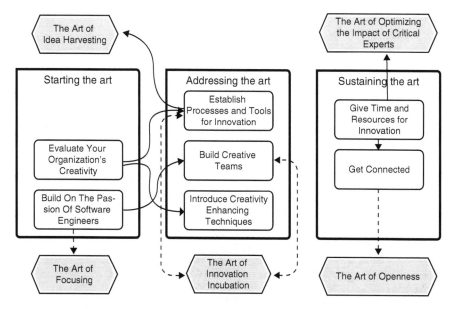

Fig. 2.17 The art of innovation stimulation and the activities involved

Challenge or *involvement* refers to the degree to which people are involved in daily operations, long-term goals and visions. High involvement indicates motivated and committed people.

Freedom describes the independence and autonomy that people have in the organization with regard to their work.

When *trust* or *openness* is high in the organization, people are more willing to share their ideas and to be frank and honest in their relationships with other people in the organization.

Idea time is the time that people can use to elaborate on new ideas.

Playfulness or humour is indicted in spontaneity and ease at the workplace, and these are conductive to innovation.

Idea support refers to the way in which new ideas are treated and people react to each other's ideas.

Risk-taking describes the tolerance of uncertainty and ambiguity, for example, whether people can make decisions without being completely certainty and having all the necessary information.

Debate refers to open disagreements between viewpoints and ideas. Debate contributes to sharing and combining different points of view and knowledge.

Conflict refers to emotional tensions in the workplace. If conflict is high, people fight and plot against each other, which is naturally bad for creativity and productivity in general.

Amabile's Componential Theory of individual/team and organizational creativity (1997) identifies three main components in both of these areas. Individual/team creativity is needed for organizational creativity, and the organization's actions determine whether this creativity flourishes in practice.

The components at individual and team level are expertise, task motivation and creativity skills. The *expertise* component refers to knowledge and skills in the actual professional field in which innovation is looked after. There are two types of *task motivation*: extrinsic and intrinsic. Extrinsic motivation refers to factors like rewards or pressure, and intrinsic motivation refers to personal motivation to work because the person finds the work interesting, exciting and personally challenging. *Creative thinking skills* refer to the cognitive style that favours taking new perspectives on solving problems. Creative thinking skills depend, to some extent, on personality characteristics like independence, self-discipline, orientation towards risk taking, tolerance of ambiguity, perseverance in the face of frustration, and a relative lack of concern for social approval (Amabile 1997). The components of the work environment are *organizational motivation, resources* and *management practices* (Amabile 1997).

Ekvall (1996) and Amabile (1997) have both developed questionnaires that measure factors that their respective models of organizational creativity describe. In Moultrie and Young (2010), shortened versions of these question sets are presented, capturing the main aspects of these theories. Using these questionnaires, organization members can tell to what extent they agree with the presented claims. The results give an overall view of the way people in the organization see the current situation in the company, helping to pinpoint the areas to be improved.

2.9.2.2 Build on the Passion of Software Engineers

Software developers are often highly committed and proud of their work. This can be seen in many open source projects in which developers participate and cooperate in their own time to contribute to a common goal. These open source projects are also proof that it is the person's intrinsic motivation that counts.

This is also in line with the previously mentioned Amabile's Componential Theory of organizational creativity. According to this theory, expertise and creativity skills define what a person *can* do, and the third component, task motivation, defines what a person *is willing* to do. There are two types of motivation: extrinsic or external, and intrinsic or internal. *Intrinsic* motivation is partly a personality issue, but social environment can also have a significant, either positive or negative, effect on a person's level of intrinsic motivation (Amabile 1997). As intrinsic motivation is hard to produce from the outside, it is important to hire people with high intrinsic motivation.

Extrinsic motivation can be used, to some extent, to increase motivation, but it cannot compensate for a lack of intrinsic motivation. It is also important to know that extrinsic motivation measures may even reduce intrinsic motivation. Rewards, recognition, better resources, more independence and frequent feedback on work are examples of extrinsic ways of motivation that are also likely to support and boost intrinsic motivation.

Giving software engineers the opportunity to explore new areas supports motivation and increases the likelihood of them coming up with new ideas. In any case, software engineers often work independently and are constantly making decision that, on the whole, may have a big impact on the final result. When intrinsic motivation and freedom can be aligned with your company's goals to bring true value to customers, much creative energy will be available in the company.

2.9.2.3 Establish Processes and Tools for Innovation

Processes and tools, as well as communication and discussion skills are needed for creativity to bloom. Processes and tools do not make innovations, though a well-defined process for evaluating ideas has been found to stimulate innovation (DeSouza et al. 2009).

New innovations are hardly produced by one person alone. Collaboration and communication are therefore crucial throughout the innovation process. Even though new ideas often require an idea owner or champion who pushes the idea forward in the organization, the idea can only be developed in collaboration with different parties. This development work requires good communication skills. Mock-ups, demos and other concrete results are examples of so-called boundary objects that capture different people's ideas and knowledge in one artefact and make communication between different partners easier. Managers should encourage their people to maintain formal and informal interaction, active listening and constructive controversy. It is also important that managers themselves show, in their everyday activities, that they value innovations and new ideas.

There is an optimal amount of discussion and debate. Closing the discussion too quickly is dangerous because important views of people with different knowledge and backgrounds may be missed, though discussing too many things or for too long without making decisions is also counterproductive and should be avoided.

Another important issue is to realise the difference between productive *debate* and *conflict*. There are different types of conflict. *Task conflict* refers to disagreements relating to work content and includes differences in viewpoints, ideas and opinions. *Emotional conflict* is characterized by anger, frustration or hostility among or between individuals on a personal level. *Process conflict* refers to disagreements over the approach to the task, the desired group processes and the method the group chooses to follow. The first type has been found to have a positive outcome on some research, but the last two clearly have a negative impact on the performance and creativity of an organization (Isaksen and Ekvall 2010).

No organization is completely free of personal tension and conflict, and a complete lack of conflict would probably indicate a complete lack of involvement in the work. The managers' task is to introduce actions to alleviate possible tensions and provide training to people to teach them to focus on task conflict away from a personal level.

Face-to-face discussions are important to creativity, as are various types of tools that can support the collaboration process. In a software company, people already use many tools for communication and sharing of ideas. Communication using email and various other tools is likely be fragmented, however, and does not help in the accumulation of knowledge at company level.

Asynchronous tools like wikis provide means for storing ideas and building and commenting on them in turn, whereas synchronous, real-time tools like Etherpad[11] support co-creation by people in different locations or even face-to-face meetings, making co-creation more effective.

As well as tools for direct idea collaboration, tools that support finding people with knowledge are becoming increasingly important. The bigger the company, the more tools are needed to identify people with knowledge or interest. Various kinds of *social networking tools* play a key role here.

2.9.2.4   Build Creative Teams

Much of the work that is done on creative problem solving and innovation takes place in teams. In requirements engineering, for example, creativity often takes place in a team setting (Nguyen and Shanks 2009).Teambuilding is therefore crucial, and different aspects need to be taken into consideration when innovation teams are being created. The two most important aspects are finding the correct combination of skills and knowledge in the team and making sure that the team can communicate and cooperate well.

A good starting point is to involve people with high intrinsic motivation. The team should have people with different knowledge and backgrounds in order to increase the likelihood of them coming up with creative solutions. The risk of involving people with different backgrounds is that communication between them may become more difficult. Using design-based communication methods such as rapid-prototyping, modelling, storytelling and persona-based scenarios can mitigate this risk. These methods use many human senses and are able to capture some of the complexity of the real world (Steiner 2009).

The use of Agile methods in software development is one of the ways to stimulate innovation. There are two important factors contributing to this: rapid development quickly takes requirements into prototypes that can be evaluated by different parties, and the presence of the customer in the process provides quick feedback based on real needs.

In Cotterman et al. (2009), 32 of *Business Week's* Top 100 Most Innovative companies were studied. The companies that produced disruptive innovations systematically were found to have organized innovation differently, in some ways, to the rest. One differentiating factor was that the most innovative companies had dedicated *cross-functional* groups for innovation, with members from, at least, the technical and marketing departments. They had also *trained* their people for

---

[11]http://en.wikipedia.org/wiki/EtherPad.

their chosen innovation approach and techniques, which gave team members a common language. In addition to internal participants, customers were involved in innovation processes early on. The reward system also has to support innovation, not only at individual level but also at team level.

2.9.2.5 Introduce Creativity-Enhancing Techniques

Numerous methods have been developed to boost creativity in problem-solving sessions. Some examples and practices are presented here to get stimulating innovation started. Information about these methods can be found on websites like Ideaconnection[12], MyCoted[13] and Gamestorming[14]. The frequent use of creativity-enhancing methods is more important than which methods are used.

Future foresight gathers information about future changes in the societal, economic and technical environment, and this material has the potential to stimulate creativity. One way of doing this is through *trend spotting,* which involves gathering pieces of information that may be indicative of bigger changes and new trends. They may be gathered from the web or events, by visiting innovative companies or just by observing media and life. Gathering and sharing observed things such as photos or notes is important to inspire creativity and accumulate different people's observations into a shared resource.

Future scenarios are a way of combining information and visions of future opportunities. Scenarios are typically built by first gathering information about trends and weak signals and then combining and structuring them into alternative futures. Scenarios have the potential to reveal future trends that provide new opportunities or pose threats (Meristö and Laitinen 2009, p. 16).

Brainstorming is probably the best-known method for producing creative ideas. The key is to separate idea generation from idea valuation so that participants also become encouraged to present their funny and crazy ideas. Another basic assumption is that when there is quantity there is also quality. Typically, the first ideas that come up are old, well-know ones, but as the ideation continues, new ideas will emerge. The ideation is typically performed in groups of 6 –12 people in order to bring different points of view into a single group and to give participant the opportunity to build on each other's ideas.

De Bono's *Six thinking hats*[15] is another well-known method of ideation. The hats represent different points of view, such as facts, feelings, optimism and criticality. The method can be used either by selecting different roles for different people or by going through the different points of view together.

---

[12]http://www.ideaconnection.com/thinking-methods/.

[13]http://www.mycoted.com/Main_Page.

[14]http://www.gogamestorm.com/.

[15]http://www.debonothinkingsystems.com/tools/6hats.htm.

Distant thinking models is a method that tries to create new ideas by combining the topic of ideation with some item that is not obviously connected to it. For example, if the task is to improve a sports event, a fishing trip could be selected as the distant thinking model. First, the features and associations are listed for the distant model. As the second step, wild combinations are created by attaching these features to the topic of ideation. Finally, the wild combinations are elaborated further into more practical features or applications (Ojasalo et al. 2009).

Excursion technique can be used when generating new ideas, but it is not very successful. It can be carried out by picking a random object and asking participants to start generating associations and features relating to this randomly chosen object. At a time when the listing by the associations is going well, the leader of the workshop stops and picks the latest association and asks participants to combine it with the topic of the ideation (Ojasalo et al. 2009).

Recently, *spaces* have been specially built for innovation. They are often called innovation labs. These may be built within a company for internal use or offered as a service to a house innovation session. In Madagley and Birdi (2009), the effectiveness of such a lab was studied in the UK. There seemed to be a positive impact, though the impact was dependent on several factors. The use of a special external facility gave the participants the time and place as well as the technical support and human facilitation to concentrate on creative activities.

Virtual spaces, particularly 3D worlds like Second Life seem to hold a promise for creative work. They make it possible for people to meet across distances, and a virtual world can be used to visualize such future products or services that do not yet exist in real world.

Even though the company atmosphere and people's attitudes are of utmost importance to creativity, the daily *physical environment* can also be used to enhance creativity. Space for free discussions on a comfortable sofa, and surprising creative and inspiring objects and media are examples of concrete support for creativity and innovation.

Competitions are a popular form of innovation stimulation, and there is much, though not unanimous, evidence that competition can increase innovation. Competitions may be organized internally or externally, and they can be used in connection with a short or long duration innovation activity. For example, a brainstorming session may be modified into a competition between groups in order to boost the total number of ideas created during the session.

Internal competitions may take the form of an internal challenge to solve issues that are of importance to the whole company or bring new ideas onto the table on a wide front. Internal competitions and challenges also stimulate innovation by showing the management's real support for innovation, assuming that the admitted ideas are handled in a constructive and transparent way.

When designing an actual innovation competition, many aspects need to be decided (Bullinger and Moeslein 2010). Important issues are the competition environment – is it online, mixed or offline – how strictly is the task specified, and what should be presented as the entry – is it enough to present an idea or should it be developed further into a prototype?. Another important aspect to consider is whether the participation is meant for individuals or teams and whether collaboration between contestants is encouraged. If collaboration is encouraged, it is important to support it clearly and well (Bullinger et al. 2010).

Another variant of competitions is to invite students and hackers to participate in a live *innovation camp* in which people gather during an intensive period to code together and quickly build prototypes to demonstrate their ideas.

Before launching a competition, it is important to make sure that your company really needs what the competition is asking people to produce. For example, if the competition is aimed at generating new ideas for future products or services, you need to be ready to *invest time and effort* to evaluate the results and take the most promising ideas into further development. This is likely to be more resource consuming than initially assumed.

2.9.2.6 Give Time and Resources to Innovation

As we have mentioned in the previous paragraphs, Amabile's Componental Model identifies three key elements: resources, management practices and organizational motivation. We have already talked about the last two. The *resources* element refers to different kinds of assets, such as time to innovate, people with expertise and funds (Amabile 1997).

Lack of time and *competing task* are a constant problem, and the recommendation is that the same people should not be involved in developing both existing and new products. If they are, the existing products will tend to take too much of their time, making the innovation project suffer (Cotterman et al. 2009).

In Lindeke et al. (2009), the time dedicated to innovation and cross-functional teams is pointed out as a key factor in innovation, and a model – The *Temporal Think Tank™* (T3™) – is proposed as a solution. In this model, creative people from different functions are assigned to work solely on new product development. For a small company, collaboration with other companies is suggested as a way of making it financially feasible to participate in cross-functional innovation.

Events like *downsizing* (reducing the number of employees in the department or organization) are likely to have a negative impact on creativity. The impact on creativity seems to recover more slowly than performance indicators such as productivity. The biggest drop in creativity is seen when downsizing is expected. *Disruptions* in teams, i.e., interruptions to people's normal collaboration patterns and networks, also have a negative impact (Amabile and Conti 1999).

2.9.2.7 Get Connected

Liu (2011) has looked at the way network structures affect innovation. Alliances play a key role in promoting inter-firm, information sharing and creation. A broad network connection was found to have a positive effect on innovation performance. This can be explained by the fact that a large number of network ties and being well positioned in a network improve diversified information sharing among partners. Broad connections may give unique access to a variety of information and knowledge.

Both the social network view and organizational learning theory confirm that diversity in information and knowledge access is a necessary premise of acquiring and internalizing external resources. Networks also give partners the opportunity to interact, share innovation ideas and to develop mutual understanding and trust. Innovation alliances give companies an opportunity to learn from each other and to exploit that learning in order to develop new knowledge and produce new goods and services, thus obtaining superior innovative performance.

Networking with other companies is important, not only to get new ideas and information but also to be able to meet new customer requirements and seize new opportunities quickly. In Johannessen and Olsen (2010), a claim is made that, in the future, Connect and Provide (C&P) will increasingly replace Research and Development (R&D) as a way of creating new offerings. Using the term *coopetition*, coined by Raymond Noorda, they emphasize the importance of finding new ways to operate by balancing cooperation and competition. Cooperation is needed for creating, sharing and accumulating knowledge, and some competition is necessary to keep companies active in developing their cost-efficiency.

In the context of software industries, especially web-based applications, it is often possible, without too much effort, to gather data on how people use them. This information can be vital for new innovations to be introduced into the product/ service, and it may help the company identify its lead users for closer co-development. Combining this with social media tools to collect customers' opinions and needs can be a great source of information to boost innovations.

2.9.3 Relations with Other PAs

Due to its broad scope, innovation stimulation is connected to many 'The Art of Software Innovation' -book practice areas.

The intrinsic motivation and passion for software engineers is an important asset for creativity. It is crucial that this enthusiasm is focused on things that are useful and interesting to the company and its customers. The Art of Focusing supports channelling of this creative potential in the right direction.

The activity 'Introduce innovation collaboration' supports the Art of Idea harvesting and the Art of Innovation Incubation. Collaboration and communication skills contribute to improving and combining many people's ideas and thereby lead the way to better ideas for harvesting.

The activities in 'Introduce Creativity-Enhancing Techniques' and 'Use Competitions and Games' are connected to the Art of Idea Harvesting. These activities support the actual act of generating ideas.

The need for innovation stimulation is not only about more creativity when generating new ideas. Creativity and creative problem solving are needed along the process to turn ideas into real innovations. Building Creative Teams, Introducing

Innovation Collaboration and Introducing Creativity-Enhancing Techniques are activities that contribute to the Art of Innovation Incubation.

The Art of Openness is one important way of stimulating innovation. Information coming from outside the company about users' and customers' needs and requirements is an important source of new ideas and a source of feedback during the development phase. New solutions can also be sought with the help of open innovation from users and professionals from outside the company. The Art of Openness supports the activity to 'Get connected'.

The Art of Optimizing the Impact of Critical Experts relates to the Art of Innovation Stimulation in the sense that innovation requires resources and time. The most motivated and creative people should not be completely tied to carry out urgent tasks but should also have some time and freedom to explore new ideas and opportunities.

2.9.4   Questions/Checklist

- What are the bottlenecks limiting your organization's creativity?
- Is there a common definition and understanding in your company about what is meant by an idea?
- Is the passion of your software engineers aligned with your organization's goals?
- Do the people in your organizations know how to build on each other's ideas and debate constructively? Are there opportunities for that? Are there tools to support this collaboration?
- Do your employees have good communication/creativity skills? If not, do you have any training initiative to improve this?
- Are different skills, knowledge and backgrounds represented in your innovation teams?
- What motivates people in your company to innovate?
- Which creativity techniques are used regularly in your organization?
- Would your organization benefit from setting up an internal innovation challenge or an open innovation competition?
- How do you obtain feedback from customers or potential users?
- Are your company and its people well positioned in external networks?
- Is your organization ready to start to work on ideas or new solutions that come from outside the company?

2.10   The Art of Innovation Incubation

Jose Antonio Heredia and Minna Pikkarainen

2.10.1   Introduction and Scope

Imagine that you are the CEO of a software company. You launched a product successfully a while ago, released version after version, and gradually captured more market share. Still you do not feel comfortable: new, unexpected players emerge on the market, sometimes with unconventional solutions or business models. They undermine your position and eat away your top line. You realize that your current way of innovating (incrementally producing release after release) will never yield drastic or radical innovations. The art of innovation incubation comes down to this: how can I organize my company so that there is room to go beyond incremental innovation?

Innovation is a series of activities from new idea to new product design, manufacture and marketing (Hui and Wang 2006). Based on the innovative activities, the innovation can be divided into incremental and radical innovation (Hui and Wang 2006). Incremental innovations are progressive and continuous innovations that are caused by the improvement of the existing products or services (Hui and Wang 2006).

For many software companies, the word "innovation" often means *adding new features to the product*. Some techniques such as *total quality management (TQM) principles, lean manufacturing techniques or six sigma techniques provide a basis to manage the incremental innovations (Dismukes, et al. 2009)*. Although, software companies are typically good at managing incremental innovations, these incremental feature additions to the existing products do not always help a software company to create growth or move into the new markets. According to Dismukes et al. (2009) *"focus on incremental innovation will be less effective and potentially counterproductive in the twenty-first century environment"*.

Radical innovations are fundamentally different to *incremental innovations* (Hui and Wang 2006). Therefore, it is not surprising that for many software companies it is quite a new game to manage radical breakthrough innovations that will launch the company into new markets and enable rapid growth or a high return on investment. As a consequence, many software companies are now forced to leave their comfort zone of incremental innovation in search of more radical innovations.

Anyone who has purchased a cell phone in the past few years can see how quickly new types of phones are launched on the market (Chesbrough 2006b). However, radical changes to cell phones (e.g. invention of the phone itself) happen only very occasionally. Typically, *radical innovations* are linked to the entry into new and emerging markets and the adoption of new technologies. In fact, for new industry, radical innovations are often the gateway to new successful markets. (Hui and Wang 2006).

Historically, radical innovations emerged rarely and took decades to reach the market (Dismukes et al. 2009). Nowadays, however, the possibility of using software technologies, more rapid telecommunication, and the open innovation environment (see The Art of Openness practice area) have significantly increased the commercialization time of radical innovations (Dismukes et al. 2009). The faster time to market of radical innovations has also increased the need of software companies to establish more systematic ways of managing radical innovations (Tellis et al. 2009). In this new situation, the companies simply cannot simply rely on incremental innovations. Sometimes a company only needs one successful radical innovation to guarantee a leading position in the market (Kim and Mauborgne 2005). After a long period of incremental innovation, we have seen software companies investing a large amount of money in incubating radical innovations. Sometimes these large-scale initiatives are successful, but too often they fail, causing the company loss in terms of their investments. The reason for the situation is that either the emerging ideas are poorly conceived or the projects are not properly managed (Tucker 2008).

In some studies, 'incubation project' refers to those projects that were novel for the company and required significant investments from critical experts (Leifer 1998). In the context of this chapter, we will use the term *incubation* to refer to the process of realizing radical innovations. We refer to an *Incubation project* as a project in which a radical idea is turned into a profitable business solution.

An incubation project can give several outputs for a company. In reality it may be a new product or service, a new product line or even a new spin-off company. Incubation projects are typically characterized as projects that begin with a high-level technological uncertainty and risks. While working with software companies, we have observed that the typical deployment of an incubation project requires many organizational changes and some increase in the company competences:

- **Incubation projects require a different organization**: If they are not incorporated into a distinct organization or venture, incubation projects have to fight for internal funds on the same terms as other incremental investments in the core business. As maintenance of the actual business is often seen as critical to survival, incubation projects may only receive marginal funds.
- **Incubation projects require different skills**: Companies may have to look for different skills that are not available inside the company. In the case of incubation projects that involve the adoption of new technology, particular technological skills need to be acquired. In the case of an incubation project, attempts to enter a new market and find the necessary entrepreneurial competence for the new endeavour may be a challenge.
- **Finding the right window of opportunity**: It is important that the incubation project is launched at the right time and in the right market segment. If the radical innovation enters the market too early, it may be difficult to find other complementary players to support the innovation development. If the radical innovation enters the market too late, there is a risk of losing the opportunity because the market has already been taken by the competitors (Kim and Mauborgne 2005).

- **Incubation projects require networking competence**: Internal and external networking is critical to the success of an incubation project (Chesbrough 2006b). Internal networking is necessary to ensure that the radical idea is communicated appropriately. External networking permits access to complementary resources but requires careful management (see the Art of Openness practice area, Sect. 2.6, in this book).

For software companies, it is therefore important to understand which management practices they should apply to incubation projects. How can these initiatives be made shorter, less expensive and less uncertain?

2.10.2 Activities of Radical Innovation Incubation

There are several ways of carrying out incubation projects depending on the target markets and the radical idea itself. According to our observations, however, the incubation projects needs to be addressed with the following activities:

1. Radical idea opportunity spotting
2. Experimenting
3. Uncertainty management
4. Business model design
5. Venturing
6. Incubation climate and environment building.

In the following sections, the Art of Innovation Incubation steps are explained further (Fig. 2.18).

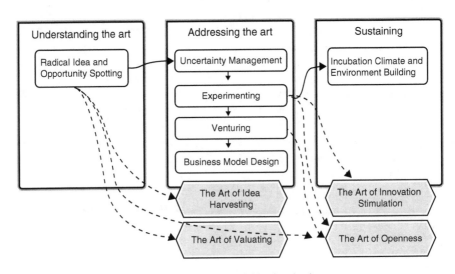

Fig. 2.18 The art of innovation incubation and activities involved

2.10.2.1 Radical Idea and Opportunity Spotting

It is mentioned in the Art of Idea Harvesting practice area (see Sect. 2.4) that the amount of radical innovations do not necessary correlate with the general amount of produced ideas because the probability of ending up with radical ideas does not usually increase with the quantity. Radical ideas can also merge as part of the idea capturing process. It is important for software companies to be able to separate radical ideas from incremental ideas.

Radical breakthrough innovation assessment is a method of evaluating if your idea is radical or not. With a brief look to the literature, we can find few examples concerning radical breakthrough innovation assessments. For example, a company called General Electric developed a light bulb guided by effective technological and cost assessment (Dismukes et al. 2009). Setting of assessment criteria is important for the companies to understand if an idea is radical or not. Often these criteria are company-specific but related either to the new markets or to technologies.

- Market-related criteria: Are your competitors doing similar things? Is your idea addressing a completely new market?
- Technology-related criteria: The *radicalness* may be based on the technical content and the ways in which an invention's technological content differs from the already existing technological state of the art (Dahlin and Behrens 2005).

2.10.2.2 Uncertainty Management

Incubation projects have a high degree of uncertainty, from the technical as well as the marketing side.

Uncertainty Related to Market Transformation

Compared to incremental innovation, radical innovations demand more expensive and time-consuming market studies. Moving to a new market can be difficult. When marketing a radical innovation, it is impossible to predict which will be the successful market segment in the future (Leifer 1998). Each market segment is different and requires separate analysis of the customer and user values and needs in the specific market sector.

There are two sources of great uncertainty related to the market transformation. Firstly, companies lack the necessary knowledge for moving to the new market segment. Secondly, they lack communities of key players and customers in the new market sector.

> "For example, moving from the telecommunication sector to the automotive field demands a huge amount of knowledge about the safety standards and key car manufacturers in the automotive field."

Uncertainty Caused by New Technology Adoption

In incubation projects, some of the critical and central technologies may be new or need to be developed during the incubation project itself. It is uncertain whether the technology idea will work, whether the technology itself can work, or whether there is a product market based on the particular technology.

Most incubation projects require a flexible management style (e.g., agile), due to the uncertain nature of the technologies. Another way of dealing with uncertainty is experimentation, as it is a core instrument for understanding risks caused by launching radical innovations. Experimentation can be used as a way of reducing market risks by checking if the developments are aligned with the market (i.e., potential users') needs and expectations.

Product development involves thousands of decisions. In incubation projects, in particular, the decision-making process needs to be managed explicitly. For example, Leifer (1998) argues that decision-making is more difficult in the early phases of radical innovation than in the corresponding phases of incremental innovation: *"decision making is associated with uncertainty and ambiguity in the context and situation requiring decisions" (Leifer 1998).* The uncertainty is caused by a situation in which it is difficult to ascertain whether the technology will work and which are the customer segments. Ideally, decisions should be delayed until the very last moment in order to maintain flexibility as long as possible and have all available information on which to base the decision.

2.10.2.3 Experimenting

Pursuit of knowledge is the rationale behind experimentation, and all experiments yield information that comes from understanding what does and does not work. For centuries, researchers have relied on systematic experimentation, guided by their insight and intuition, as an instrumental source of new information and advancement of knowledge. Nevertheless, experimentation has often been expensive in terms of the critical expert's time involved, even if it has been essential for innovation (Thomke 2003).

Effective experimentation should not be a random walk of trial and error. There should be integrity in experimentation that needs to be understood. At the same time, experimentation trials need to be coordinated with the objectives of the enterprise and integrated into the overall innovation process.

In software companies, different kinds of experiments can be envisioned:

- Experiments to test new technologies
- Experiments to evaluate a new product concept
- Experiments to understand the product market fit (Blank 2006)
- Stress testing: overloading a machine to see what breaks [note. You also do stress testing when doing incremental innovations as a footnote]

A common way of experimenting in software companies is to build fast and sometimes small-scale prototypes (Thomke 2003). A prototype is a version of a product with reduced features and limited functionality for the purpose of validating key concepts. Typically, prototypes are built to understand the constraints of the radical innovation idea. They enable faster time to market and lower development expenses. Depending on the type of company and the new product, techniques for developing the prototypes may vary (Thomke 2003). Examples of the different types of prototyping techniques are Mock-ups, Beta testing (Neff and Stark 2002), perpetual beta, Living Lab (Følstad 2008), A/B testing,[16] lead users (von Hippel 1986) and pilots. Early prototypes can be as simple as sketches of screens, storyboards or slide presentations. These can usually be made quickly. More mature prototypes include html mock-ups, mash-ups and patchwork prototypes (Thomke 2003).

Approximately 80% of software features are rarely or never used (Hibbs and Sullivan 2009). One way to solve this problem of unused features is to increase the involvement of users in software product development, which is why many software companies organize experiments in which they involve their customer base.

> Google Inc., for example, nowadays runs 50 –200 software experiments at any given time. In one case, Google asked selected users how many search results they would like to see on a single screen. 'More', said the users, 'many more'. So, Google ran an experiment that tripled the number of search results per screen to 30. The company found that traffic declined. What happened? On average, it took about a third of a second longer for the search results to appear – a seemingly insignificant delay, but one that nonetheless upset many of the users. The greater number of results also made it more likely that a user would click on a page that did not have the information he or she was seeking.

For experimentation to be a reliable and effective element of company decision-making, companies need to create an infrastructure for making it happen. They need training programmes to sharpen competences, software to structure and analyse the tests, a means of capturing learning (Thomke 2003), a process for deciding when to repeat tests, and a central organization to provide expert support to all of the above.

For instance, Living Labs are environments for innovation and development in which users are exposed to new ICT solutions in (semi-)realistic contexts (Følstad 2008). A Living Lab is about experimentation and co-creation with real users in real life environments in which users, together with researchers, firms and public institutions, look for new solutions, new products, new services or new business models.

> For example, the Finnish telecom giant has created a lead user community called Nokia Beta Labs that has been given the opportunity to pre-test and give feedback on new products and services that have not been launched on the public market and are still under development. This not only provides Nokia with critical and valuable information on new offerings that are developed but also strengthens its customer relationship with those customers who are qualified to become part of the community.

As more people become involved in experimentation, companies will need to change their focus on education and training efforts for innovation. Instead of merely getting workers to interpret large volumes of data creatively, companies will need to help them develop the skills to design rapidly and provocatively.

---

[16]http://en.wikipedia.org/wiki/A/B_testing.

2.10.2.4 Venturing

Venturing is the process of creating and evolving a venture. The term *venture* is often used to refer to a risky start-up or enterprise company. Ventures can range from internal corporate ventures through joint ventures to spin-offs (Burgelman 1984). Corporate ventures are more appropriate when organizations need to exploit internal competence while retaining control over the business. Joint ventures and alliances involve working with external partners and therefore imply autonomy.

A spin-off of a new business is convenient when there is little relatedness between the core competences of the organization in which the idea originated and the new venture (Tidd and Bessant 2009). One type of venture that is often used by software companies is a community venture. In this situation, multiple software organizations create a community together and bring innovation to the market as an ecosystem. Innovation ecosystems take many forms. Instead of using the closed innovation approach, the companies in the innovation ecosystems search inside and outside the company to find the best resources and business models. Knowledge shared inside the community ventures can be significant especially for new start-up companies and spin-offs (Stuer et al. 2008).

The open source movement is a specific way of launching ventures in the software development field. Most software innovations seem to occur in a social context. In Denning's (2004) words, software innovation has a "social life". An example is the Apache Software Foundation[17] with its suite of products for software developers and administrators. In this community, the developers are also expert users with a strong need for new product features to manage their own work lives.

Some examples of the open source movement, successful communities such as GNO,[18] Mozilla[19] and Eclipse foundation,[20] have a significant impact on innovation. For example, Eclipse is an industrially driven community involving more than 100 companies, universities and contributors. Many of these communities follow various incubation processes. In the first phase, the sponsor evaluates the proposals which are either accepted or rejected. In the second phase the actual incubator checks the project status. At this stage the project is rejected, continued or engaged with other projects. Both proposal evaluation and project status checking can be seen as an entry point to the idea valuation.

2.10.2.5 Business Model Design

A business model is a translation of the strategic issues, such as strategic positioning and strategic goals, of the company into a conceptual model that states explicitly how the new business functions. The business model serves as a building plan that allows the business structure and systems that constitute the company's operational form to be

---

[17]http://www.apache.org/.

[18]http://www.gno.org/gno/.

[19]http://www.mozilla.org/projects/.

[20]http://www.eclipse.org/.

designed and realized. Business model implementation and management include the 'translation' of the business model as a plan into more concrete elements such as an organization (e.g., departments, units, teams), business processes (e.g., workflows, responsibilities) and infrastructure and systems (e.g., rooms, hardware) (Brews and Tucci 2003). Furthermore, the implementation of the business model must be financed through internal or external funding (e.g., venture capital, cash flow).

A business model describes how a company creates, delivers and captures value. Osterwalder's Business Model Canvas (Osterwalder 2010) is a useful strategic management tool that allows the development and adaptation of business models to changes in the business environment. The Business Model Canvas is divided into nine building blocks that together outline the business model elements of the company's business:

- Key Activities
- Key Resources
- Partner Network
- Value Proposition
- Customer Segments
- Delivery Channels
- Customer Relationship
- Cost Structure
- Revenue Streams

Recently, business model design has moved from traditional business model creation to identification of different business model innovation opportunities (Loebbecke and Soehnel 2010). One example of an innovation that provides an opportunity to design new business models is eBooks. In general, there are several players along the value chain of the eBook business. For instance (Loebbecke and Soehnel 2010):

- "Authors are willing to adopt eBooks and the possibilities of self-publishing when they benefit from increasing revenue shares and audience sizes"
- "Traditional publishers receive economic benefits from ePublishing, as manufacturing costs decrease due to the digital delivery and elimination of the printing process"
- "Consumers can enjoy a recognizable look and feel as reading an eBook has become almost as comfortable as reading a traditional book."

Amazon differentiated themselves from their competitors by utilizing the new business model innovation integrated with a new technology solution. They created a Kindle Shop containing more than 4,00,000 eBooks. Books can be downloaded free using a Whispernet mobile data connection. Users are more likely to make impulse purchase decisions using the mobile device (Loebbecke and Soehnel 2010).

2.10.2.6 Incubation Climate and Environment Building

Companies need a great deal of information before they can make decisions about radical innovations. In incubation projects with high uncertainty, the requirements may often change once development has started.

Three broad strategies exist for increasing development flexibility: adopting flexible technologies, increasing management flexibility and exploiting product architecture as a tool to increase development flexibility. One way to manage uncertainty is to reassess the requirements and design uncertainties after each milestone, development cycle or sprint.

> Example: In the Internet-software industry, a common practice is to build a low-function-ality version of the product, put it into customers' hands at the earliest possible stage and adopt an iterative approach to adding functionality. It illustrates the importance of having a development team with experience of multiple projects and implies the creation of a product architecture that facilitates flexibility.

A good practice in incubation projects is to allocate contingent resources or buffers to respond to unexpected difficulties and delays (Loch et al. 2006). This allocation could even be as much as 50% in projects with high uncertainty (Shenhar and Dvir 2007). Oliveira (2009) conceptualized a project as a process whose goal is to reduce uncertainty. Ideally, it should start by addressing market uncertainty, for example, clarifying customer requirements. The process of learning customers' needs and acquiring the necessary technological capabilities gradually turns incubation projects with high uncertainties into projects with lower uncertainty levels.

One problem with radical innovations is that typically the breakthrough does not produce return of investment until years later. To support the funding of incubation projects, software companies can tap into the many funding opportunities that support radical innovations in the domain of software engineering. Examples of such European research programmes that support incubation projects in software companies are ITEA 2,[21] Artemis,[22] FP7,[23] Medea,[24] Eniac[25] and Celtic[26].

2.10.3 Links to Other Practice Areas

There is a link between the following practice areas:

The Art of Idea Harvesting

The art of incubation has an impact on the Art of Idea Harvesting practice area. Radical innovations can be collected and stored in the same way as with incremental ideas, but their origin and identifier are likely to be different.

---

[21]http://symposium2009.itea2.org/.

[22]http://www.artemis-ju.eu/.

[23]http://ec.europa.eu/research/fp7/.

[24]http://www.project-medea.eu.

[25]http://www.eniac.eu.

[26]http://www.celtic-initiative.org/.

The Art of Idea Valuation

Valuating radical ideas can be even more challenging than valuating incremental ideas. This is because decision-making difficulty is associated with an increase in the degree of uncertainty and ambiguity in the decision- making context. Decision about radical idea launching can change the whole future of the software company.

The Art of Openness

The Art of Openness practice area provides companies with activities for enhancing competitiveness using external knowledge. In the case of radical innovation the utilizing of external experts is often even more important than in the case of incremental innovation. Thus, being successful with incubation can require some of the activities in the Art of Openness practice area to be addressed.

The Art of Innovation Stimulation

Innovation stimulation is an important way of supporting company innovativeness, increase the opportunities of the companies for radical innovation creation. Incubation projects need to be stimulated in a particular way. Insights can found in the chapter on the Art of Innovation Stimulation.

The Art of Optimizing the Impact of Critical Experts

In the case of radical innovation, the companies need an ability to reconfigure resources to match to the needs of the new situations. Each radical innovation is different. Each time when the radical innovation are valuated, there is need for the different competences from inside and outside of the software company.

2.10.4   Questions

- What does radical innovation mean to your company?
- What does incubation mean to your company?
- How do radical innovations differ from incremental innovations?
- How do you manage incubation projects today?
- How do you deal with risk today?
- How do you manage uncertainty?
- What could *venturing* mean in your context?

2.11   The Software Innovation Canvas

Minna Pikkarainen, Wim Codenie, and Leire Orue-Echevarria

At this point in the book, we have explored the eight practice areas. Together, they introduce 47 practices for software innovation. The Software Innovation Canvas consolidates this in a single drawing (see Fig. 2.19). The canvas provides an overview of the activities that you, as a software company, can consider to innovate in your software. You can use the canvas as a kind of compass to help you to find the right direction for your journey towards improved software innovation.

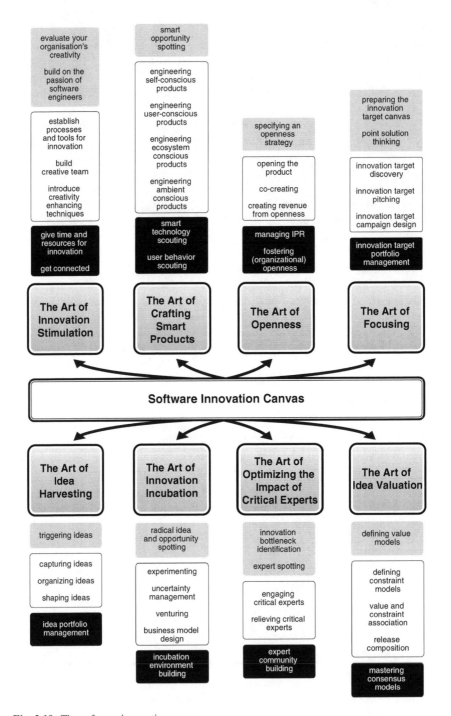

Fig. 2.19 The software innovation canvas

As a company, software companies can use this canvas several ways. For example, software companies that are highly engineering-driven today can use the canvas to explore how to become more innovation-driven. Non-software companies that consider including software in their product offering can use the canvas to explore the various innovation opportunities that software can offer.

Perhaps the most important use of the canvas is as an instrument for innovation improvement. In several of the industrial cases described in this book, the innovation canvas was used to improve the innovation capabilities of software companies. For example, in Metso (sect. 3.6), VTT coached several innovation improvement projects.

In software process improvement literature, deployment paradigms such as QIP (Basili 1989), and IDEAL (McFeeley 1996) have been widely used to support improvement actions in software engineering. It was noticed ,while working with companies, that innovation improvement involves the five key steps that have similarities with the traditional software process improvement approaches. The steps are as follows:

Step 1: *Set goals and choose practice areas for your improvement activities.* Metso had two innovation targets. The first target was to make the customer idea management even more efficient and provide quicker responses to customer requests and wishes. The second target was to find more systematic ways to manage innovation in the software context by defining and deploying a new software tool to support identified innovation actions and improvements. Based on these targets, three practice areas were selected as a focus for the innovation improvement activities: the art of idea harvesting (sect. 2.4), the art of valuation (sect. 2.5) and the art of openness (sect. 2.6), as the goal of the study was to look at the customer communication aspect of idea harvesting and valuation.

Step 2: *Understand how you are going to deal with the activities today (as-is).* At Metso, VTT's staff carried out nine interviews aimed at company sales, marketing and product management. For the interviews, a set of questions related to the art of idea harvesting, valuation and openness were adapted to be better suited to Metso context. Remove:, was used. To help you as a company define your own questions we provide a set of questions at the end of each practice area that you can use as inspiration.

Step 3: *List the challenges you currently experience in the area of this activity.* At Metso, VTT researchers recorded all the interviews, analysed them and summarized the results in a presentation that was later shown to the company's sales, marketing and management. Examples of the challenges in the analysis are listed below:

- The marketing and customer support staff do not use the innovation tool (the potential of customers is not made full use of when making business plans and roadmaps).
- No feedback on ideas, and the innovativeness/motivation of the creativity of the actors is disappearing.

- Ideas and customer demands are sometimes documented vaguely (not focused), making the analysis difficult.
- Idea evaluation and prioritization are time-consuming due to the lack of collaboration.

Step 4: *Examine the improvement needs in your company in terms of these activities*. This book provides 21 industrial cases about software innovation (sect. 3). The cases are provided to help software companies to define innovation improvements / targets. In Metso case, VTT researchers used some cases presented in this book as inspiration for the improvements identification. For example, the Steria case (Steria, 'Focusing Innovation in a Large ICT Company') was used as an inspiration to organize a workshop in which the innovation targets were defined for the selected Metso programme. In addition, some experiences from the Mobideas case ('Mobideas – Co-creating B2C software together with end-users') were used to identify ideas on how to improve innovation openness. While your company situation will undoubtedly differ from that faced by the companies in our experience reports, some aspects of their experiences are likely to be relevant to your context.

Step 5: *Prioritize and plan*. In the Metso case, a workshop was organized on software innovation challenges and improvements during the workshop. VTT researchers presented the results of the key innovation challenges and needs and collected feedback from Metso's sales, marketing and management. At the same meeting, the marketing, sales and management at Metso had the opportunity to vote on the priorities of the innovation ideas and improvement needs in the area of software innovation. More information on the results of the case can be found from the section 3.6 'Harvesting product ideas as part of a global innovation process' in this book.

The canvas is not only useful to industry; it may also be relevant to the research community. The innovation canvas and experience reports can be used as inspiration to start new research initiatives in the domain of software innovation. The practice areas and activities from the canvas can be investigated from the research perspective: *What does this activity mean from a research perspective?* The experience reports introduced in the following chapter can provide support to find some new practical angles for research in the domain of software innovation.

The research on software innovation is still relatively new, which means that all aspects of software innovation may not yet be addressed in this canvas. In fact, we may have missed some activities or even practice areas. If you as a representative of a software company have any ideas on how to develop this further or if your research or practice generates new software innovation angles, please feel free to discuss it with us and others in the SinnoBok. Org community.

References

Aarts E, Harwig R, Schuurmans M (2001) Ambient intelligence. In: The invisible future: the seamless integration of technology into everyday life. McGraw-Hill, New York

Alastair J. Gill, Darren Gergle, Robert M. French, and Jon Oberlander. 2008. Emotion rating from short blog texts. In Proceeding of the twenty-sixth annual SIGCHI conference on Human factors in computing systems (CHI '08). ACM, New York, NY, USA, 1121–1124. DOI=10.1145/ 1357054.1357229 http://doi.acm.org/10.1145/1357054.1357229

Almirall E, Casadesus-Masanell R (2010) Open versus closed innovation: a model of discovery and divergence. Acad Manage Rev 35(1):27–47

Amabile TM (1997) Motivating creativity in organizations: on doing what you love and loving what you do. Calif Manage Rev Fall 40(1):39–58

Amabile TM, Conti R (1999) Changes in the work environment for creativity during downsizing. Acad Manage J 42(6):630–640

Ancona D, Bresman H, Kaeufer K (2002) The comparative advantage of X-teams. Sloan Manage Rev 43(3):33–39

Bartels AH (2009) Smart computing drives the new era of IT growth. Forrester Research, Cambridge

Basili, VR (1989) Software development: a paradigm for the future. In: COMPSAC'89 conference, Orlando, pp 471–485. IEEE computer society

Beck K (1999) Extreme programming explained: embrace change. Addison-Wesley, Reading

Beck K, Fowler M (2001) Planning extreme programming. Addison Wesley, Boston

Begel A, Phang KY, Zimmermann T (2010) WhoseIsThat: finding software engineers with codebook (research demo). In: Proceedings of the 16th international symposium on foundations of software engineering (FSE), Association for computing machinery

Berners-Lee T, Hendler J, Lassila O (2001) 'The semantic web'. Scientific American Magazine. http://www.sciam.com/article.cfm?id = the-semantic-web&print = true. Accessed 26 Mar 2008

Blank S (2005) The four steps to the Epiphany. Published September 2010 Edition. Cafepress.com

Blank SG (2006) The four steps to the epiphany (9780976470700) Cafepress.com

Blank S (2011) Customer development is not a focus group. http://steveblank.com/2009/11/30/ customer-development-is-not-a-focus-group/. Accessed Mar 2011

Blue Ocean Strategy: How to create uncontested market space and make competition irrelevant, Harvard Business School Press

Boudreau K (2006) Does "opening" a platform enhance innovative performance? Panel data evidence on handheld computers. Working paper, Massachusetts Institute of Technology, Boston, and HEC, Paris

Brews PJ, Tucci C (2003) Building internet generation companies: lessons from the front lines of the old economy. Academy Manage Exec 17(4):8–23

Brooks F (1995) The mythical man-month: essays on software engineering, anniversary edition. Addison-Wesley, Reading

Bullinger AC, Moeslein KM (2010) Online innovation contests – where are we? In: Proceedings of the sixteenth Americas conference on information systems (AMCIS), Lima

Bullinger AC, Neyer A-K, Rass M, Moeslein KM (2010) Community-based innovation contests: where competition meets cooperation. Creativ Innovation Manage 19(3):290–303

Burgelman R (1984) Managing the internal corporate venturing process. Sloan Manag Review 25 (2):33–48

Burt RS (2003) Social origins of good ideas. University of Chicago Press, Chicago

Chesbrough H (2003a) Open innovation: the new imperative for creating and profiting from technology. Harvard University Press, Boston

Chesbrough HW (2003b) The era of open innovation. MIT Sloan Manage Rev 44(3):35–41

Chesbrough HW, Vanhaverbeke W, West J (2004) Open Innovation: Researching a new paradigm, Oxford University Press. ISBN: 0-19-929072-5 978-0-19-929072-7

Chesbrough HW (2006a) New puzzles and new findings. In: Chesbrough HW, Vanhaverbeke W, West J (eds) Open innovation: researching a new paradigm. Oxford University Press, Oxford, pp 15–33

Chesbrough H (2006b) Open business models, how to thrive in the new innovation landscape. Harvard Business School Press, Boston

Clegg D, Barker R (2004) Case method fast-track: a RAD approach. Addison-Wesley, Reading

Conati C, Chabbal R, Maclaren H (2003) A study on using biometric sensors for detecting user emotions in educational games. In: 3rd workshop on affective and attitude user modeling, Kluwer, Pittsburgh

Cotterman R, Fusfield A, Henderson P, Leder J, Loweth C, Metoyer A (2009) Aligning marketing and technology to drive innovation. Res Technol Manage 52(5):14–20

Dahlin KB, Behrens DM (2005) When is an invention really radical? Defining and measuring technological radicalness. Res Policy 34(2005):717–737

De Jong JPJ, Vanhaverbeke W, Kalvet T, Chesbrough H (2008) Policies for open innovation: theory, framework and cases, research project funded by VISION Era-Net, Helsinki, Finland

Dehoff K, Neely D (2004) Innovation and product development: clearing the new performance bar. Booz Allen Hamilton publicatie. http://www.boozallen.com/media/file/138077.pdf. Accessed Mar 2011

Denning PJ (2004) The social life of innovation. Commun ACM 47:15–19

DeSouza K, Dombrowski C, Awazu Y, Baloh P, Papagari S, Jha S, Kim JY (2009) Crafting organizational innovation processes. Innovation: Manage, Policy & Pract 11:6–33

Diener K, Piller F (2010) The market for open innovation: increasing the efficiency and effectiveness of the innovation process. RWTH-TIM Group, Aachen

Dismukes JP, Lawrence K, Miller JA, Bers J, Sekhar A, Shelbrooke AE (2009) Accelerated radical innovation (ARI) methodology validation. In: PICMET 2009 Proceedings, Portland, Oregon, 2–6 Aug 2009

Dooley KJ, Corman SR, McPhee RD (2002) A knowledge directory for identifying experts and areas of expertise. Hum Syst Manage 21(4):217–228

Eggermont LDJ (ed) (2002) Embedded systems roadmap 2002. Technology Foundation, Utrecht

Ekvall G (1996) Organizational climate for creativity and innovation. Eur J Work Organ Psychol 5 (1):105–123

Farhoomand A (2007) Opening up of the software industry: the case of SAP. Comm Assoc Inform Syst 20(1):800–811, http://aisel.aisnet.org/cgi/viewcontent.cgi?article=2632&context=cais

Fellowforce (2011) www.fellowforce.com. Accessed Mar 2011

Følstad A (2008) Living labs for innovation and development of information and communication technology: a literature review. Electron J Virtual Org Netw 10:100–131 (Special Issue on Living Labs)

Fortuna L, Graziani S, Rizzo A, Xibilia MG (2007) Soft sensors for monitoring and control of industrial processes. Springer, London

Fraser J (2005) Inspired innovation: how Corel is drawing upon employees' ideas for user focused innovation. In: Proceedings of the 2005 conference on designing for user experience, San Francisco, 3–5 Nov 2005 (Designing for user experiences, vol. 135. AIGA: American Institute of Graphic Arts, New York, p 40)

Gassmann O, Enkel E (2004) Towards a theory of open innovation: three core process archetypes. In: Proceedings of the R&D management conference, Sesimbra, Portugal, 7–9 July 2004

Gill AJ, Gergle D, French RM, Oberlander J (2008) Emotion rating from short blog texts. In: Proceeding of the twenty-sixth annual SIGCHI conference on human factors in computing systems (CHI '08), ACM, New York, pp 1121–1124, doi: 10.1145/1357054.1357229. http://doi.acm.org/10.1145/1357054.1357229

Granovetter MS (1973) The strength of weak ties. Am J Sociol 78(6):1360–1380

Greenspun P (2002) Managing Software Engineers. http://philip.greenspun.com/ancient-history/managing-software-engineers

Greenstein S (1996) Invisible hands versus invisible advisors: Coordination mechanisms in economic networks. In: Noam E, Nishuilleabhain A (eds) Public networks, public objectives. Elsevier, Amsterdam, pp 135–160

Hohmann L (2006) Innovation games: creating breakthrough products through collaborative play. Addison-Wesley, Upper Saddle River

Hibbs C, Sullivan SJM (2009) The art of lean software development: a practical and incremental approach, O'relly media, US

Hui Q, Wang Q (2006) Radical innovation or incremental innovation: Strategic decision of technology-intensive firms in the PRC. IEEE, 1-4244-0286-7/06/$20.00

IBM Wiki Central. https://www.ibm.com/developerworks/wikis/display/idctest/IBM + Wiki + Central. Accessed Mar 2011

Ideastorm. http://www.ideastorm.com/. Accessed Mar 2011

Innocentive (2011) www.innocentive.com. Accessed Mar 2011

Interpersonal Ties. http://en.wikipedia.org/wiki/Interpersonal_ties. Accessed Mar 2011

Isaksen SG, Ekvall G (2010) Managing for innovation: the two faces of tension in creative climates. Creat Innovation Manage 19(2):73–88

'It's a smart world', special report. The economist. http://www.economist.com/node/17388368. Accessed Mar 2011

Johannessen J-A, Olsen B (2010) The future of value creation and innovations: Aspects of a theory of value creativity and innovation in a global knowledge economy. Int J Inform Manag 30:502–511

Kano N et al (1984) Attractive quality and must-be quality (Japanese). J Jpn Soc Qual Control 14 (2):39–48

Karlsson L (2006) Requirements prioritisation and retrospective analysis for release planning process improvement. PhD Thesis, HUT, Department of computer science

Kim WC (2005) Blue ocean strategy: how to create uncontested market space and make competition irrelevant, 1st edn. Harvard Business Press, Boston

Kim   WC: http://www.amazon.com/Blue-Ocean-Strategy-Uncontested-Competition/dp/1591396190. Accessed Mar 2011

Lehtola L (2006) Providing value by prioritizing requirements throughout product development: state of practice and suitability of prioritization methods. Licentiate Thesis, HUT, Department of computer science

Leifer R (1998) An information processing approach for facilitating the Fuzzy front end of breakthrough innovations. IEMC'98 Lally School of Management and Technology Rensselaer Polytechnic Institute, 110 8th Street, Troy, NY 12180

Lewis R (2008) IBM gambles on a shift from the KM model. http://www.knowledgeboard.com/item/2860/23/5/3. Accessed Mar 2011

Lindeke RR, Wyrick DW, Chen H (2009) Creating change and driving innovation in highly automated and lean organization: the temporal think TankTM (T3TM). Robotics Comput Integr Manuf 25:879–887

LinkedIn. http://www.linkedin.com. Accessed Mar 2011

Liu C-H (2011) The effects of innovation alliance on network structure and density of cluster. Expert Sys Appl 38:299–305

Loch CH, DeMeyer A, Pich MT (2006) Managing the unknown: a new approach to managing high uncertainty and risk in projects. Wiley, Hoboken

Loebbecke C, Soehnel A, Weniger S, Weiss T (2010) Innovating for the Mobile End-User Market: Amazon's Kindle 2 Strategy as Emerging Business Model, International Conference on Mobile Business (ICMB) and Global Mobility Roundtable (GMR), IEEE, Athens, Greece, June, 337–344.

Madagley W, Birdi K (2009) Innovation labs: an examination into the use of physical spaces to enhance organizational creativity. Creativ Innovation Manage 18(4):315–325

Maiden N, Robertson S, Robertson J (2006) Creative requirements: invention and its role in requirements engineering. In: Proceedings of the 28th international conference on software engineering (ICSE '06), ACM, New York

Mauborgne R (2005) Visit Amazon's W. Chan Kim Page. Accessed Mar 2011

McAfee A (2009) Enterprise 2.0: new collaborative tools for your organization's toughest challenges, 1st edn. Harvard Business School Press, Boston

McConnel S (2011) Origins of 10X – how valid is the underlying research? http://forums.construx.com/blogs/stevemcc/archive/2011/01/09/origins-of-10x-how-valid-is-the-underlying-research.aspx. Accessed Mar 2011

McConnell S (2006) Software estimation: demystifying the black art. Microsoft Press, Redmond

McFeeley B (1996) A users guide for software process improvement. Carnegie Mellon University, Pittsburgh

Meristö T and Laitinen J (ed) (2009) INNORISK: The fountain of new business creation. Corporate foresight group CoFi/Åbo Akademi University. ISBN: 978-952-12-2265-8, 978-952-12-2266-5 (electronic version). Turku. 35 p

Moultrie J, Young A (2009) Exploratory study of organizational creativity in creative organizations. Creativity and Innovation Management 18(4):299–314

Neff G, Stark D (2002) Permanently beta: responsive organization in the internet era. Center on Organizational Innovation, Columbia University, New York

Nguyen L, Shanks G (2009) A framework for understanding creativity in requirements engineering. Inform Softw Technol 51:655–662

Norman DA (1998) The invisible computer. MIT Press, Cambridge

O'Reilly T (2005) What is Web 2.0. Design Patterns and Business Models for the Next Generation of Software, p. 30. Munich Personal RePEc Archive

Ojasalo K, Moilanen T, Ritalahti J (2009) Kehittämistyön menetelmät. Uudenlaista osaamista liiketoimintaan. WSOYpro. 181 p

Oliveira J, Mattos V, Laufer A, Moreira de Souza J, Miranda PE (2009) A KMS to support collaborative innovation - The design of the Brazilian Solid Oxide Fuel Cell case. CSCWD'2009. pp. 630–635

Ostenwalder A, Pigneur Y, Tucci CL (2005) Communications of AIS, volume 15, article clarifying business models: origins, present, and future of the concept

Osterwalder A, Pigneur Y (2009) Business model generation: a handbook for visionaries, game changers, and challengers. Modderman Drukwerk, Amsterdam

Osterwalder A, Pigneur Y (2010) Business model generation. Wiley, ISBN 978-0470876411

Paasi J, Luoma T, Valkokari K, Lee N (2010) Knowledge and intellectual property management in customer-supplier relationships. Int J Innovation Manag 14(4):629–654

Pikkarainen M, Boucart N, Biot O, Codenie W (2009) Innovation with software is different. ITEI newsletter 1/2009. ITEI research project

Piller F, Ihl C (2009) Open Innovation with customers – foundations, competences and international trends. RWTH ZLW-IMA, Aachen

Poppendieck M, Poppendieck T (2006) Implementing lean software development: from concept to cash. Addison-Wesley Professional

Poslad S (2009) Ubiquitous computing: smart devices, environments and interactions, 1st edn. Wiley, Chichester

Prahalad CK, Ramaswamy V (2004) The Future of competition. Harvard Business School Press, Boston

Quora. http://www.quora.com. Accessed Mar 2011

Regnell B et al (2001) An Industrial case study on distributed prioritisation in market-driven requirements engineering for packaged software. Requir Eng 6(1):51–62

Reinig BA, Briggs RO (2008) On the relationship between idea-quantity and idea-quality during ideation. Group Decis Negot 17:403–420

Release Planner (2011) Release planner tool. www.releaseplanner.com. Accessed Mar 2011

Rohrbeck R (2010) Harnessing a network of experts for competitive advantage: technology scouting in the ICT industry. R&D Manage 40(2):169–180, http://dx.doi.org/10.1111/j.1467-9310.2010.00601.x

Rowe G, Wright G (1999) The Delphi technique as a forecasting tool: issues and analysis. Int J Forecast 15(4):353–375

Rutkowski A-F, Saunders CS (2010) Growing pains with information overload. Computer 43 (6):94–96. doi:10.1109/MC.2010.171

Sarma A, Maccherone L, Wagstrom P, Herbsleb J (2009) Tesseract: interactive visual exploration of socio-technical relationships in software development. ICSE '09 proceedings of the 31st international conference on software engineering. Vancouver, Canada, 16–24 May 2009

Satyanarayanan M (2001) Pervasive computing: vision and challenges. IEEE Pervasive Comput 8 (4):10–17

Scrum Schwaber K, Beedle K (2002), Agile Software Development with Scrum. Upper Saddle Riven, NJ. Prentice Hall http://www.controlchaos.com/. Accessed Mar 2011

Sebe N, Cohen I, Gevers T, Huang T-S (2004) Multimodal approaches for emotion recognition: a survey. In: Proceedings of the SPIE internet imaging, San Jose, pp 56–67

Sebe N, Sun Y, Bakker E, Lew MS, Cohen I, Huang TS (2004) Towards Authentic Emotion Recognition. In: IEEE SMC International Conference on Systems, Man, and Cybernetics, pp. 623–628

Serrano N, Ciordia I (2005) Bugzilla, ITracker, and other bug trackers. IEEE Softw 22(2):11–13. doi:10.1109/MS.2005.32

Shenhar A, Dvir D (2007) Reinventing project management. Harvard Business School Press, Boston

Spithovena A, Clarysse B, Knockaert M (2009) Building absorptive capacity to organise inbound open innovation in traditional industries. Technovation 30:130–141

Stackoverflow. http://stackoverflow.com/. Accessed Mar 2011

Steiner G (2009) The concept of open creativity: collaborative creative problem solving for innovation generation – a systems approach. J Bus Manage 15(1):7–33

Stryszowski P (2009) OECD organisation for economic co-operation and development/Douglas Lippoldt (2009) Innovation in the software sector. Edition. OECD Publishing, Paris

Sun G, Chen J, Guo W, Liu KJR (2005) Univ. of Electron. Sci. & Technol. of China, Chengdu, China. Signal processing techniques in network-aided positioning: a survey of state-of-the-art positioning designs. In: Signal Processing Magazine, IEEE. Issue Date: July 2005. Volume: 22 Issue:4, page(s): 12–23. ISSN: 1053-5888 DOI: 10.1109/MSP.2005.1458273

Surowiecki J (2004a) The wisdom of crowds – why the many are smarter than the few. Doubleday/Anchor, New York

Surowiecki J (2004b) The wisdom of crowds: why the many are smarter than the few and how collective wisdom shapes business, economies, societies and nations. Little Brown, New York

Technorati. http://www.technorati.com/. Accessed Mar 2011

Tellis G, Prabhu J, Jaideep C, Chandy Rajesh K (2009) Radical innovation across nations: the preeminence of corporate culture. J Mark 73:3–23

Thomke S (2003) Experimentation matters: unlocking the potential of new technologies for innovation. Harvard Business Press, Boston

Tidd J, Bessant J (2009) Managing innovation, 4th edn. Wiley, Chichester

Tourwe T, Codenie W, Boucart N (2009) Bringing software innovations to market in release-driven organizations, building blocks of agile innovation. BookSurge Publishing, Charleston

Tourwe T, Codenie W, Boucart N and Blagojevic V (2009) Demystifying release definition: from requirements prioritization to collaborative value quantification. In: 15th international working conference on requirements engineering: foundation for software quality, Amsterdam, The Netherlands

Tsiporkova E et al (2006) Multi-step ranking of alternatives in a multi-criteria and multi-expert decision making environment. Inf Sci 176(18):2673–2697

Tucker RB (2008) http://www.amazon.com/Driving-Growth-Through-Innovation-Robert/dp/1576751872. Accessed Mar 2011. (Driving growth through innovation, Berrett-Koehler Publishers)

Valacich JS, Dennis AR, Nunamaker JF (1992) Group-size and anonymity effects on computer-mediated idea generation. Small Group Res 2:1

von Hippel E (1986) Lead users: a source of novel product concepts. Manag Sci 32(7):791–806. http://www.jstor.org/stable/2631761. Accessed Mar 2011

von Hippel E (2005) Democratizing innovation. The MIT Press, Cambridge

Weiser M (1991) The computer for the 21st century. Sci Am 265(3):94–104

Wenger E, McDermott R, Snyder WM (2002) Cultivating communities of practice. Harvard Business School Press, Boston

Yang G-Z et al (2006) Body sensor networks. Springer, London

Yimam-Seid D, Kobsa A (2003) Expert finding systems for organizations: problem and domain analysis and the DEMOIR approach. In: Sharing expertise: beyond knowledge management. MIT Press, Cambridge, pp 327–358

Chapter 3
Industrial Cases About Software Innovation

In this part of the book we will present 21 different experience reports that are implementing part of the software innovation canvas. They can inspire you how actual companies partially implemented the activities of the software innovation canvas.

3.1 Steria, Focusing Innovation in a Large ICT Company

Pierre Paelinck

3.1.1 Challenge of the Company

As an IT services provider, Steria Benelux develops and integrates information systems and technology solutions for the public sector and for medium to large-sized private companies (active in various fields such as banking, utilities, security ...). Delivered solutions often focus on business transformation systems that help customers improve their productivity, streamline their infrastructure and revisit their business processes. Achieving such goals on a large scale requires Steria to make innovation a self-sustaining enterprise capability and a tangible core value.

Like many other companies delivering IT services through projects, Steria is facing a number of challenges that impact its approach to innovation.

First, most of the solutions delivered by Steria are developed in the frame of projects, and many of the project teams are deployed at customers' premises. This geographical dispersion of Steria's project teams limits opportunities for interactions between them and therefore impedes profitable cross-fertilization of ideas. Emerging Web 2.0 technologies were felt to be a convenient way of aligning several local initiatives.

Second, in a company as big and diverse as Steria (220+ employees for Steria Benelux), inviting all employees to submit their ideas into an 'idea box' kind of

M. Pikkarainen et al. (eds.), *The Art of Software Innovation*,
DOI 10.1007/978-3-642-21049-5_3, © Springer-Verlag Berlin Heidelberg 2011

database would quickly become unmanageable: the sheer size of the company would quickly mean that one to two full-time people would be needed to screen ideas, to handle the volume of ideas alone. Due to the great diversity of profiles, projects and interests at Steria, it would quickly become apparent that many of the submitted ideas were not in line with the company's vision. This great number of all-over-the-place ideas would eventually kill the initiative: people submitting ideas expect feedback and are particularly interested in what happens to their ideas, but in a pool of hundreds, if not thousands, of ideas, their individual ideas would not receive much attention. People would soon lose interest and abandon the idea box.

Third, having highly creative teams or individuals is definitely not a guarantee of implementing profitable innovative solutions. Crashing together seemingly unrelated themes, insights or domains and thereby expanding the creativity scope opens up new opportunities for the company. On the other hand, innovation also needs to be structured in some way to avoid chaotic and sometimes out-of-scope ideation. There is therefore an urgent need for an effective balance of open-mindedness and visibility of the way innovation is handled in the organization.

These important industrial challenges resulted in two major objectives that were addressed by the ITEI project and that motivated Steria to take part in it, structurally improving the creativity of software engineering and optimizing the critical impact of expert-driven innovations.

3.1.2 How the Case Was Executed

In order to achieve the first goal, a visionary model was developed by Sirris and thoroughly tested to deal with innovations in software product development in a service-oriented company. The goal was to adapt the model and use it within the company-specific context through several industrial cases. The model, depicted in Fig. 3.1, is based on a number of new concepts (Innovation Target, Innovation Space and Innovation Room), which must improve the creative process in software-intensive product development significantly.

The second objective of our case study, optimizing the critical impact of expert-driven innovations, further elaborated on the above-mentioned developed concepts. In combination with an open innovation work method, a community was set up that works according to the *publish & subscribe* principle. A platform for experts, external or internal to the organization, gave it the opportunity to '*register on time*' in the development process, making it possible to maximize the impact of its interventions on the whole life cycle of the development process.

Steria successfully tested the applicability of the innovation model proposed by Sirris in its specific context through a number of dedicated experiments focusing on the various components of the model. These experiments were supported by the proof-of-concept application Ideathlon developed by Sirris and IdeaSniffer developed by the text mining company Mentis (Fig. 3.2).

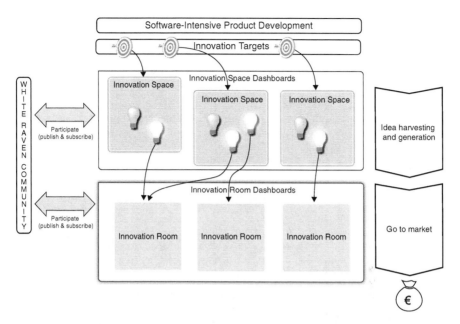

Fig. 3.1 Innovation targets at Steria

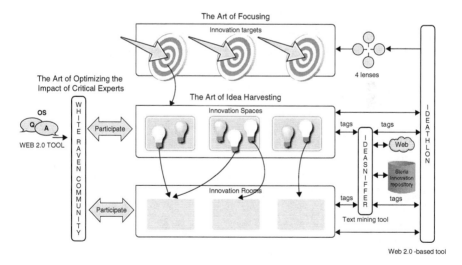

Fig. 3.2 Tool support for innovation targets at Steria

The first experiment was intended to think out an effective methodology to avoid the scenario of a rambling and never-ending innovation process. Steria, in close collaboration with Sirris, opted for an approach directly inspired by 'The Art of Focusing' practice area of 'The Art of Software Innovation' – book and relying on the definition of Innovation Targets using Ideathlon. By first carefully defining a *target* for the innovation, Steria aimed to focus and channel the creativity of its staff on a topic of high interest and value to the company. This innovation target is expressed in such a way that it becomes a measurable and concrete goal at which to aim, yet leaving enough room for creativity to flourish. An example of such an innovation target identified by Steria was 'Define 5 initiatives to increase our customer intimacy'. People were supported in establishing Innovation Targets by making use of the method of the four lenses (Skarzynski and Gibson 2008). The latter turned out to assist people in broadening their scope of thinking and sharpening the formulation of these targets. More traditional brainstorming sessions were also used as either input or output to Ideathlon to make the whole process of Innovation Target identification more performant and to allow for direct interactions between people.

The second experiment investigated the use of the open-source software OSQA (http://www.osqa.net/) to obtain a better insight into the concept of White Ravens and to assess to what extent such Web 2.0-inspired tools can help identify these experts and involve them in a Community of Practice. More specifically, this experiment had to do with the 'Art of optimizing the impact of critical resources'. The Community focused on agile methodologies and lean concepts in software engineering and has been working for several months. It initially demonstrated the effectiveness of Web 2.0 tools in opening innovation to 'hidden' experts: a range of ideas is produced by people with a variety of profiles and backgrounds, people can contribute on a voluntary basis, wasted time solving a problem or moving an innovative idea forward is drastically reduced, and the opportunity to set up knowledge maps and channels is useful for speeding up innovation ...

The last experiment, in close connection with the 'Art of idea harvesting' explored the potential advantages of coupling a Web 2.0-oriented tool such as Ideathlon with a text-mining-based tool such as IdeaSniffer to stimulate ideation in an Innovation Space. *Ideathlon*™ (Ideathlon) is a proof-of-concept online *Innovation Space* in which staff are invited to *post*, *like* and *discuss* ideas. This online platform allowed the distributed staff of Steria to participate in the ideation around the innovation targets. Integration with email and iGoogle (iGoogle) provided more engagement. Through the use of advanced semantic technology, relevant information from the Internet was brought into the innovation spaces, providing background information and inspiration for the teams. In fact, tags were associated with ideas posted by people on Ideathlon and fed into a text mining tool acting as an 'idea sniffer' on the web. Using statistical and semantic mining techniques, the information found on the web was clustered in categories with ideas containing not only similar words but also similar meaning. Coupling Ideathlon with a text mining-based tool effectively sustained innovation by discovering unknown information, something no one yet knew, so it could not have be written down yet. Given the nature of innovation space in Ideathlon, this experiment showed that the technological goal of text mining offers attractive benefits. In particular, text mining can play an important role in deriving greater understanding of these data or uncover non-trivial relationships in these data.

3.1.3   Lessons Learned – Solutions

This research project allowed Steria to draw several lessons that will have an impact on its approach to innovation.

A first lesson is that focusing most efforts on ideation initiatives and pushing up the supply of ideas (this can be observed with Ideas/Suggestion Boxes leading to a whole bunch of ideas and eventually to a withering of the innovation effort in the long run) is not the right approach: what the company is really looking for through innovation is not just many ideas. There should be an organizational framework for ensuring that ideas are aligned with the business strategy and objectives. That is why the very front-end of the innovation process must be devoted to defining Innovation Targets: it is only when we have gathered a collection of inspiring Innovation Targets and insights that the ideation work can start on a sound basis.

The experiments carried out during this project showed that the innovation process should be supported by computer applications such as Ideathlon as well as by more conventional creativity techniques involving face-to-face interaction (like brainstorming). This allows everyone to contribute according to her or his personality and demonstrates that innovation should engage as many minds as possible across an organization. Failing to drive and manage the demand side of innovation, e.g., the reflexive pull for new ideas within and across the company, can rapidly lead to the innovation momentum vanishing. We also observed that these two approaches can be used in any sequence to favour cross-fertilization during ideation.

The ideation phase (in which ideas are generated according to the Innovation Target) should be a sequence of divergent (ideas are freely produced) and convergent (ideas are screened) steps. Using a Web 2.0-based application like Ideathlon allows easy feedback about posted ideas and makes iterations quick through these two phases. Working in this way provides the innovation process with some agility.

The last experiment combining Web 2.0 and text-mining-oriented technologies is a first demonstration of the opportunities offered by semantic networks. It is anticipated that innovation will take full advantage of the Web 3.0 features.

3.1.4   Managerial Implications

Innovation has to be built into the company DNA progressively and should become part of the organization's bloodstream by being fitted into all daily activities (as Steria does with quality and customer service, for instance). Considering innovation as a sporadic activity does not sustain enough momentum to deliver profitable results. Innovation has to be woven into the everyday life of Steria just like any other embedded organizational capability. Innovation should not be in addition to operational activities – they should be interleaved.

For today's companies that are active in the field of services, innovation also consists of providing support to their customers to make changes and improvements in their own way. We are therefore increasingly involved in a classical supplier-customer scheme towards a more collaborative model in which suppliers help their customers to be more creative and to implement new ideas. This is only possible in as far as both partners show aptitude to open innovation and are willing to explicitly share information and remove organizational roadblocks to it.

The management also has to shift a number of prevailing paradigms within its organization: from a need to know to a need to share, from a 'Not Invented Here' syndrome to a 'Proudly Found' one, from individual stars to performing teams.

3.2 Mobideas, Co-creating B2C Software Together with End-Users

Kaisa Koskela, Pirjo Näkki, and Minna Pikkarainen

3.2.1 Challenges Related to B2C Software Development

There is clear empirical evidence of the high value of user involvement in new product development (Lilien et al. 2002). Users can be involved as partners in co-creation, which means that they participate in interactive value creation from the early phase of the innovation process (Piller and Ihl 2009).

When developing consumer-oriented, out-of-the-box software and, especially, web services, however, the potential end-users are often not known in advance. Even if the company wants to involve end-users in the innovation process, it may be difficult to find the most innovative users. It is not clear to the companies who they should involve in which process phases and what kind of benefits participants would gain from co-creation.

In addition, in global business, end-users can be distributed geographically and by time. It is therefore challenging to co-create with end-users in software innovation processes using traditional user-centred design methods that build mainly on face-to-face communication.

The special characteristics of software bring new kinds of opportunities for co-creation activities. Demo releases can easily be shared through the web and be tested by users anywhere and at anytime. The agile software development process also enables quick changes in the product based on user feedback.

3.2.2 How the Case Was Executed

The purpose of the Mobideas case was to explore how out-of-the-box, consumer-oriented software could be co-created with end-users. During autumn 2009 and spring 2010, selected users participated in the case as active innovators and designers of a new software product from early idea generation to prototype testing. The exact product idea was left to be invented and decided on by the users, and only a loose domain of 'mobile social media' was given for the project.

In order to find the users with most ideas and motivation to participate in the software innovation process, we used the lead user approach developed by von Hippel (1986, 2005). Lead users are individuals who are at the leading edge of an important trend in a specific marketplace or product category and who anticipate relatively high benefits from obtaining a solution to their needs. For these reasons, lead users experience needs earlier than the rest of the market and are more likely to innovate if they do not find a ready-made solution to their needs.

The lead users of mobile social media were identified based on an online survey and open online idea generation on the Owela online co-creation platform (http://owela.vtt.fi). The identified lead users were then invited to participate in the product concept design and software development phases. In order to reach and involve the very disperse user group with the other actors of the process, Owela was used as a communication tool between the lead users, software developers and facilitators.

The software development was done using agile software development practices, meaning lightweight and iterative development with the emphasis on customer involvement and continuous communication (Williams and Cockburn 2003; Larman and Basili 2003a). The method that was used in the Mobideas case is called Scrum. It starts with planning and product backlog creation, followed by 1-month sprints (i.e., iteration) and finally ends up at the post-game phase with intermediate releases (Abrahamsson et al. 2002). The framework for the lead-user-driven innovation process is illustrated in Fig. 3.3.

3.2.3   Lead User Identification

Approximately 600 persons answered an online survey about their social media use. The questionnaire was designed to explore the possible lead user characteristics of the respondents in the context of mobile social media. The survey was conducted for a random sample of Finns via email and posted to a few existing social media services (e.g., Qaiku).

The survey showed that almost all (94%) of the respondents had used social media services and that nearly half (49%) used social media services daily. The use of mobile social media services was not as common. Only 26% of the respondents had used social media through a mobile device. This supports the assumption that using social media services through a mobile phone can be seen as the underlying trend that is only common among leading edge users of social media.

After filling in the survey, the respondents had a chance to register in the online space on Owela to continue the ideation. More than 200 respondents registered in the Mobideas workspace in Owela and approximately 100 of them participated actively in the first idea collection round. The idea collection was open for 2 weeks and resulted in 80 ideas, 500 comments and 870 idea evaluations.

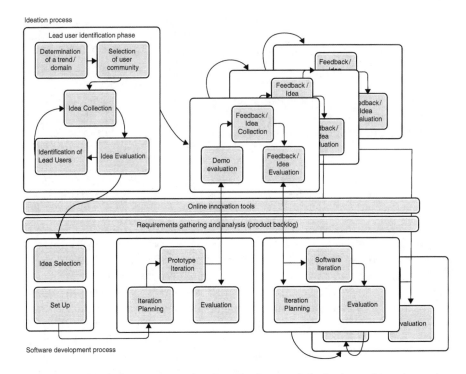

Fig. 3.3 The Mobideas process was based on the framework for lead user driven innovation (Koskela et al. 2009)

Of the 200 users, 56 were selected as participants for the lead user group in the second idea generation round. Several selection criteria were used to test the different kinds of lead user identification methods. The first group of users was selected based on the quality of its ideas, and the second group was based on the intensity of the lead user characteristics. The quality of the ideas was evaluated by the users themselves using three valuation criteria: newness of the idea, usefulness of the idea and commercial potential of the idea. As a comparison, the developers and facilitators also evaluated the ideas using the same three criteria as well as the additional criterion of feasibility of the idea. Altogether, 21 users were selected for the next phase based on the idea valuation. In addition, 35 users were selected by their lead user characteristics. The measured characteristics were forerunner position of the user in using mobile social media, anticipation of high benefits when acquiring a new solution and progressive adoption behaviour.

3.2.4 Idea Generation and Product Concept Design with Lead Users

A second idea generation and product concept design phase was conducted with the selected lead users, of whom 30 participated. In this phase, the lead users were asked to write stories of everyday situations and generate new service ideas based on the recognized needs. Synchronous chat sessions were also organized in order to generate more ideas together with other lead users. Based on the users' rating, business interests and available resources, five ideas were selected for development at concept level. The lead users then chose the final product concept to be implemented in the software development phase.

3.2.5 Lead users Drive Agile development

The agile development was performed by four student programmers. The actual implementation of the two selected concepts was done in six iterations of 2 weeks each during a 4-month period (November 2009 to March 2010). The product backlog was iteratively updated and prioritized based on the feature suggestions and voting by the lead users in Owela. Furthermore, the design decisions were continuously made based on the communication by the lead users and the developers.

During the actual agile development phase, the lead users were actively involved in Owela, where they suggested new features, created user interface layouts, tested the prototypes and gave feedback of the developed product features.

The developers communicated with the users via Owela. For example, they reported the development progress in a blog and chats. With regard to the Art of Innovation Incubation (experimentation activity), software has unique implications. The nature of the software made it possible to release a demo version in Owela after each iteration. As a result, the users had the opportunity to test the demo versions online by themselves or in chat sessions at the same time as other participants while the developers could give direct feedback. Figure 3.4 illustrates the communication channels between the different participants.

3.2.6 Lessons Learned

The users' overall experience of participation in the co-creation process was very positive. The people who choose to participate in the project were interested in social media and already had ideas for new services. For them, the idea generation phase was therefore the most inspiring part of the project. We claim that the participation experience would have been different if there had been a product idea already at the beginning and the users had only been involved in developing the idea further and in testing the prototype versions. Hence, it is important to consider how much freedom for creativity is given to the end-users when they are generating ideas. Based on the goals set for the idea generation and for the users selected to participate, more focused idea harvesting is sometimes required and a looser frame for ideas sometimes works better.

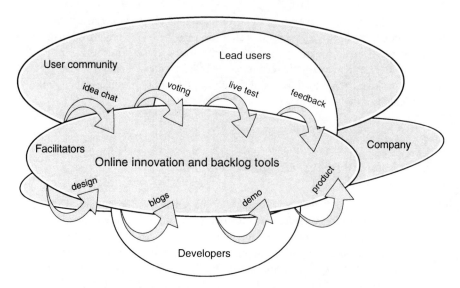

Fig. 3.4 Online innovation and backlog tools were used for communication between lead users, developers and facilitators

The other thing that made participation rewarding and interesting for the users was the continuous development of both the ideas and the prototype. The collaborative idea generation and, especially, the chat sessions were pleasant experiences when users could also learn from others. In the development phase, users were delighted to see that their ideas really became a functional prototype and that their feedback affected the end result. Stories of everyday life situations, real-time collaboration with other users and developers, as well as continuous changes in the product based on feedback stimulated new ideas.

The roles in this study essentially differed from the traditional user-centred design projects, as no designer or usability specialist was directly involved in the process. These tasks were partly managed by the developer team, though the user group also acted as a 'crowdsourced' designer and took collaborative responsibility for the usability of the product. Design decisions were made based on collaborative voting by the users, which meant that instead of a clear vision of the product, the average count was trusted.

For the users, the most confusing and frustrating parts of the process were the ones that they considered too 'technical'. These included giving feature suggestions and user interface sketching. The main reason for the frustration was that some users felt that they should have been able to think about the big picture of the software, consider technical aspects and understand other users' needs to be able to complete the tasks. They did not feel capable of doing this. The few users who participated in the user interface sketching, however, liked it. Thus, some tasks could be important to user motivation, although they would not provide such valuable data for the development.

Although the project was not confidential and the idea generation and software development could have been done openly, the closed workspace proved to be a good choice. Belonging to the active user group was seen as a commitment to being involved throughout the development process. Some users even apologized if they were unable to participate in certain process phases.

Throughout the process, the expected contributions from the users were small enough to make the participation feel fun and not like work. Some users even mentioned a kind of addiction to checking new ideas in the Mobideas workspace in the intensive phases of the process. For passionate users, the breaks between different tasks or new demo versions were sometimes too long. Email reminders of the new tasks and updates were appreciated and the pace of emails (approximately 5–6 per month) was seen as appropriate.

In the end, the facilitation of the process was quite challenging. Facilitators had to struggle with the contradiction of guiding the users sufficiently while not being too compelling. Clear articulation of the questions and guidelines is especially important when using online tools, and all the users should understand the tasks in the same way to prevent frustration.

Key elements that need to be considered when co-creating with end-users in software innovation and the development process:

- Provision of continuous feedback and updates for the users to keep them motivated.
- The tasks assigned to the users should not be too technical in nature.
- The sense of belonging to a selected user group made the users more committed to participating actively throughout the process.
- The expected contributions from users should be small enough to make the participation feel fun and not like work.
- The facilitation of the process is very important; special attention should be paid, especially to clear articulation of the tasks and guidelines.

How the presented challenges/lessons learned are related to the 'The Art of Software Innovation' -book practice areas

The co-creation of out-of-the-box, consumer-oriented software with end-users, as described in this article, is one specific form of the Art of Openness: the company opens certain phases or the whole innovation process to a group of users who can also participate in the decision-making related to the new product. Lead user-based idea generation is one example of the Art of Idea Harvesting: using innovative users to create new product ideas. In this case, the users did not only provide ideas but also everyday life needs and problems that could be used as Idea stimulation for the company employees who could develop new solutions based on user needs. The Art of Innovation Stimulation also played a big role in planning how to motivate and reward end-users for participating in the co-creation activities.

In this case, the activities related to the Art of Idea Valuation were partly crowdsourced for the users, who evaluated each other's ideas. The facilitators and developers also participated in the idea valuation using the same online tools for idea rating. The agile software development process, with short iterations, provided good practice for the Art of Innovation Incubation: after each release, the users could test and comment on the actual software prototype online via Owela. This way, developers received regular feedback from the users and could develop the prototype continuously based on real user feedback.

3.3 Movial, Case of Innovation Improvement

Suvi Keinänen and Kaisa Koskela

3.3.1 Challenge of a Company

Movial is globally recognized for its user experience design expertise and long-term experience of working with different Linux platforms on embedded devices. By delivering highly intuitive and compelling user experiences, Movial has become the trusted source for enriching the way people interact every day. Consequently, being innovative is very important to the company. It was clearly recognized, however, that several challenges were related to the innovation activities in the company. As Movial lacked the resources and expertise to make a critical analysis of the way the company created new business opportunities by innovating and pinpointing challenges, it brought in innovation experts from VTT to provide an objective analysis of the situation.

3.3.2 How the Case Was Executed

The software innovation assessment method used in Movial is developed in the ITEI project by VTT and based on the eight 'The Art of Software Innovation' -book practice areas (Pikkarainen et al. 2010a). The assessment was made by conducting a wide set of interviews in the company. The interviewees were chosen from several organizational units in order to ensure a broad and truthful picture of the innovation activities within the company. After careful analysis, the results indicated that the innovation practice areas that required most attention were the Art of Focusing, the Art of Idea Harvesting and the Art of Innovation Incubation.

Based on the assessment, VTT provided Movial with a set of innovation improvement suggestions. The results and improvement suggestions were shared and discussed in a day-long workshop in the company. Employees across the company were present at the workshop. The employees had been selected to form a team that was motivated and committed to driving the recommended changes inside the company. At the end of the workshop day, the team had gone through the assessment results, discussed them and made decisions about how to take the suggestions further in the organization.

3.3.3 Lessons Learned and Solutions

The software innovation assessment revealed that Movial has innovative and experienced employees who have many ideas. The company was failing to take this potential into use, however, as there were no goals and procedures for innovation. In other words, the employees did not have the means to take their ideas further. Most employees also felt that being innovative was not something that they were meant to be, as targets and encouragement were missing.

Due to the lack of a systematic procedure for collecting ideas and managing them, many ideas just disappeared. Consequently, there was no history of previous ideas or innovations (e.g., problems solved in different customer organizations), or formal decisions on whether the ideas were going to be analysed further, and there was no documentation on the decisions. This also meant that no feedback was given to the individuals from whom the ideas had originated. As a result, the company suffered from a major lack of motivation to generate new ideas.

Movial decided to start improving innovativeness in the organisation by focusing into the following areas.

1. Innovation requires time and commitment – allocate it

The Movial team understood that if innovation was something that was to be pursued in the organisation, innovation-related activities needed to become an acknowledged part of the employees' work time and should not be seen solely as something that they do on their own time.

2. Innovation requires clear goals and targets – set them

The assessment indicated that clear innovation goals and targets had not been defined. This created confusion among the employees. In fact, the common impression was that the goal was not to create new ideas for the moment.

3. Ideas require active collection and handling – manage them

The biggest challenge relating to idea harvesting was the shortage of an appropriate and commonly accepted tool for gathering and handling ideas. The employees also felt that they did not receive any feedback on the presented ideas. As a result, not many wanted to generate ideas in the first place.

4. Ideas have to be transformed into services and products – create opportunities for them

It was also rare for an idea to progress further and to reach implementation as no systematic processes for idea incubation existed. Movial started to actively look for opportunities to improve this, internally and from the partner networks.

3.3.4   Managerial Implications

Innovation improvement brought about many changes at Movial. It was about learning new things and new ways of working. Movial established a specific team that consists of motivated individuals for innovation management activities. Each team member had specific tasks to perform and enough resources and time to carry out the assigned tasks. When the innovation team learned about the innovation assessment results, it realized that it faced major changes. The first priority of the team was to assess and choose the company-specific innovation tool(s) and define the basic processes for collecting and handling ideas in the organization. Based on the improvement suggestions, a detailed innovation improvement strategy was drawn up, including a follow-up process for progress. Some of the items that were considered important in order to succeed in improving software innovation and innovativeness in Movial are listed next.

Innovation improvement requires motivated individuals to drive the change
It is not only the initiation of innovation activities that counts; there must also be individuals to drive them further. A dedicated team that drives innovation throughout the organization is important. No improvement happens without motivated individuals who plan and iterate the innovation improvement changes.

Common terminology makes it easier to communicate about innovation
In Movial's case, in order to implement the improvement suggestions, the established team needed to learn to discuss innovativeness, innovations, the innovation process, innovation tools and other related areas with each other. The team created a common terminology to help in discussions about mythical, perhaps even scary, 'innovation' and to bring it closer to practice and individuals as well as their daily work. The common terminology and deeper understanding gained of innovation has helped the company to implement improvement activities as well as to identify further problems, and discuss and tackle them.

Communication must flow bottom-up and top-down in the organization
Movial's case shows the importance of supporting communication flows of ideas and thoughts inside the company. In order to proceed with implementing the improvement suggestions, Movial's innovation team created open and semi-open forums for interactive discussions so that ideas and thoughts had an opportunity to come out and flourish in the organization. This way, the right people could hear and act on the ideas and thoughts.

External expertise facilitates innovation improvement
In Movial, external experts helped to discover the innovation-related challenges in the first place. When using external expertise, it is easier to make the management committed and make communication on innovation challenges not fall under internal politics or blaming, instead external support should help to keep the topics the top priority. By setting up a specific improvement suggestion, the external experts also allowed Movial to focus its improvement efforts more effectively.

During the innovation assessment and improvement process, awareness of innovation increased dramatically in Movial. The company gained the ability to discuss this critical element of its business, set clear goals for the innovation activities, seize moments to introduce new ideas in the company and opportunities to process them further. It has also become clear that innovation awareness and improvement activities need be continuous in the company and re-activated on a regular basis, especially as new employees enter the company.

3.4   Movial, Selecting Innovation Tools

Suvi Keinänen and Kalle Karinen

3.4.1   Challenge in a Company

New, innovative ideas are important to Movial, as they are to any software business organization that wishes to exist in the current, fluctuating software industry. Despite the importance of managing novel ideas, Movial had trouble capturing new, innovative ideas from coffee table discussions, and corridor and online conversations. The ideas were only discussed, as the company lacked sophisticated means to catch, manage and develop them into innovations. Furthermore, if ideas were captured, they remained in just one geographic location. As Movial has remote teams in Palo Alto (USA), Helsinki (Finland), Iasi (Romania) and Taipei (Taiwan), the importance of capturing and sharing ideas between remote teams is even greater than if it only had a team in one location. As the company had problems just managing ideas in a single geographic location, it had a great need to manage new ideas between teams in such a way that ideas could flourish into innovations. Lost ideas and market opportunities were the key motivational factors to improving Movial's practices to support the passage of ideas into innovations in the company. This is a case story about the way Movial selected innovation tools to support the process of managing ideas and turning them into innovations in its organization.

3.4.2   How the Case Was Executed

In the beginning, Movial had no particular method for selecting an innovation tool. When we look back, however, we can discover that we followed an iterative process: understand user needs, run innovation tool pilots, look back and try to learn from exercises and experiences, analyse outcomes and do our best to deploy the outcomes in practice. This was our approach to discovering the suitability of different innovation management tools to meet the needs of our organization. The following sections will provide more details on how we carried out the case.

We gained an understanding of the basic user needs by arranging several big and small workshops. In these workshops, we used a variety of methods to identify the needs. We considered the key methods for gathering user needs to be group discussions, individual and group interviews, open area forums and observation of the daily work of a few key individuals. We also ran pilot projects for different, existing idea management tools to test their suitability for us.

Based on the outcome from the workshops and, in general, from gathering user needs, we started to form broader thoughts on the innovation tools fit for our organization. First, if the organization was already running well and was continuously able to seize new business opportunities, the assumption was that the right innovation flow existed in the organization. Thereby, what was really needed was to discover the patterns that would bring the best out of the innovation flow and support that with the right set of tools. Second, when working with innovation-related things, we were working with areas that created new business and wealth for the organization and its future. When we summed up the innovation tool selection for this, we found that we were selecting tools that formed the organization's technological basis aimed at supporting the day-to-day creation of the future of the business. The process was thereby greater than just choosing a tool that gathered ideas from the front line of innovation and made it easier to manage the ideas for products, services, processes and practices that support business being conducted. Third, in order to ensure that the innovation tool supported the organization's needs, it had to adapt smoothly to the business process itself as well as to the hands of the users.

We finally gained a deeper understanding of the organization's tools, business process, ideation flow and innovativeness via iteration in several workshops, simply by discussing with members of the organization how they completed their daily work, which tools they used and what they were missing that could ease their working. After understanding the current state of the variety of tools used and the gaps between the tools and users (organization members), we formed an overall picture to which an innovation tool was then supposed to fit. Although we had identified the innovation tool gap in the organization at that time, we realized that we were still missing something. The reason was that we were unable to really confirm that a tool could suit our use to such an extent that we could safely deploy it in our teams' daily use.

After a few discussion sessions on the new challenge, we decided to try a user-role-driven approach to overcome the challenge. We decided to split the organizational innovation flow into the following user roles: idea originator, idea seeker, idea reviewer and idea manager. These finally helped us to discover the fit between the user requirements and the different innovation tools.

The innovation user roles that Movial used were as follows:

1. Idea originator – anyone who comes up with a usable idea, within or outside a project
2. Idea seeker – someone who is looking for ideas or innovation for a project
3. Idea reviewer – anyone who gives feedback on the idea
4. Idea manager – someone who maintains the idea bank

The innovation roles that we used were based on observations that: although all the organization members can innovate, only a small percentage (approximately 5–20%) is active and actually comes forward with ideas. Even though most of the members seemed to keep their ideas to themselves, unless they were asked to bring them up, they still gladly commented on the ideas of active innovators when they were given an opportunity. Our rough estimate was that 10% of an organization's members are active idea originators and 90% reviewers. These 90% are a big resource that can be used by offering them a tool that will make their entry into the innovation process as easy as possible.

We realize that this is a simple approach to the roles and that there are innovation models with more fine-grained roles. These top-level roles cover the company's basic innovation process, however, and support it in the beginning before going for a more complex approach. The roles have considerably different goals: the important thing for an idea originator is to attract attention to his/her ideas and to be able to easily present them. An idea seeker needs to find the right people who have relevant expertise and experience. Idea reviewers want to take part in discussions on ideas already presented and an idea manager needs tools to keep the idea flow clean and up to date. The goals identified here are the basis of a list of use cases that the innovation tool needs to support. Innovation tool providers usually provide a list of the features of their tool. This list of use cases was compared with the feature list to see how well the tool matched the organization's innovation needs.

Based on the outcomes of the innovation tool selection process, we developed a 'user role vs. innovation tool' matrix to discover the fit of innovation tools vs. the innovation tool needs of the organization. In the matrix, the required innovation tool features (innovation tool requirements) are gathered from real user needs of real innovation actors. The matrix lists the requirements for each use case. When a tool is evaluated against it, the tool evaluator can quickly understand if the tool fits the organization's needs and how close the fit is (does not fit at all, fits quite well, perfect match). The matrix quickly shows which of the features of the innovation tools fit the organization and which do not. With the help of the matrix, it is a fairly straightforward process to rule out innovation tools that do not fit the organization's need (Fig. 3.5).

3.4.3 Lessons Learned and Solutions

We believe that understanding and being able to communicate the basic innovation flow from the organization is the key starting point for innovation tool selection. It provides a complete understanding of the environment the innovation tools were intended to fit and a view of where the innovation flow is likely to fluctuate in the future.

In order to figure out the flow, we considered it important to interview individuals about their daily work. We got to know the different team members better, their challenges in the work and how a tool may help them to innovate better.

	Tool 1	Tool 2	Tool 3	Tool 4	Tool 5
Main use cases					
Search for a suitable idea	bad	bad	medium	medium	good
Find persons to produce the idea	good	good	bad	bad	medium
Manage the received idea	bad	bad	medium	good	good
Submit idea	bad	bad	medium	good	good
Participate in idea discussion	good	medium	bad	medium	medium
Review idea	medium	medium	medium	medium	medium
Keep idea forum usable	bad	bad	medium	good	medium
Main functionality					
Search method for ideas	bad	bad	medium	medium	good
Communication method between users	good	medium	bad	medium	medium
Commenting / sharing method	medium	medium	medium	medium	medium
Idea forum / bank	bad	bad	medium	medium	good
Other functionality					
Idea voting	bad	bad	?	bad	medium
Real time discussion / meeting	good	bad	bad	bad	medium
Privacy / security	medium	medium	good	good	good
Including files (images, diagrams)	bad	medium	medium	medium	medium

Fig. 3.5 'User role vs. innovation tool' matrix

During the process, we received an improved understanding of where in the organization ideas originate and how they are processed by different individuals. This more detailed information helped us to verify that the understanding gained of the innovation flow was correct, and it also helped us to learn to eliminate unnecessary practices and habits from the process.

In addition, one important area for us was admitting that we did not progress well enough, although we had gathered a large amount of organizational knowledge for the case. This helped us to discuss and consider alternative approaches to progress further. We discovered user roles as the helping factor for us to move on.

Movial is continuously pushing to introduce new ideas to the market and industries in which it operates. It is critical for the company to ensure that this process flows smoothly to ensure the future of the company, as its business is based on this. When Movial learned about the need to improve the collection of ideas and purposeful management of them towards innovations, it understood that this tool selection process could have a harmful impact on the business if the tool selection failed. The team focusing on selecting the tool was challenged by two key questions: 'how could it find the right innovation tools for the organization's use?' and 'how could it ensure the acceptance of innovation tools by the different team members?'

These questions were not as easy as they might initially have seemed. First, Movial's organization is full of software developers and user experience designers who can create and develop such tools themselves – how can the focus of the business be retained while simultaneously looking for the innovation tool-related needs of the organization? Second, the innovation tools market offers several different tools, which does not make finding the right innovation tool easy; it only increases the amount of tools to examine. Third, possibly the quickest way to discover an innovation tool is to select a tool that is marketed as 'solves-all-your-innovation-related-problems', push that into the organization and make everyone use it. As quick as it may sound, this approach is probably the quickest way to failure as it provides no means to ensure user acceptance of the tool. The fourth alternative is to go on to study the organization's idea flow to business opportunities in more depth and discover the right innovation tools that best support the flow.

3.5 DS2, the Idea Management Process

Urko Rueda, Raul Soriano, Juan Sánchez Díaz, Oscar Gómez, and Pepe Fuster

3.5.1 Description of the Company

Design of Systems on Silicon S.A. (DS2), founded in 1998, was the first to develop and market Power Line Communications (PLC) chipsets and is the leading supplier of silicon and software for PLC. DS2 technology is widely used in many markets and runs on any type of wire in the home: electrical wiring, coaxial TV cable or phone line.

The company plays an important role in driving the development of Industry Standards to ensure that consumers, equipment manufacturers and service providers can benefit from fully interoperable wireline networking products. DS2 executives contribute to various international standardization committees including IEEE, ETSI, CENELEC, CISPR and ITU-T G.hn.

3.5.2 Challenges – Innovation strategy by DS2

The company's market coverage enforces a fast product development environment. To manage innovation in this environment, time is needed to identify ideas throughout and even beyond the organization: not only ideas related to product development but also those related to management procedures. Thus, time is a key issue. The time lag from ideas harvesting to ideas incubation is critical, as the final objective is to reach the market with the right product on time.

To manage emerging ideas, companies must identify and implement a methodology to ensure that the best and brightest ideas are not lost. In many respects, these ideas are the company's treasure. Correct management of them is critical to innovative companies like DS2.

3.5.3   Case Objectives

The company's goal is to seek continuous improvement in processes and projects. In particular, it wants to achieve a user-driven innovation management process. The case is aligned with three of the practice areas defined in this book:

- The Art of Idea Harvesting: avoid losing ideas
- The Art of Idea Valuation: avoid choosing the wrong ideas for development and paying insufficient attention to potentially interesting ones

The case focused on defining the procedures the company will require to manage ideas. Academic researchers helped DS2 identify critical requirements. These will be used to respond to the key questions and define methods and procedures to improve idea management in the company.

3.5.4   Initial State

Prior to this case study, the company did not assign enough resources to innovation due to the market time restrictions, by which products had to be ready according to the very strict timelines. It was acknowledged inside the company, however, that ideas were continuously emerging.

The DS2 business is submerged in a rapidly changing environment in which technology and competitors are continuously evolving to produce better products to solve customer requirements. This changing environment reduces the time dedicated to important activities within the company, for instance, the management of ideas. As ideas can come from different sources across and beyond the organization, it can be difficult to harvest and incubate them. Some possible causes that can drive innovation to failure are reflected in Fig. 3.6. In this sense, DS2 requires effort to be put into the work of defining a methodology and process to help it become more efficient in front of the market.

The objective of DS2 was to combine different tools to meet the needs of the company. There was a requirement from the Engineering Department for ideas to be collected using agile tools, for example, Wiki tools. The wikis help the engineers to drive the new ideas that arise during the software and hardware development process. DS2 wants to use a social wiki (maybe social Web 2.0) in which different roles and procedures can easily be defined to manage the new ideas among all the engineers. These agile tools should help harvest the ideas and evaluate them until they are properly mature. The Quality Department, however, required an advanced documentation management tool so that mature ideas can be translated into formal documents.

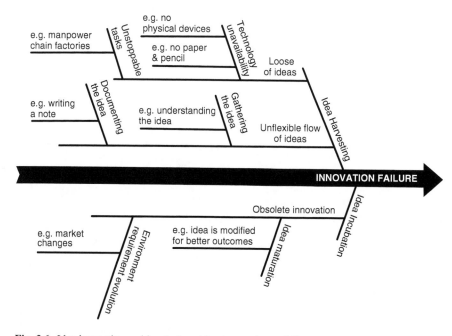

Fig. 3.6 Idea harvesting and incubation drive innovation to failure

3.5.5 How the Case Was Executed

DS2 has worked on a process for idea management using the Business Process Management Suite (BPMS)[1] by AuraPortal. The suite was used to deploy a suitable experimental portal for idea management that helped to drive ideas for product services. This is the first pilot project in terms of idea management that has been carried out within DS2.

The DS2 requirements were clarified and the use cases defined in several meetings with the UJI,[2] AuraPortal and UPV-ProS.[3] A process model, in Fig. 3.7, was built and improved for the idea management process using the Business Process Modeling Notation (BPMN[4]) standard.

To deploy it as an executable process, the model was translated to the specific notation of AuraPortal's BPMS suite, as displayed in Fig. 3.8. Although the models are equivalent, some specific components are used for further detail in the process.

The improvements from this process are aimed at allowing developers to share ideas with their work community. The organization carries out idea harvesting

---

[1]http://www.auraportal.com.

[2]http://www.uji.es/.

[3]http://www.pros.upv.es.

[4]http://www.bpmn.org/.

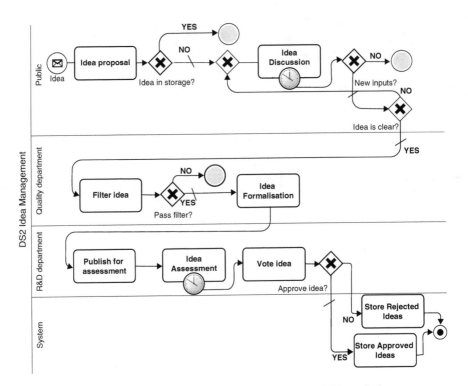

Fig. 3.7 Design of the process for idea management through the BPMN standard

campaigns to stimulate idea generation (though users can also propose the start of a new campaign). It is performed through a web portal with information from the campaign launched, including a summary of the state: proposed ideas, ideas for discussion, accepted ideas and incorporated ideas. There is also information about completed campaigns with success cases of ideas embodied in the company.

The company has an internal public platform for proposing ideas, Fig. 3.9, because ideas can come from different sources across and beyond the organization. The web portal gathers the identification of the entity that proposes a new idea (e.g., internal staff, partners or customers). It also collects the title and description of the idea and its optional procedure to carry out the idea. Ideas can also only be accessed by authorized users, i.e., customers do not see the ideas of internal staff.

Once a new idea proposal has been made, a discussion period initiates when the idea is explored, until it is clearly understood and defined. Next, a filtering process is started by the Quality Department to ensure the idea meets the minimum requirements for public inspection. The idea then undergoes a formalization process and is published for assessment. Ideas can be edited using a wiki tool. Each user has control of the grade of the share of his/her own proposals. Formalized ideas are defined more clearly and seen as enabling better decision-making on innovation. Although the idea is saved in the document's library and can be queried during the process, it can also be made public to the relevant persons.

Idea Management

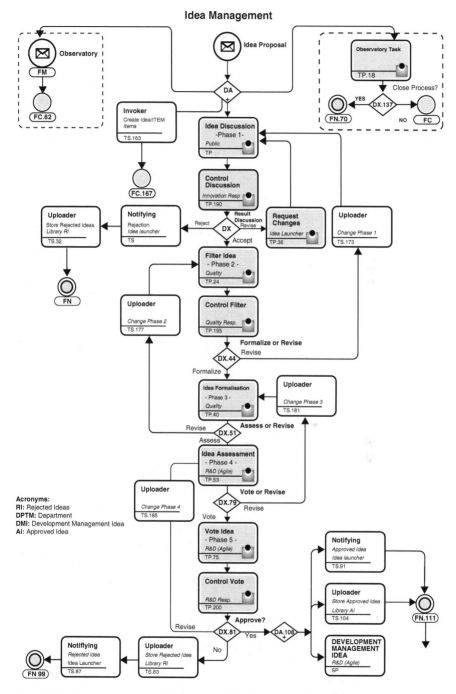

Fig. 3.8 Deployment as an executable process through AuraPortal's suite notation

Fig. 3.9 User interface for idea harvesting

During the assessment period, users who have been granted permission may consult and, if necessary, modify the proposal. Those responsible for approving ideas for incorporation into products, services or business processes can report the conclusions they deem appropriate. To favour idea queries, ideas are classified by different criteria, such as the type of innovation and the nature of the idea.

After the assessment, the idea is voted on for approval. Comments can be added to the vote whenever necessary. Ideas are evaluated and ranked in order based on the interest expressed by the community of colleagues. If the idea is approved, it is stored and may be annotated to the project to which it is related. Once the idea is included in the commercial offer, the state of the idea becomes incorporated. In the meantime, the idea is in a development state.

3.5.6 Lessons Learned – Solutions

Three lessons were learned from this experiment.

- **Lesson 1: The need for mobile support for idea harvesting.** Harvesting ideas under agile and flexible conditions, as in the DS2 case, requires appropriate methods to enable a dynamic flow of ideas and safe persistence so that they are not lost. A related method is discussed in Seyff et al. (2009). It involves a tool-supported contextual method that enables requirements elicitation in the *Austrian Alps* to discover the stakeholder's requirements for a ski tour navigation system. The tool is based on a Mobile Scenario Presenter (MSP) for mobile devices that need to model the domain and support on-site analysts in contextual requirements elicitation. If applied to the innovation context, an analogy would be a web portal for idea management, such as this pilot case, which can be made accessible through the use of mobile devices. These devices would then allow idea proposals to be registered as they emerge. A much simplified interface for fast ideas submission is needed to avoid breaking their flexible flow and minimizing the chance of losing them.
- **Lesson 2: The need to synthesize idea information.** There are situations in which technology, or even paper and pencil, are not available. An example can be found in manpower chain factories. An alternative approach is therefore needed, for example, a synthesis perspective on the ideas. Synthesizing implies the ability to infer relationships between sources of information. The basic skills needed are summarizing to understand the information and focusing to select the information from each source that best builds ideas. Mechanisms such as synthesizing keep a good balance between idea generation and idea storage, as the less information the easier it is to understand and remember. Less time is then needed to store the ideas, fostering a flexible flow of ideas. People's skills (memorizing, focusing, etc.) can be taken into account and roles can be assigned to further improve ideas harvesting. It is therefore important to understand what must be collected as well as when to collect it.
- **Lesson 3: The need for traceability**. Changing environments and ideas maturation introduce modifications to the ideas requirements. This has a negative influence on business capabilities to transform ideas into market solutions. If the environment (the market) changes, one consequence is that ongoing and implemented ideas can fall into a state of unsatisfied requirements. Unless they are adapted to the new requirements, the ideas will lose value and become invalid or useless. To enable fast adaptation in this context and drive innovation to succeed, it is a prerequisite to maintain the traceability of the innovation. This is similar to other disciplines in software engineering (Gotel and Finkelstein 1994; Cleland-Huang et al. 2005; Khabbazi et al. 2009) in which a management process must be present to deal with software evolution. Nonetheless, the fundamental innovation processes related to harvesting, valuation and incubation should be flexible enough to allow fast adaptation of ideas to changes in environmental requirements.

3.6 Metso, Harvesting Product Ideas as Part of a Global Innovation Process

Jukka Kääriäinen and Antti Välimäki

This case describes how Metso tackled the challenges of idea harvesting in a global innovation environment.

3.6.1 The Challenge of Harvesting Product Ideas in a Global Innovation Environment

Nowadays, the innovation process is very important to companies. Best-practice companies value effective collection and evaluation of product ideas. Based on systematic idea collection and evaluation, these companies develop more new products to sell than typical companies do. Product ideas have to be collected, evaluated and incorporated into roadmaps and product development faster and more efficiently than before, also in a global development environment. Metso had the challenge of systematizing and improving product idea collection and management in a distributed development environment. Globalization forces companies to find ways to overcome geographical barriers. Information technology offers excellent means to achieve this goal. In this case, the company implemented a new innovation management database with practices to cope with the challenges.

3.6.2 How the Case Was Executed

The case study was carried out at Metso. Metso is a company operating in the field of automation industry. The company operates in a multi-site environment and, in the future, the work related to product ideas and features will globalize even more to cover several countries. The challenges of the global development environment were therefore studied, and solutions to overcome the challenges were defined and implemented.

Metso developed a new innovation management database based on the current state analysis (Välimäki and Kääriäinen 2007). The applicability of the solution was analysed based on data received from a questionnaire sent to the users of the innovation management solution (global Notes innovation management database and practices). The questionnaire asked about the users' satisfaction with old and new innovation management solutions. The questionnaire was sent to persons who were active users of the innovation management solution and therefore capable of assessing the impact of the new solution on their work. This questionnaire was part of a larger case study aimed at analysing and improving the whole innovation management process at Metso (Pikkarainen et al. 2010b).

3.6.3   Lessons Learned – Solutions

In the old solution, product ideas were in e-mails, text files, presentation templates, etc. Increasing efficiency demands and a shift towards a distributed development environment, however, requires a centralized database for collecting, managing and sharing ideas, features and requirements. The new solution comprises a global Notes innovation management database and practices for its use. A common global Notes-based innovation management database was taken into use by the product and project management to support ideation. The new solution has many advantages compared with the old one. The new solution provides secure global access to the database regardless of time and place. Product ideas are fed into the database as Demands with a pre-defined form, including information concerning, for instance:

- Idea Identification: *Idea ID, status, Author, Responsible Person, Contact Person*
- Demand Description: *Title, Description and Benefit, Other Comments*
- Product Family: *Target Product Family*
- Requirements and Priorities: *Required by, Importance for Requester, Target Release, Business Impact, Cost Estimation*

The tool contains the different views of information based on the needs of the teams, project managers and product management. Furthermore, it now allows product ideas, features and their related information to be visible globally in real time, including links between different items. Possible future improvements relate to, for instance, more systematic use of the database among all the relevant stakeholders and feedback mechanisms for idea originators.

The users of the Notes-based innovation management solution were asked about their satisfaction with the old and new innovation management solutions. The results emphasize the importance of a centralized product idea management database that can be used around the world. The summary of the ratings, based on the innovation management process phases, is presented in Fig. 3.10. The results indicate that the respondents are more satisfied, especially in the early phase of the innovation process, i.e., 'The Art of Idea Harvesting'.

3.6.4   Managerial Implications

Customer-orientation is fundamentally based on successful knowledge management between customers, sales, and the research and development department. Efficient processes and tools are needed, as well as commitment by top management to provide resources and possibilities to implement an efficient innovation management process.

The global innovation management database proved successful at Metso. An efficient process and database for collecting product ideas, transforming them into realizable features and assigning them to practical development projects is

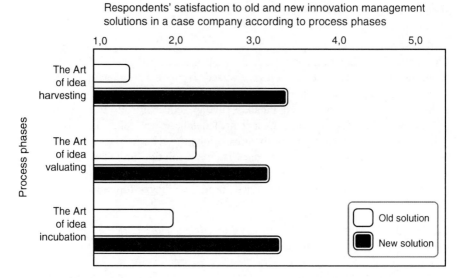

Fig. 3.10 Respondents' satisfaction (mean value) with old and new innovation management solutions in a case company (1 = poor, 5 = excellent)

essential to effective product development. It is therefore important that tools that support the innovation process are in active use by all the relevant stakeholders. The company believes that the solution is moving in the right direction, even though there are some issues that need to be tackled in future improvements. The company is familiar with the Notes technology and the application was therefore fairly easy to implement. The users were also familiar with the terminology, and look and feel of the solution. This facilitated the successful deployment of the solution.

3.7 Financial Company, Customer Values and Innovation

Oza Nilay

3.7.1 Challenge of Aligning Innovation with the Company's Capabilities and Customer Values

Before jumping into innovation activities, it is important to understand how specific improvement initiatives will impact the companies' capabilities and customer values. The dilemma is classic and ongoing. Senior management is puzzled by the return on investment of innovation initiatives and often lack the visibility of how investment in innovation brings the yields demonstrated by middle management (which runs the innovation programmes). Middle layer management (such as programme managers) tends to have a constant struggle convincing senior management that innovation programmes are needed to improve certain capabilities and often lack an understanding of the clear impact of innovation initiatives on customer values. The workforce at junior level (e.g., engineers who actually contribute significantly to the companies' capabilities) actually knows the real problems and scope of improvement in several capability areas. They often lack the ability to align the improvement opportunities properly with their capabilities, however, and are unable to convince middle management (which has its own driving agenda with a positive view of 'contributing something good'). The story could be much more complex however. In essence, at times, technology companies lack the ability to see the whole value chain of innovation programmes and the respective initiatives.

3.7.2 How the Case Was Executed

A case study was conducted to align agile practices with innovation enablers and customer values. The case study was conducted using a moderated workshop and post-workshop analysis of the collected data. Data were collected in the form of two matrices during the workshop. One matrix included a comparison of agile practices against innovation enablers and the second matrix included innovation enablers compared with important customer values. The result from the case was a list of innovation enablers that have a high potential impact on those agile practices that are important for addressing customer values. The tailored version of Quality Function Deployment (QFD) was used to conduct the alignment analysis.

The case study started with a moderated workshop of participants from different software functions, from management and coordination to core development. The workshop took approximately 3 h. As a first alignment exercise, a matrix (such as that in Fig. 3.11) was developed, showing agile practices that potentially have a high impact on customer values. Customer values and agile practices were discussed and prioritized with group exercises. The cumulative high impact of agile practices was measured and prioritized accordingly. In the second alignment exercise, the prioritized, high-impact agile practices were then aligned against innovation enablers. Innovation enablers were also discussed and prioritized using a group exercise. The second matrix was developed (as shown in Fig. 3.12), showing the cumulative high impact of innovation enablers against the high impact and prioritized (according to their respective impacts on customer values) agile practices. The patterns from the matrix were extremely useful for seeing the impact of specific innovation enablers on certain agile practices.

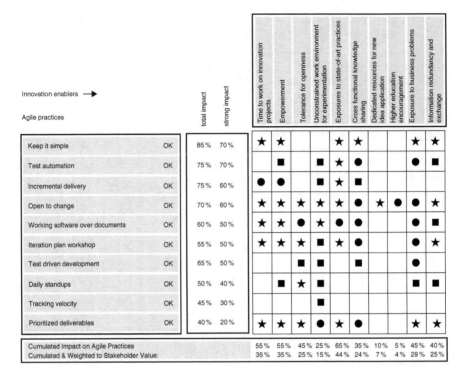

Fig. 3.11 Excerpt from one of the workshops in which the impact of innovation enablers was reviewed against high impact agile practices

3.7.3 Lessons Learned – Solutions

The case proved that with proper alignment, companies can make strategic and more informed choices when investing in improvement initiatives. It was interesting to learn that certain agile practices that were thought to have a high impact on customer values did not initially have a high impact when they were aligned with the innovation enablers and customer values. The workshop conducted for alignment also greatly helped the participants to understand the potential impact of a specific enabler. In the next phase, we took the results of the alignment exercise and conducted a company-wide survey to validate the findings and find possible deviations from the results of a wider audience. Finally, based on the survey results, we selected three innovation enablers (with the highest possible impact ratio) and developed a set of actions that would help to address a specific enabler. To hold an alignment workshop, please contact the author of this chapter.

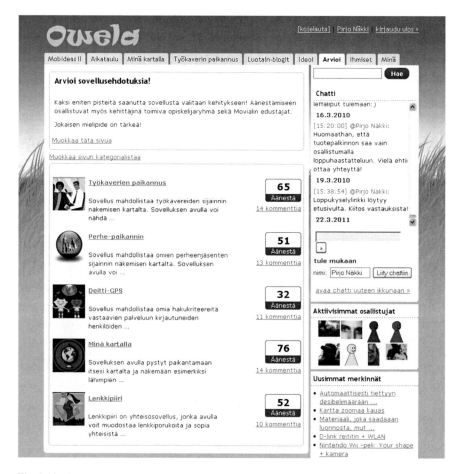

Fig. 3.12 End-users comment and rate concept designs in the Owela online co-creation platform

3.8   Owela, Online Co-creation with End-Users

Kaisa Koskela and Pirjo Näkki

3.8.1   Challenge of Co-creation with End-Users

Customers and users play a major role when looking for innovation outside a company's boundaries. This vast crowd of people represents huge innovation potential. Many companies struggle to harness this resource to its full potential however. In the software domain, co-creation with users is especially challenging in the now much dispersed consumer markets in which potential end-users are distributed both geographically and by time. As a result, traditional co-creation methods that rely on face-to-face communication cannot easily be applied. Online tools, especially social media, provide new opportunities for reaching end-users and involving them in co-creation activities.

3.8.2   How the Case Was Executed

A case study was conducted to explore the benefits and challenges of online co-creation when developing a web service. The innovation project started by recognizing user needs and it continued for several months until the implementation of the software. An online co-creation platform Owela (http://owela.vtt.fi) was used as the co-creation platform for all the participants, including the end-users, software developers and facilitators. The online workspace provides structured and easy-to-use tools for different phases of software design. The users did not have to participate in any face-to-face meetings.

In the beginning of the case study, a selected group of users was invited to participate in a software development project. A software development team was involved that worked according to the agile software development practices. The users were actively involved throughout the development process via Owela. They wrote user stories, generated new service ideas based on their own needs and rated the ideas, chose the concept for prototyping and prioritized features to be implemented in the web service. The users also participated in the testing of the prototype demos of the web service and provided feedback to the developers by leaving comments and improvement suggestions, and by communicating directly with the developers in live chat sessions.

3.8.3   Lessons Learned – Solutions

The case proved that online tools help overcome some of the challenges related to co-creation with end-users distributed geographically and by time. The Owela platform enabled continuous user involvement and direct communication between the end-users, software developers and facilitators. This way, the real user needs acted as the drivers of the decision-making and development work throughout the project. The agile development cycles, with continuous updates and interaction, worked as a mechanism to keep the users motivated and involved throughout the 4-month development phase.

The users felt very motivated when they saw how their ideas and feedback were taken into account in the each release of the prototype. The developers also considered the user feedback beneficial. It inspired them to deliver better solutions after each release.

The online co-creation platform proved to be an effective and pleasant way to involve users in the new software development process. It enabled the users to have a more active role and participate in several phases of the process. Giving the users a more active role and direct communication did not mean that the managing the process was simple however. Instead, the facilitator's role in the process was essential in order to guarantee active participation by the users and mutual understanding between the users and developers.

3.9   Inno-W, Practical Open Idea Management, Case Finnish Forestcluster

Paula Jalo and Henry Palonen

3.9.1   Challenge of Open Idea Co-creation

The world's strongest knowledge-based wood processing cluster is located in Finland. In order to keep this position, continuous innovation and renewal is needed. Forestcluster Ltd is an innovation company established to network and enhance top-level research and innovation in the Finnish forest cluster. Forestcluster Ltd's target is to double the value of forest cluster products and services and establish a successful, constantly developing forest cluster in Finland whose products and services are among the most sought after in the world. The major companies in the Finnish forest cluster (UPM-Kymmene, Stora Enso, Metso, Kemira and Andritz) together with the research organizations (VTT, Finnish Forest Research Institute and four Finnish universities) are the owners of Forestcluster Ltd. Research in the forest cluster focuses on the Strategic Research Areas (SRA): *Intelligent and resource-efficient production technologies, Future Biorefinery* and *Customer solutions for the future.* Many of the new innovations in the forest cluster are based on ICT (e.g., developing embedded software in paper machines).

When so many parties are involved in innovation, the challenge is to gather all the good ideas, thoughts and proposals in one place and not lose any important data. New open-source-based software technology (Web 2.0) has created novel opportunities to solve the above-mentioned challenges. It offers solutions and services based on collaboration platforms. The Web 2.0 community platform connects customers, suppliers and partners in the innovation process, enabling openness in all business interfaces. Inno-W's community-based online portal has been introduced as a solution for information sharing and idea management in the forest cluster.

In addition to the initial idea collection phase, it is also important that the online portal support further steps in the idea management, such as idea assessment and formation into actual projects. The challenge is to make the different parties exchange ideas and knowledge among themselves and to motivate them to do so. The first step in motivating people to use the online portal for distributing ideas and proposals is to offer them user-friendly software. The second step is to motivate and encourage them to open communication through an online portal.

3.9.2 How the Case Was Executed

The case study was carried out in the Forestcluster Research Portal, which is one of the development and testing environments, and it includes open and semi-open innovation platforms. The Finnish Forestcluster Research Portal is designed to help researchers in Finland and abroad to prepare for the implementation of the Finnish Research Agenda (NRA). Skilled people and a well-functioning education system are key factors to the success of the Finnish forest cluster at present and in the future. Universities and research organizations play an important role in the cluster's cooperation. Therefore, it is important that they can share and distribute their ideas among themselves through the Forestcluster Research Portal. In this case, Inno-W's research focus was on supporting open innovation through the idea process and the decision-making process.

The Forestcluster Research Portal enables the innovation process through open, semi-open and protected ideas (Fig. 3.13). The creation of open ideas is the first phase of the idea process, and it takes place on open wiki pages such as open idea platforms (Discussion forum) on which any licensed user in the portal is able to create ideas. Semi-open ideas or project proposals are created through formal wiki forms in password-protected areas. They are always made by certain experts and they therefore concern certain subjects or research fields. At this stage, experts can develop ideas and concepts further together in a highly collaborative environment as well as develop ideas for project proposals. Many of the semi-open ideas that have been created in the Forestcluster Research Portal have and will be developed through a formal innovation process.

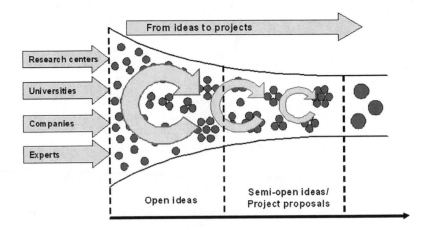

Fig. 3.13 Innovation process, from ideas to projects

The current outcome shows that the open idea platform of the Forestcluster Research Portal, designed for open brainstorming and discussion, has not yet been in frequent use for creating actual new ideas. The semi-open idea forum has been useful for discussions and answering the questions inside the programs. IPRs have been defined in consortium agreements, and all the ideas are then only open to consortium members. Members of the programme can easily share their ideas and strengthen the collaboration on the semi-open idea platform. The platform has facilitated interaction in, e.g., developing new innovations based on new software in paper and bio-energy processes and utilities – especially between different companies and universities.

The platform for project proposals has been in more active use. Proposal management includes a total of 118 proposals from different companies and universities. Forestcluster's research programmes are the main users of proposal management. Intelligent, resource-efficient production technologies (EffTech) are a good example of a programme that has used proposal management. EffTech's first Proposal Management included 32 proposals from 14 companies and universities. The second EffTech New Ideas round included 40 proposals from 12 companies and universities. All the proposals were evaluated by expert groups that viewed the proposals and entered their scores and comments using specific criteria. After the evaluation, the summary of evaluations and charts showed the total scores and comments (Fig. 3.14). Eight of the proposals were approved, and these eight are now actual projects of the EffTech programme.[5]

3.9.3   Lesson Learned – Solutions and Managerial Implications

The results of the case study show that it is important to have tools and solutions that support the idea management process by the Forestcluster Research Portal. The focus was on finding solutions that support teamwork even better in the idea process in the forest cluster and all other strategic industry clusters. At present, it is obvious that idea processing is happening in all areas of the Forestcluster Research Portal. Participants are voting and commenting on new ideas on the open pages. The best idea generation happens on the internal project pages (semi-open ideas) among project members however. The collection of new ideas through closed proposal forms and the evaluation of these proposals have progressed gradually. The culture in which experts process and discuss new ideas together is lacking. People want to take credit for ideas and they do not see the added value of cooperation. People want to process their ideas alone not by working in teams. If the commenting on

---

[5]More information from http://www.forestcluster.fi/d/content/intelligent-and-resource-efficient-production-technologies.

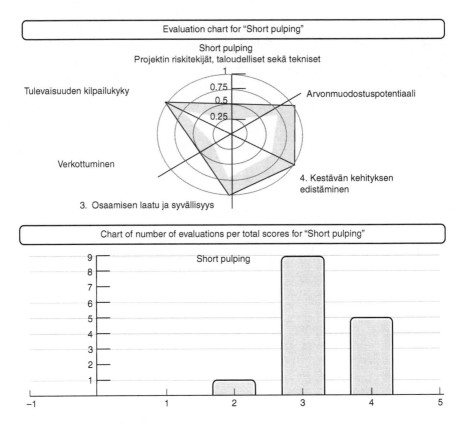

Fig. 3.14 Idea evaluation charts

ideas is not tied to the programme process, including agreed voting and commenting on dates, people do not respond to these separate ideas. The question is whether the lack of cooperation is just something that is related to the Finnish culture and academic work culture or if it could be alterable by the Forestcluster Research Portal idea process tools.

The above-mentioned EffTech proposal is a good example of how Web 2.0 solutions have facilitated and enriched the idea management process for programmes that include different companies and universities. The Web 2.0 solutions have not only helped companies to make new proposals but also expert groups to evaluate proposals. Evaluators have also presented their development ideas regarding the idea management system, thereby helping Inno-W to develop the idea management system. The real use of the idea management system and the feedback from users are the key to developing a successful and user-friendly system. Software development has brought different companies closer together. Companies that have not used an open idea forum or idea/proposal management have missed the opportunities that social media offers, e.g., collaboration, changing of ideas, brainstorming with other users and effective proposal management.

3.10   Mahiti Infotech, Open Source as an Innovation Enabler in India

Katja Henttonen

3.10.1   Challenge of Using Open Source Software in Software Business

Involvement in open source software (OSS) projects is often raised as a 'classic' example of applying the Art of Openness to the software business. In the case of the outside-in approach, a company sources intellectual property (IP) from OSS communities. Typically, the main goal is to save R&D expenses and/or achieve a shorter time to market. In the case of the inside-out approach, a company turns an internal development project into an externally visible OSS project. Such an OSS 'spin-out' may create a demand for other products or services that a company sells or support strategic goals such as standards creation. OSS communities can also be platforms for *open co-creation* in which diverse stakeholders join forces to achieve a common R&D goal and pooled contributions are made available to all.

Many software companies are still wondering what OSS could offer to their business in practical terms. With regard to inbound IP flows, they are often concerned with the lack of control over externally developed OSS technology and/or their own ability to add value to a product that is already widely available free. In turn, outbound IP flows seem to require significant investment in non-revenue-generating activities and, thus, companies have justified concerns about affordability and difficulties capturing indirect returns. The question 'what is there to gain' is especially relevant to small and medium-sized enterprises (SMEs), as they can hardly expect to rearrange global markets with their OSS investments, at least not in the same way as IBM and some of the other 'big players' have famously done.

3.10.2   How the Case Study Was Executed

We performed an organizational case study of an Indian software SME called Mahiti Infotech (Henttonen 2011), which derives significant value from OSS involvement. The objective was to understand better how OSS has helped the case company improve its innovative capability and differentiate itself from competitors. Data collection involved interviewing directors and developers in the case company, reading company documentation and monitoring employee interaction with OSS communities on the Internet. Two qualitative methods were employed to analyse the data. First, Value Network Analysis (Allee 2003) was employed to model how open innovation works in the case company. Second, a thematic coding method was used to analyse the company's experiences of open innovation.

Mahiti Infotech is headquartered in Bangalore and it employs 70–90 people. It bases practically all of its offerings on OSS and has reportedly been soundly profitable for the past 8 years. The company employs a *customized product development model:* it develops 'semi-finished' products, often co-creatively with OSS communities, and later adds value by customizing them to the needs of individual end clients. The tailored products go to market either as bespoke software or through the application service provision (ASP) model. Technical consulting provides additional revenue streams.

The case study exemplifies the way primary software companies can benefit from OSS-based innovation processes. When using OSS, Mahiti integrates elements from the different openness approaches: outside-in, inside-out and open co-creation. The benefits are discussed briefly below.

3.10.3   Lessons Learned

With limited financial and human resources, the case company must in-source commodity software from outside in order stay at the technological forefront. Sourcing it from OSS communities has several advantages. The company can modify the software freely without being confined to vendor-designed interfaces or configuration options. It can therefore add more value to OSS products than a non-vendor can typically add to proprietary products. In the absence of licensing fees, it can also keep a bigger proportion of the revenues from the added value. OSS also makes customized software affordable to new consumer groups, e.g., small and domestic non-profit companies and thereby expands the size of the bespoke software markets in the region. As the case company does not distribute packaged software, OSS licensing terms have little or no implications for their business.

In addition to in-sourcing, the case company releases any 'surplus' intellectual property that it owns. Whenever it has a piece of source code that has reached the end of its life cycle, it makes it freely available on SourceForge or a similar OSS platform. The cost of open sourcing is very low in this case, but sometimes there are surprising benefits when the IP 'gets a new life' in the OSS domain. For example, the company open sourced a very small business software program, a leave management system that was only meant to be used in-house. Later, it was contacted by a big foundation that had downloaded the software from the Internet and wanted to have it extended. The company gained a very important customer in this way, but the marketing effort consisted only of a few mouse clicks.

Mahiti also plays a globally important role in the development of some OSS products, e.g., the Plone content management system. By participating in open co-creation, the company gains a degree of control over product development decisions and can accumulate the type of in-depth expertise that is only available to a vendor in the world of closed source software. Significant promotional benefits of OSS participation were also reported. Most importantly, the company becomes seen as a 'shaper' of technology. 'They [customers] come to us because they see us as people who vision the [OSS] product and not only as people having [third-party] expertise on it', explains a marketing director. The OSS communities are also specialized social networks in which 'word-of-mouth' travels quickly: recommendations by other OSS community members bring many customers.

3.10.4   Managerial Implications

*   In-sourcing software from OSS communities can be a viable option to 'buy or build'. If a company avoids investing in commodity software, resources are freed for more innovative activities. Increased affordability to end customers may also create new markets.
*   It is rarely worthwhile to 'sit on' surplus intellectual property. OSS communities provide a channel for releasing IP that no longer creates value in-house. If the released IP creates value elsewhere, there is a change to claim a portion of that value.
*   OSS co-creation blurs the boundary between a software vendor and a third-party service provider. It can open up new opportunities for those third-party software companies that wish to upgrade in the value chain but lack the resources to develop their own products from 'scratch'.

3.11   Answare, Idea Generation Within the Company's Human Resources

Eduardo Riol

Traditional brainstorming methods have evolved and adapted to a more competitive and dynamical environment: new ideas should be collected, discussed and applied in a standardized and well-managed way. A proposal for the best method of Idea Harvesting within a Company's Human Resources must prove to be reliable and robust enough to ensure this issue without losing flexibility.

3.11.1   How the Case Was Executed

The framework we are about to expose consists of three phases: Detection, Management and Decision. The first takes place when an issue that needs to be faced – e.g.: business opportunity, lack of resources, etc.- is noticed and a solution is required. Typically companies have an innovation responsibility person who reports the issue to the organization. This is called Detection phase. During the

Ideas Management phase, a responsible person then takes charge of organizing the meeting by supplying the team with the necessary resources and support (Fig. 3.15).

The main phase of the framework is Decision. It supports three different sub-processes to harvest ideas. The responsible person from the Management phase referred to previously takes charge of selecting one of the sub-processes, depending on the problem context and its knowledge. An experienced responsible person is therefore needed for this phase (Fig. 3.16).

The L-M-N method is the first possible choice for Idea Harvesting. It is based in the idea of 'L' people discussing 'M' ideas during 'N' minutes. It obliges everyone to participate in the brainstorming, provide new ideas and/or comment on others', so it would fit in well in less experienced teams (Fig. 3.17).

Each participant writes an idea on a sheet of paper, and when a previously established time has passed, she or he passes the paper to the next teammate. When each participant reads her or his mate's paper, the participant chooses between commenting on the other's ideas and writing a new idea on the paper. The process ends when everyone has seen every paper.

The Metaplan has a more flexible frame, but it cannot prevent one participant from refusing to join the discussion.

Participants take part freely in the discussion. When the responsible person asks for a new idea, everyone is able to add her or his own idea, wait to comment on another's idea or just keep quiet.

The 6 Hats method, a thinking methodology for group discussion based on the interpretation of several roles, requires more training and fits well when the team is experienced and motivated (Fig. 3.18).

The person responsible for the meeting starts by notifying the first hat/role, choosing between one of the following: black/critical, blue/pragmatic, green/creative, red/emotional, white/objective and yellow/optimistic. Each participant assumes her or his role and follows the discussion under that hat. Ideas are discussed and comments are added until no one has anything more to say. The hat is then changed and previous ideas are discussed under the new role. New ideas can also be added. The discussion finishes when every hat has been worn.

Finally, regardless of the chosen branch, a balloting process between all the participants is launched to obtain a list that has been sorted out with the generated ideas, which must be checked by an authorized committee.

3.11.2   Lessons Learned – Solutions

The case has been tested in Answare in a variety of issues and has proved that Idea Harvesting might take place in many fields, like eHealth, Telecommunications, Mobile Applications, Tourism, Energy, etc. Nevertheless one of the most important fields of application is the company itself: the people who work together as a team seeking common objectives may have many unexploited ideas that can be of great interest to harvest, manage and analyse. Everyone in the organization should feel

Idea Generation

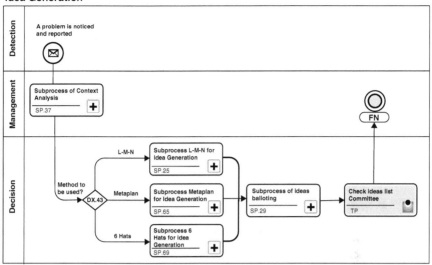

Fig. 3.15 General process of idea generation

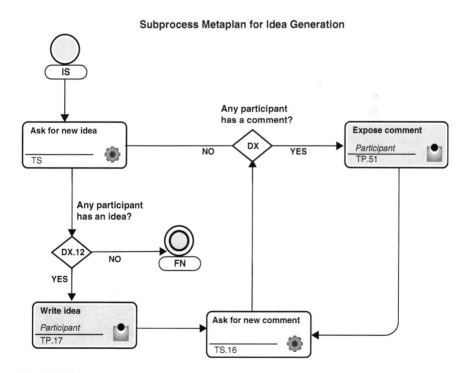

Fig. 3.16 Sub-process metaplan

Subprocess L-M-N for Idea Generation

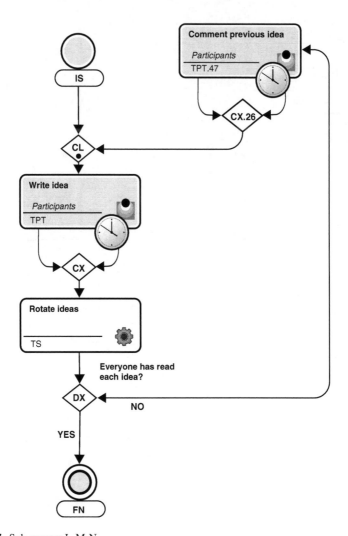

Fig. 3.17 Sub-process L-M-N

free to expose her or his worries and possible solutions. A good process or set of processes is needed to ensure an accurate atmosphere and motivation to develop this framework.

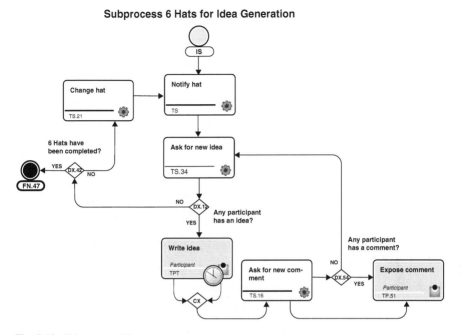

Fig. 3.18 Sub-process 6 hats

3.12   Sisteplant, Idea Valuation

Ander Gorostiza

Sisteplant is a Spanish management software vendor that offers two standard products: a maintenance management software program called Prisma and a manufacturing execution system called Captor. A new release of both products is delivered every year. At Sisteplant, the software development is based on Scrum, an iterative, incremental framework for agile software development.

3.12.1   Challenge

Sisteplant's product competitors are developed by multinational companies like SAP, IBM, Oracle, etc. Sisteplant's main competitive advantage is its large customer base (more than 1,000), which is centred mainly in the Spanish market. To beat the competition, Sisteplant must focus on knowing its current and future customers' needs.

Participation by local customers in product evolution is something that competitors cannot provide, and it increases the customers' involvement with the product and satisfaction with the company.

The company's available development force is much smaller than that of its competitors, however, so it is essential that it prioritizes its efforts.

3.12.2   How the Case Is Executed

Each product has a Product Owner who collects and prioritizes the requirements for the product. Next, versions of both standard products are developed every year. Releases are offered to customers with an after-sales contract.

The requirements for new releases are taken from three sources:

- Every customer may contribute by sending new requirements.
- The Product Owner may contribute by studying competitors.
- Internal stakeholders may contribute requirements that have come up during the process of implementing the product.

With all these requirements, the Product Owner builds a list called the Product Backlog. A prioritization criterion is needed so that development can be carried out in a logical order.

The Product Owner prioritizes this backlog based on the productivity of the requirement:

$$\text{Requirement Productivity} = \frac{\text{Requirement Expected Benefit}}{\text{Requirement Development Effort}}$$

How the requirement expected benefit is measured

The Product Owner needs to know the real benefit that this requirement provides for current and future customers.

Every year, Sisteplant Customers hold an Annual Users Club meeting (or to be precise four meetings, in: Spain, Portugal, Brazil and Mexico). At this meeting, requirements collected during the year are presented to the plenary. Each customer selects five main requirements ordered according to its opinion. With this information, an ordered list is built and each requirement is given a score.

How the requirement development effort is measured

The Product Owner needs to know how much real effort is needed to implement the requirement. The whole development team participates in the estimation process for each requirement. A voting system is used.

In the estimation process, some previously estimated processes (called master processes) are taken into account. Each process type (report, graphics, etc.) should be reflected by at least one process master.

For the estimation process, each requirement effort is compared against the effort for the master (two times, three times ...). The risk and complexity introduced by the new requirement should be taken into account (it is not the same modifying a satellite process as a nuclear process).

How the requirement productivity is measured

With the Measuring Requirement Expected Benefit and Requirement Development Effort Product, the Owner can measure the Requirement Productivity and prioritize the product backlog.

3.12.3 Lessons Learned – Solutions

Customers are our main source of requirements. They live with our products (successes and failures) every day, so it is a must to consider their opinions.

It is essential to have objective prioritization criteria when development resources are limited so that productivity can be maximized.

Everyone (internal and external) thinks that his/her requirements are the most valuable. It is highly motivating to include a requirement, but it can be very frustrating to reject one. The prioritization criteria must be clear, objective and known.

If a customer sees that an idea is included in the product, you will gain a supporter of your product.

It is important that developers participate in the evaluation effort. The expected measured effort will be more precise, though it is more important that the developer's commitment increases, as his/her opinion is taken into account.

3.12.4 Managerial Implications

The company understands the customers' needs and knows that its effort is aimed at real requirements. Resource productivity is optimized, so size limitation can be afforded.

3.13 Polar Elektro, InnoCoop – A Method to Support Innovation

Mikko Järvilehto and Jouni Similä (University of Oulu)

3.13.1 Innovation competition and the InnoCoop Method

InnoCoop (Innovation Coopetition) is an innovation method that incorporates features from innovation competitions, strategic consulting, business events, brainstorming workshops, staff recreational events and organizational surveys.

An innovation competition (Innovation_competition in Wikipedia) is a method or process in the industrial process, product or business development. It is a form of social engineering that focuses on the creation and elaboration of the best and sustainable ideas coming from the best innovators. Innovation competitions are sometimes organized by a third party (an intermediator) instead of the focal company or innovator community.

Innovation competitions (and coopetitions) are seen as a solution to the following major industry challenges: ineffectiveness of traditional market research; the structural innovation gap that exists between customers, R&D departments and other organizational units; the closed innovation paradigm; and the low amount, quality and variance of innovation opportunities.

The aims and design principles of innovation competitions are noted in the literature as follows:

- Encourage Adidas users to participate in an open innovation process to inspire creativity and increase the quality of the submissions.
- Constraints are an invaluable tool for fostering creativity. Idea Crossing's contestants are bound by rules and they strive to strategize optimal solutions to meet a competition's goal.
- Generate innovations, process and product ideas for SAP Research and Development through an IT-supported ideas competition among the SAP UCC Community. The concept aims to provide an interface to SAP Human Resources processes in order to identify the most promising students for VCs.
- Siemens Corporate Technology held an idea competition to help bridge the innovation gap that exists between different R&D departments and operational units. The company learnt that idea competitions can be a first step towards more comprehensive innovation processes.
- Innovation competitions are useful for generating radical ideas for the development of new products for the service industry.

3.13.2 Theoretical Background and Development

InnoCoop is based on theories about effectiveness, efficiency and adaptability (Deming 1986; Juran and Godfrey 1998; Terwiesch and Ulrich 2009), openness (Chesbrough 2003, 2006; Chesbrough et al. 2006), agility (Agile Manifesto; Larman and Basili 2003b), games and competition (Caillois 2001; Amabile 1996; Terwiesch and Ulrich 2009), creativeness and group flow (Csikszentmihalyi 1990; Csikszentmihalyi 1996; Sawyer 2008) and scientific validity (Amabile 1996; Piller and Walcher 2006; Yin 2009; Whyte 1991)

InnoCoop is developed collaboratively by an international, cross-disciplinary research team consisting of experts from engineering, business, software and social sciences at the University of Oulu, Finland. In order to ensure scientific validity of the InnoCoop method, comparative case studies are being conducted using a participatory action research approach.

3.13.3 Why Does InnoCoop Work?

As InnoCoop bundles traditionally separate activities into one single process, it creates synergy between those parts.

InnoCoop optimizes individual and team creativity through time constraints, rich audio and visualizing stimuli. It enhances motivation through individual and team competition. InnoCoop optimizes a requisite variety of team composition and visualization of the problem domain. As with traditional brainstorming, InnoCoop aims to create as many ideas as possible. InnoCoop uses multi-level filtering in order to track down exceptional innovations. Innovation elaboration is supported by external domain experts.

3.13.4 InnoCoop in Figures

InnoCoop normally includes 2–5 facilitators, 10–30 innovators, 2–5 teams and lasts from 8 to 24 h. InnoCoop uses external jurors to evaluate the ideas. InnoCoop is also scalable to a large-scale seminar-format, which can involve a multitude of participants.

3.13.5 InnoCoop in Polar Electro Ltd

A comparative case study of the InnoCoop method at Polar Electro Ltd. can be found in Järvilehto et al. 2010. The results confirm that InnoCoop is more effective than traditional market research; InnoCoop overcomes the structural innovation gap that exists between customers, R&D departments and other organizational units; and InnoCoop increases the amount, quality and variance in innovation opportunities. InnoCoop produces more holistic product concepts, involves management in participation, is active in terms of working methods, offers more surprise elements and produces more creative ideas. The traditional method produces singular but concrete ideas and is more passive in terms of working methods.

3.13.6 What Kind of Results Can InnoCoop Deliver?

InnoCoop process can be used to develop solutions for a selected domain, e.g., business models, product or service concepts, and strategy plans. It can also be used to foster a more creative/innovative working culture (Fig. 3.19).

3.14 Invicor, Flying Start to Merge Three Organizations

Petri Morko

The InnoCoop-based Innovation Tournament is an open, agile and scalable IT software-supported method for managing strategic challenges. It has been tested in many strategic management situations such as the ones below.

InnoCoop Process*

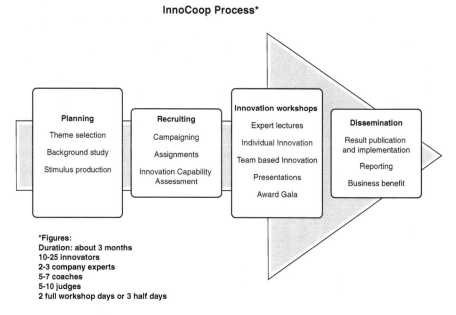

Fig. 3.19 InnoCoop process

The Innovation Tournament in new business creation: How do you create an outstanding new business in 2 days in an open-innovation fashion based on the existing knowledge of your organization? The organization knew that it had huge business potential. The big question was: How do you transform it quickly and efficiently into a new business? The Innovation Tournament was the chosen method, and it resulted in:

- Three new horizontal businesses based on existing knowledge
- Revenue expectations of 150 M€, equalling 25% of today's revenue
- First pre-orders placed
- A few customer meetings scheduled

Destia Innovation Tournament, autumn 2009

The Innovation Tournament in ecosystem creation: How do you create a new national level innovation programme that needs an ecosystem and broad commitment at national level? The Innovation Tournament was the chosen facilitation method for a high-level strategy and design workshop. The Finnish Agency of Technology and Innovations invited the Finnish Ministry of Education and Culture, the Finnish National Board of Education, the Confederation of Finnish Industries, FinPro – Future Learning Finland, companies and other important parties from the learning ecosystem. The Innovation Tournament resulted in:

- A versatile and multi-angle programme plan from nothing to the 0.5 version
- Mutual vision
- High-level commitment to the programme

- Enthusiasm and team spirit to continue the work

Tekes Learning Environment Innovation Tournament, spring 2010. Note: the Finnish Technology Agency for Research and Innovation (Tekes) launched the programme on 16.2.2011 under the name Learningsolution 2011–2015.

The Innovation Tournament in management transformation: How do you start the strategic transformation of management in large organizations? The Innovation Tournament was the chosen method. During the 5 h, approximately 150 top managers from the city of Helsinki innovated cross-organizational services and management processes. Innovation Tournament resulted in:

- Cross-organizational teams
- Eight cross-organizational service initiatives
- Rough action plans

Helsinki City Innovation Tournament, winter 2011
For more information: petri.morko@invicor.com, www.invicor.com

The Innovation Tournament examples above may provide you with an understanding of what an agile strategy management tool Innovation Tournament is. The next case example is introduced at a more detailed level for greater understanding.

Case Example: A flying start for an organization merge – Case Business Oulu Innovation Tournament 2010

The case study was executed by Invicor Ltd (www.invicor.com). Invicor Ltd provides **Invicor Innovation Tournament™** services and **Invicor Tournament Management Suite™** software. Both are applications of the multidisciplinary InnoCoop theory.

3.14.1 Challenge

Three different organizations would be merged in the next 7 months. The challenge was highly complex and multidimensional.

- All three organizations had different customer segments, organizational cultures and expectations for a common future.
- The personal uncertainty over their existing positions influenced their attitudes and work motivation.
- The organizations had not worked together.
- A new strategy for a soon-to-be-merged organization was created by the strategy group, but it was not communicated.

Traditional management methods were considered inefficient for this case. The InnoCoop-based Invicor Innovation Tournament was selected to provide a systematic toolset to resolve the knots and find the lurking business potential in this change. Openness, a multidisciplinary management approach and innovate ways of working aimed to promote the forthcoming change as an opportunity.

Picture 3.1 The innovation tournament challenges empower participants

3.14.2   How the Case Was Executed

A case study was conducted to explore the benefits of a collaborative and IT-aided strategy management method in a context of radical change in existing business operations and environments. The rules of ordinary business operations were temporarily suspended and replaced with the rules of the tournament. The tournament created an alternative world, a model world. The following states were carried out:

1. Design of the tournament and agreement on tournament goals. This stage aligns the tournament with the main strategic goals and creates the necessary understanding for the customer organizations on how to use the tournament. The tools used are interviews and web-based questionnaires.
2. Preparation and pre-assignments. This stage includes the service design for the Innovation Tournament: preparation, pre-assignments and main tournament days. The Scrum methodology is used for fast iteration and late decisions to understand the core of the challenge and the required tournament design principles. In this state, **Invicor Radical Generator**® software is used to create innovative and radical design combinations for the tournament.
3. This stage prepares and trains the tournament participants' mindsets (players, judges, coaches and stimulus creators) for the tournament. This is usually done with the help of www.innovillage.net, which offers a suite of tools for the management of Innovation Tournaments.
4. The fourth state includes tournament days during which a set challenge is opened, explored and closed. Some of the teams use Invicor Radical Generator for more radical solutions. Finally, the report and conclusions are created.

Picture 3.2 Mission accomplished – energized and open tournament players bursting with joy!

3.14.3 Lessons Learned – Solutions

Synergy and openness of interest groups and partners accelerated by an innovative and collaborative management method play a major role in successful and efficient business re-engineering. Success is based on the following:

- Versatile and heterogenic tournament participants are needed to create a fast and adaptive business and operational changes.
- Organizations should be encouraged to open the challenge to business partners and customers. To manage this fuzzy, open situation, a stimulating, systematic, energizing and brave management method is needed.
- Strategy management and innovation IT tools can increase the productivity and quality of Innovation Tournaments significantly, and there are still more requirements for the use of the software in the Innovation Tournaments.
- One 'shot' of an Innovation Tournament is not enough. To get the best out of the change, collaborative events should be repeated frequently to keep up the pace.

Perhaps the best lesson learned is the joy and energy of the participants.

The tournament participants rated the tournament 4.5 out of 5.0. Some comments included:

- 'Excellent days'
- 'Nice experience. Recommended.'
- 'Different, interesting way of working. Fun.'
- 'Excellent energy'
- 'Participants were exhilarated and open'

'The Innovation Tournament brought us exactly what we needed in this state of new organization creation. On a scale of 4–10, I give you 10+,' said Juha Ala-mursula, Head of Business Oulu (former Head of base station R&D, Nokia Siemens Networks).

For more information: petri.morko@invicor.com

3.15 Tecnalia, the Art of Innovation Stimulation

Iñaki Etxaniz

Tecnalia Research & Innovation is a Spanish applied research centre with the aim of generating, developing and transferring technology to local industry. It is organized in several divisions containing a total of 13 business units, made up of multi-disciplinary teams oriented to different strategic sectors such as Telecommunications, IT, Energy, Automotive, etc.

3.15.1 Challenge

Given the nature and mission of the research centre, one of its main objectives is to perform high level research. Technology transfer is made through R&D and Innovation projects with companies and consulting services without losing contact with the market demands. It is not always easy to maintain a good trade-off between these two sides, and it can have an important impact on the results of the company.

After an internal assessment, the Telecom Unit noticed that the distribution of its capabilities regarding these two axis was not ideal: essentially, after a period with plenty of work and personnel expansion, the technological expertise was lower than desired (see Fig. 3.20).

3.15.2 How the Case Was Executed

A plan was established, with the goal to increase the technological excellence of the unit in the near future. In addition, also the long-term market excellence needed to be raised. The underlying idea was that the creation of a team of high-level researchers would foster the innovation in the unit through the establishment of close relationship with external organisations like universities and R&D departments of technologically advanced companies. In short, this is a step towards a more open innovation paradigm.

The initial step consisted on recruiting three new researchers that were going to work solely in the generation of innovative ideas for the unit. These could be ideas for solutions to existing problems, ideas for new products or services; or

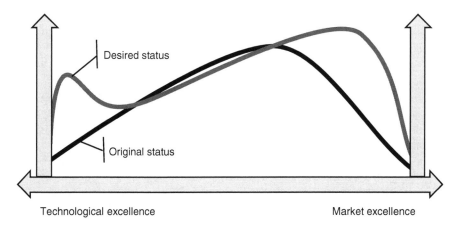

Fig. 3.20   Technological versus market expertise

improvements in state-of-art algorithms and technologies. These new researchers formed a dedicated group for innovation.

The skills of the new researchers were distinctly different from those of typical employees. They were doctors, and more theoretical and mathematical oriented than the rest (which were mainly telecommunications engineers).

Because of that, some training in telecommunications was necessary at the beginning, which also reinforced the cross-functional orientation of the unit. These employees dedicated 100% of their time to find new promising research fields to investigate. They didn't participate in other projects related with existing products.

These people were intrinsically motivated for the kind of work they were hired to perform. But also some external motivation was considered. The reward system included attending important conferences, visits to universities abroad, part-time teaching at university, or participating in international scientific forums. But the most important motivation came from the creative work, and the feeling that they were useful for their colleges solving his problems.

3.15.3   Lessons Learned – Solutions

Some lessons can be pointed out after almost 3 years since the start. The main conclusion is that to obtain good results in a global market, serious and simultaneous betting in several fronts is needed. In this case the bet was relatively modest despite the changes it introduced in the internal organization, and the obtained results are positive and in accordance: papers have been published in prestigious journals, several patents have been granted, and some agreements signed with university departments.

The investment in expert staff and reserving about 10% of the total work capacity of the unit to innovation is a necessary condition to increase the innovativeness, but it may not be sufficient. Among the positive things, we can remark that changes in the organization were well accepted by the staff, and that the cooperation between the different teams was productive.. However, the feeling about the success is cautious: "it is work in progress, we can do it better".

There are some ideas for improvement. An attractive career plan has to be defined in order to maintain the enthusiasm and motivation for innovation. Also, a deeper and more precise evaluation of the achievements is seen desirable by both the management and the staff. This evaluation has to be based not only on the most direct results like patents, publications, and contacts, but also on other measurable results like agreements signed with universities or companies, and the number of assets and products achieved as a result of the proposed innovations.

Also, everyday working practices need some revision. Informal interaction among colleagues was usual. However, the "innovation group"experienced some lack of formal and regular contact with the rest of the unit, in which they could be informed about technical problems other teams face or new challenges to consider.

Another aspect, related with finding and selecting research fields, is that the researchers would like to have closer contacts with customers. Not only to gather information about their requirements for new products, but also to collaborate in problem solving. This is the part of the market excellence that needs to be improved. The question to formulate here is: does it worth to achieve an innovation if no client is interested in it?

In research, sometimes you have to abandon some line of work after a while, because no clear results have risen. This leads to frustration, but it is something that researchers can *accept*. It is worse when an innovation is achieved, but company management decides not to continue with it due to possible commercial conflicts with existing clients. This kind of a thing should have been detected earlier.

To finish, the innovation teams have the time, but they would also appreciate a bigger budget that allows them buying needed material, extra equipment or hire more staff to work in innovations projects.

3.16   AuraPortal, Incubating a BPMS Company

Jose Antonio Heredia

In 1981, Dr. Juan J. Trilles founded a European company called Dimoni Software devoted to the development of ERP and MRP applications for the enterprise. Some aspects of the applications were highly innovative and, due to its outstanding achievements, the company became one of the most successful and respected in the Spanish market, with an installed base of more than 6,000 customers.

In 2001, the company was acquired by a Dutch corporation. As a result, several executives decided to leave and suggested that Dr. Trilles create a new company devoted to the development of enterprise software related to Workflow, Process Management and Enterprise Content.

3.16.1   Challenge: Incubating a New Venture

AuraPortal, with €21 million in shareholders' equity, was founded in 2001 with one aim: to develop a 100% web-based business software application of a type called Business Process Management Suite (BMPS), with the name AuraPortal, at the highest technological level, including the latest standards such as the BPMN modelling notation.

The main goal was to invent a radically new concept of process design to weld the modelling and execution of processes into a single stage performed by business persons on their own without programming or intervention by IT persons.

Instead of programming processes, the IT persons could then concentrate on more technical matters such as hardware, operating systems, application integration, etc.

This original approach meant significant time savings for process design and modifications, and, above all, the vaporization of traditional communication problems between business persons and IT persons.

In short, the new concept implied that just drawing the process model with a drawing tool like Visio would be enough, once the parameters of the objects in the model were defined, to put the process into execution immediately. This goal was certainly audacious, but AuraPortal did find a way to achieve it.

The project also included:

1. The development of a Structural Platform providing a basis for enterprise operations
2. A new concept of a Business Rules System that was easier and more powerful
3. The definition of Process Patterns performing CRM operations based on BPMS, addressing the new paradigm of CRM as a set of processes modelled with BPMS

3.16.2   How the New Venture Was Incubated

In 2001, after a short period devoted to the selection of new personnel, the company concentrated on incubating the software to carry out the ideas contained in the project.

For 3 years, the personnel at AuraPortal worked intensively to come up with a new product for the market.

In April 2004, AuraPortal was presented to the public at an event with a beautiful piano concert attended by more than 500 people.

Since the date of its launch, AuraPortal has enjoyed steadily growing international success driven by satisfied customers that usually praise the names of the company and product.

In 2007, after only 3 years on the market, the analyst firm Gartner Inc. selected AuraPortal as one of the 22 best BPMSs in the world from hundreds of candidates, defining the product as an 'Example of next-generation BPMS', as stated in its Magic Quadrant graphics and report.

In 2009, AuraPortal was present in 40 countries, and more than 300 customers were working with its BPMS solution.

In 2010, AuraPortal was established as a bicephalous company with its headquarters split between the USA (Boston) and Europe (Holland) while its software development facilities are mainly concentrated in Spain and India.

Today, the name AuraPortal is widely recognized as being synonymous with confidence and modernity.

The company tries to foster a stimulating climate that motivates the generation of new idea streams to include in the product and services. The source of ideas not only proceeds from internal inspiration but also from suggestions and new requirements from customers and partners.

Ideation channels (formal, informal and IT supported) are in place for circulating, evaluating and filtering the idea stream towards the Analysis Committee, which established the product development plan. The Analysis Committee steers the innovation process with strong leadership from the Chief Executive. The leadership clearly establishes the focus and targets for the company, with closely market-oriented criteria.

Once the ideas have been approved, a process of continuous experimentation with feedback from the users is carried out. Information generated during the execution of the idea is supported by its own BPM platform. The analysis and development teams are highly flexible and dynamic and do not depend of critical individuals who could act as bottlenecks.

3.16.3 Lesson Learned

During the new venture incubation, AuraPortal has learned that innovation should be a continuous endeavour. For this reason, AuraPortal is opening the innovation process by participating in collaborative R&D projects with partners, customers and research institutions, although it keeps the core of the company's knowledge assets closed. Participation in this kind of project is seen as strategic to the enterprise. It also contributes to the company's innovative image.

The company has set up a project web portal in which potential users and distributors can be involved in the different research and innovation projects, as the initial idea through proposal development, financing search, initial prototypes and training until the final product is released to the market.

AuraPortal is now experimenting with open innovation with pilots in two applications domains. One is aimed at developing an Energy Management Information System, in collaboration with its partners and customers. The other is an application to manage the innovation projects itself using internal social networks.

These experiments are being developed in collaboration with a university and 20 partners worldwide. Each one has prepared a virtual workspace on the portal to experiment with user cases using the Living Lab technique.

In parallel with these strategic innovation projects, the company has assumed the need to provide an increased value proposition for its end-users with more customized solutions. The business model design consists of providing the platform and supporting the technological partners to develop customized solutions.

3.17   Sisteplant, Experiment of the Mobile Devices

Iñaki Etxaniz

When mobile devices started to become widespread, Sisteplant saw the opportunity to improve its products with the introduction of such tools. Sisteplant is a software-intensive company that provides solutions for manufacturing and maintenance process optimization. One of its flagship products is its maintenance management software (CMMS), mainly sold in the Spanish and South American markets.

3.17.1   Challenge

The maintenance tasks were typically carried out by mobile workers who received their task orders from a central management office. The task list was set at the beginning of the day and delivered to each worker. In the best case, these tasks would affect the same building, but the most likely case was that the workers had to travel between several places or even from one city to another.

The introduction of a mobile device in the workers' equipment would give immediate advantages to the user: more flexibility, control of the workers and their tasks, improved response to unexpected maintenance issues, etc. The cost of developing such a solution could be high, however, and some questions remained to be answered, such as the operational costs, the real benefits to the user company, the reaction of mobile workers to the new gadget that they would have to learn to use, etc.

3.17.2   How the Case Was Executed

Tecnalia-Information and Interaction Systems were called on to support Sisteplant in the definition and implementation of a pilot project in order to test the use of the mobile devices with its maintenance software product. The technical solution was defined by the research centre based on state-of-the-art mobile device technology, data communication protocols, mobile operating systems and geographic information systems. The expertise of the maintenance business was provided by the company with a detailed specification of its processes and the data related to the task orders.

Different devices where tested to find the most suitable one in terms of features, usability and cost. A software solution was implemented, consisting of one central operation point in charge of scheduling the task orders, their distribution and control and five devices that received the orders and let the worker fulfil them in the field. The system was tested at no cost for 3 months by a client company that provided its feedback on the experience.

3.17.3   Lessons Learned – Solutions

The overall impression of the client was very satisfactory. Despite the fact that it had to learn to use a new system, the benefits were noteworthy, namely:

- A better plan for preventive maintenance
- Faster feedback on tasks carried out in the field
- Control of the time spent by workers on each task
- Location of workers known in real time
- Better reaction to unforeseen maintenance problems
- Less paper needed to carry out task information, for technical manuals and to fulfil the results

Not all the feedback was positive however. It also reported issues that need to be re-evaluated or solved. For example, mobile workers were afraid of using the device because of the control of their working day it provided to the company; the GPS system did not work as well as expected in some urban areas and even worse inside the buildings; the user interface was not very friendly due to the small screen of the device.

All in all, the trial results were very positive as they confirmed the added value that such a mobile solution could provide for the maintenance product. At the same time, some drawbacks of the experimental system were detected that have to be addressed if a future system is to become commercialized. Finally, the feedback provided the users' real feelings about the innovation with their pros and cons.

The experience of the pilot case, performed with real users, was crucial to the company in its strategic reflections. It demonstrated the usefulness of the approach and paved the way for later inclusion of the features into one of its key products. This enhanced the product and gave it a competitive advantage, provided extra value to clients and new features that led to better planning, more control of mobile workers in the field, faster reaction to clients' problems and real-time feedback on the work status.

3.18   Metallurgy, Example of Experimentation

Iñaki Etxaniz

Tubos Reunidos (TR) is an industrial group working in the metallurgy industry. In the area of seamless pipe construction, the group is the main manufacturer in the Spanish market and one of the leading companies in the world. The group works for clients in sectors such as drill activities, and petrochemical, automotive, energy and construction industries. The manufacturing process normally involves hot finish milling or cold drawing.

3.18.1   Challenge

The hot rolling process of seamless steel tubes sporadically produces different marks and surface defects that are difficult to detect in hot conditions. These defects were only detected after a number of value-added fabrication steps had been completed, and several tons of material were involved.

In its quality improvement programmes, TR noted the importance of detecting these defects as soon as possible and to include this point in the quality control system. To help it with this issue, it contacted *Tecnalia Research & Innovation*, with whose machine vision group it had a long collaboration history.

As said, the idea was to detect defects as soon as they were produced, but the working environment conditions were extremely hard in the inspection zone: high temperatures, humidity and the presence of oil vapour and dirt. To make it worse, the project team had no samples of the usual defects in order to detect them with software algorithms.

3.18.2   How the Case Was Executed

The Tecnalia research group designed a new innovative inspection method for quality control in close collaboration with the manufacturer. The new equipment was installed at the exit of the push bench, just where the defects originated. It consisted of a frame with the necessary equipment placed just after the zone of the hot rolling stands. As the implementation of a complete solution would require considerable effort due to the required equipment, security aspects and necessary workforce, the company decided to test the viability and reliability of the proposed solution with a small-scale, low-cost system. A platform comprising a frame with a single matrix camera, a white light and optical filters, all inside a protective enclosure, was installed for 3 months at the company's factory.

3.18.3   Lessons Learned – Solutions

Thanks to this experimental system, the first samples of surface defects on the pipes were obtained: material detached/pasted, holes in the tube, roll marks ... During the test, a number of risks and areas of improvement for the final system were also detected, namely, illumination was improved using redundant laser lights to achieve a monochromatic light; high-speed linear cameras were introduced in the final system for better resolution; three cameras instead of one covered the complete pipe surface; a refrigeration system was implemented to keep the system cold; an external cleaning system was also designed; and an optical fibre Ethernet system was installed to transfer the captured data 100 m away up to the processing unit in a safe place.

In the end, a new and innovative inspection method was designed, installed and tested for the main area of activity of the company. The quality system was improved, automatically detecting defects that were hardly detected before. And, last but not least, this control was made earlier in the manufacturing process, making it possible to discard the faulty pipes immediately. This saved time and money because, prior to the project, up to 20 t of material could be post-processed before the defects were detected.

Harnessing the fact that an image database was used, defect traceability was implemented. An on-line remote inspection stand was also implemented. The defects information is now integrated into the company's productions information system.

3.19   NSN, the Art of Transforming Ideas into Market Solutions

Jarkko Hyysalo

3.19.1   A Challenge in Innovation Treatment

Different types of innovations require different practices and processes to be realized, and choosing the right approach is crucial to success. In routine situations, decision-making is straightforward and either skill- or rule-based. Innovation projects are characterized by uncertainty however. The more radical the innovation, the more uncertainty is involved, and effort dedicated to controlling the unexpected is required. When managing the innovation uncertainties, three key aspects need to be covered: financial, market and technical data. The provision of proper data and a structure for decision-making is the main challenge to be solved.

3.19.2   How the Case Was Executed

A series of case studies was conducted to explore how the challenges should be tackled. The cases started with the identification of the industrial needs and continued over several months until a suitable solution was found. The solution is a tool developed in the ITEI project for managing the innovation lifecycle workflow and controlling the decision criteria of each decision point and milestone. The interface provides access to several tools and methods for analysing different aspects of innovation and implementation at six conceptual levels from each relevant stakeholder's point of view.

In the beginning, the idea was tested with small groups of users to see how the idea was accepted. The development was started with full-on effort, with positive results. Various stakeholders of the innovation process participated in testing the prototype of the tool. Iterative and incremental development was run intensively in a plan-do-check-act manner until the prototype was sufficiently mature to be taken into limited use in the organization. Positive reactions support the full deployment of the tool.

3.19.3   Lessons Learned – Solutions

The main benefit of using the tool is the ability to align financial, market and technical data related to innovation and other ideas and needs for decision-making purposes. Secondarily, innovation/feature communities can be identified via inter-related tasks, providing a list of relevant stakeholders and of tasks that need to be done. It also helps to deliver the data and work objects from one stakeholder to another, thus creating a workflow for the implementation of innovations on innovation incubation and other ideas.

3.20   Keraben, the Human Driven Dynamic Workflow Experiment

Jose Antonio Heredia, Antonio Estruch, Luis Guaita, and Miguel Angel Bengochea

Keraben Group is a Spanish industrial company devoted to designing, manufacturing and commercializing ceramic products and complementary products such as special ceramic pieces, whirlpool systems, bathroom furniture, etc. Innovation is one of the pillars on which the competitive strategy of Keraben rests. Keraben is therefore making a special effort to develop its own technology, apply new technologies to productive processes and participate in research projects that take it to a higher level of innovation and differentiates it from its competitors.

Some of Keraben's projects have been launched as a result of 'in-company ventures' or 'spin-outs'. In this context, 'Spin-out' is understood as a 'virtual' small company within a large company, which differs from a 'spin-off' in that it remains closely tied to the parent company and, in most cases, shares administrative and sometimes operational services. The Spin-out enjoys the benefits of the company's greater resources and brand recognition, granting the management

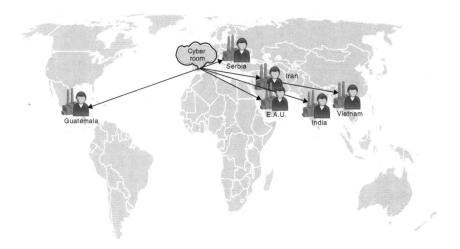

Fig. 3.21 Global environment of Keraben

team more autonomy to operate as an independent company. All the support from the parent company is provided with the explicit purpose of helping the spin-out grow. Keraben Ceramics Engineering (KCE), within the management of the Keraben international productive collaboration projects, is a fine example of a successful Keraben spin-out (Fig. 3.21).

The business model is based on establishing a joint venture between Keraben and the local partner to manufacture high-level ceramic tiles with Spanish designs to be promoted and distributed within the partner's local and neighbouring markets.

3.20.1 Challenge

Keraben needs a software solution that helps the organization achieve the main goal of setting up manufacturing-commercial cooperation relationships with partners established in the country of destination, whose manufacturing and technological capacities are suitable for making Keraben's products with the knowledge of Keraben technicians. Pulling people together who are scattered across the globe and making them work together as a cohesive unit may pose several managerial and technical problems.

To support this process of company internationalization, a solution is needed in which it is possible to track all the activities performed by people involved in each of the internationalization projects and also manage shared content, such as typical office documents and all product manufacturing-related documentation and product designs with image files, which can be very large in size. The aim of this information collection is to create a knowledge base to improve similar internationalization projects in the future.

Bearing in mind that the people participating in this process are distributed geographically around the world and may belong to Keraben itself, or other organizations with several new partners, they must all be capable of interacting with the software solution with adequate security and confidentiality through the Internet. The core group of activities performed to manage this context can be shared between multiple internationalization projects. In general, each case requires customization and inclusion of new activities, or removal of those activities that will not be used. The decisions that must be taken during the execution of these projects are initially not completely determinate either and may vary over time.

3.20.2 How the Case Was Executed?

A series of experiments was carried out for Keraben. During the experiments, different software solutions were proposed for use in order to find one that fit as closely as possible to the previously introduced requirements. Initially, a Microsoft SharePoint-based solution was proposed for use as a content management system that could be accessed through the Internet, offering a basic level of site configuration and customization. To provide the required security, a Virtual Protected Network (VPN) connection was also provided.

3.20.2.1 Challenges of the Current System

Although the content management support offered by SharePoint was considered sufficient, when the workflow functionality was incorporated to manage the activities of each of the projects, the global solution performance became unsatisfactory. Workflow engines implemented by traditional BPM vendors, including the engine implemented in SharePoint, had to be used to offer management of well-defined, simple and structured workflows.

A high level of variability was found in the execution of the process, and the complexity of the decisions to be taken during its execution therefore forced **SharePoint** to be **discarded** as a viable solution.

Dynamic processes require modifications to be performed, not only to the process workflow model but also to its executing instances, without the need to stop and start again. The required level of flexibility and the nature of the activities to be performed make modern BPM-based systems good candidate solutions for developing process models and running them into a web-oriented BPM platform that offers a collaborative environment using the latest Web 2.0 technologies. The system selected was AuraPortal BPM.

3.20.2.2 The AuraPortal System as an Opportunity

AuraPortal is a Business Process Management platform that incorporates, in a seamless, integrated and friendly way, functionalities of Client Relations

Management, Supply Chain Management, and Content Management Systems, into one environment, all on Intranet and Extranet web portals. Its holistic conception covers not only process modelling, execution and monitoring of typical BPM tools but also a powerful communication and collaboration platform for employees and external agents (clients, suppliers, etc.), and a versatile document management system.

The Keraben case describes experiences to explore the viability of using a modern BPM system like AuraPortal to support a dynamic process like the internationalization project management process in which internal and external users execute activities that are not completely predefined and in which an entire process definition could present high variability over time.

Another opportunity to experiment arose when it was decided to offer a more socially oriented front-end to the AuraPortal interface with process workflow execution forms and tracking. IT Prosper was developing a front-end with these characteristics and was incorporated into the final solution, offering users a more attractive interface to interact with the AuraPortal functionalities and introducing concepts relative to a social network-way of working to improve interaction experience with other project participants.

Initially, the main activity to be performed was to define the requirements and let the team responsible for implementing the software solution understand the complexity of the problem and the high variability of activities and scope required by each previously documented case. Once the basic requirements were established, including the user roles of the participants, the type of information to be managed with its storage needs and a generic process model definition were determined. All of this was agreed with Keraben as a very early solution template. More evolutions of this requirements definition were proposed and discussed to try to match the basic requirements as closely as possible.

3.20.2.3 Aim of the Experiment

This experiment was carried out to introduce a modern BPM-based system to Keraben. It involved AuraPortal as the BPM solution software provider, IT Prosper as the socially oriented AuraPortal front-end software provider, University Jaume I as the team providing support for the solutions deployment and customization, and Keraben Industry Partner as the end-user checking the functionality of the solutions.

In this context, AuraPortal offered test licences for its BPM system and technical support to Jaume I University, which developed the experimental process model using the requirements established during the interviews with all the Keraben employees involved in the Internationalization project management. IT Prosper also offered its front-end solution for testing purposes.

3.20.2.4   Tasks Performed Before and During the Experiment

The experiment at Keraben was conducted in two major steps: developing a prototype and executing the experiment. The tasks performed during the experiment were:

– Preparing a hardware infrastructure to host the software solution
– Configuring the required connectivity, including internal network access and enabling secure public access through the Internet using a VPN solution
– Installing software packages (SharePoint, AuraPortal and/or IT Prosper)
– Configuring the underlying content management system (SharePoint)
– Deploying the process model on the BPM engine
– Customizing forms and web pages for use in the process execution instances
– Involving real end-users in using the software solution using real data
– Collecting and analysing all the user comments and performance indicators to detect if any functionalities needed to be enhanced

At the end of each task, a meeting was held involving the process persons: managers and engineers. In these meetings, the process persons had the opportunity to express their comments and feelings and, of course, determine the degree of success of the software solution.

The main phases of the experiment are discussed further below.

3.20.2.5   Prototype Development

Initially, SharePoint was the software solution on which the efforts focused. SharePoint's web sites were designed and configured, including document libraries and customized lists.

In order to implement the software solution, the team had the option to develop a process model as a reference model that had to be modified to be customized for each internationalization project, including new activities or modifying its execution flow. Following this approach would have required extra work, however, not only in the initial customization but also in making further modifications to the process model to fit the new activity requirements that could appear during process execution. It would have implied more support from BPM-specialized personnel and increased the overall solution cost. This was what happened when the deployment of the process into the SharePoint Web sites was initiated.

When SharePoint was discarded and the efforts were focused on the AuraPortal solution, the process model was redefined. To minimize the previously exposed problem of minimizing changes, the solution that was finally adopted consisted of a unique process model to manage internationalization projects. This process included the most important activities to be performed and introduced the project manager role to drive the execution of the process. The project manager decided which activities should be performed in each project at any time and who was responsible for each one. In this way, the modification to the initially defined flow does not require modification to the process itself. In this case, it is only necessary to make changes when new activities are added or existing activities are modified.

The new AuraPortal approach provides the required flexibility to manage almost all the different internationalization projects, offering the project manager the possibility of adapting the project management to unexpected changing conditions already during the its execution.

Finally, the IT Prosper front-end was incorporated into the solution to provide a rich user experience and improve the way participants share ideas, discussions, etc., incorporating usual social networks functionalities.

3.20.2.6   Experiment Execution

The experiments were executed following the activities previously presented for each prototype that was developed.

In this phase, early prototypes were developed, helping Keraben to determine if the true scope and objectives were achieved. Partial prototypes were developed in an iterative manner, increasing the scope of the identified activities and the potential users. This way, the required information model and all the people who could be involved in the experiment were identified.

When the model was good enough to be deployed in the AuraPortal BPM system, trials were planned to try to use some real data to simulate real work loads, and detect failures and some functional aspects that would need improvement.

3.20.3   Lessons Learned

From a purely technical point of view, SharePoint was not an adequate solution on its own for Keraben without big investment in software development. The demonstration proved that the AuraPortal BPM engine is capable of handling this kind dynamic process however.

From an organization point of view, Keraben learned the benefits of using modern BPM solutions to improve the management of dynamic projects, without all its activities predefined. It also realized that the AuraPortal system would bring them better documentation management and some improvements in distributed collaboration and overall information availability.

As a BPM software provider, AuraPortal learned that its engine is capable of handling this kind of dynamic process and of collecting new ideas to improve its product. The inclusion of the IT Prosper front-end improved the adoption of the AuraPortal tool, offering a richer user experience.

The University team members improved their skills and discipline to develop complex processes with a modern BPM system applied to real cases.

In general, CMS and BPM systems are platform products. They must be customized and personalized to fit the needs and preferences of the end-user, generally deploying web portals and process models to solve real end-user problems.

Knowledge of the problem to be solved and the level of accuracy to collect the requirements were critical to providing customization that really met the organization's needs.

In this case, the personalization in the first phase included the development of web sites and content libraries on SharePoint. Later, when AuraPortal was used and a process model deployed to help manage internationalization projects, it was necessary to design forms and reports into the tool, which also required customization. The final solution for the ceramic sector could be also personalized for use by other organizations in the same sector.

The continuous work by everyone involved in this case and, especially the active participation by Keraben staff during the design, development and deployment of the software solutions, was a critical success factor.

It is also important that all external users have access to the system during experimentation. For example, it cannot be assumed that Internet bandwidth is available in all world locations. In Iran, for example, it is not as good as would be desirable and to share large documents through the CMS is not viable in some places.

Although not all the requirements were addressed and the prototypes developed in the experiment partially covered all the possible functionality, it was possible to define the potential benefits of using the AuraPortal tool for Keraben.

3.21   Sisteplant, Making the Most of Critical People in the Company

Iñaki Etxaniz

In software engineering it is a known fact that the difference in the ratio of impact on innovation between the best and the average employee can be as high as a factor of 10. If a software company wants to boost the creativity and innovation of its product line, it therefore becomes crucial that it is able to attract and retain these critical resources.

3.21.1   Challenge

Sisteplant is a software-intensive company based in Spain that provides solutions for manufacturing and maintenance process optimization. As software development is one of its principal activities, the company is seriously concerned with the quality and expertise of its technical staff.

Skilled human resources are difficult to find nowadays, and if you are lucky enough to have such people in your organization, it is also difficult to retain them. This case study shows an example of how one software company dealt with this challenge.

3.21.2   How the Case Was Executed

Sisteplant wanted to improve its development capacity, so it hired a new employee with experience and good development skills. This employee was initially assigned to pure development tasks, but he had also shown an interest in new methodologies.

As a result, he attended courses and became certified as a Microsoft Certified Professional (MCP). Soon after, he also attained certification as a Scrum Certified Manager (SCM). In both cases, the tuition fees were covered by the company as part of the internal policy to promote studies and certification of its employees in core technologies used in product development. The underlying idea of the policy was to support employees' interests while maintaining a good internal climate.

Later, the employee suggested a change to the software development process. By then, the company considered him a very valuable resource, relying on him for the introduction of several innovations in the company. The first change was to move from artisan-like development to an agile methodology: Scrum. To support this, modern project management tools were also introduced into the software production, such as Microsoft Team Foundation Server.

3.21.3   Lessons Learned – Solutions

Due to the company's policy of fostering staff proficiency and development – to each person's potential – the role of this employee changed from just being a developer to becoming the main driving force of an organizational change inside the company that improved its productivity.

Not surprisingly, when he decided to start up his own software company, Sisteplant negotiated with him and, taking into account his recent, important contribution, decided to keep him on as a part-time employee while he worked in his new company. The added value provided by such an expert proved more important than the possible drawbacks that a part-time job in such a personal situation would produce (less time available, greater involvement in his own company, etc.).

This case is an example of how a software company managed its most valued resources in order to magnify their contribution. The principal lesson to be learned is that a company has to care about its critical resources, give them an environment in which they can feel comfortable and develop their skills to grow professionally in order to contribute their full potential to the innovation at the company.

References

Abrahamsson P et al (2002) Agile software development methods: review and analysis. Espoo, VTT Electronics 408:107

Agile Manifesto. http://agilemanifesto.org/. Accessed Mar 2011

Allee V (2003) The future of knowledge: increasing prosperity through value networks. Butterworth-Heinemann, New York

Amabile TM (1996) Creativity in context. Westview Press, Boulder

Answare. www.answare-tech.com. Accessed Mar 2011

Caillois R (2001) Man, play and games. University of Illinois Press, Urbana/Chicago (1st French edition, 1958)

Chesbrough HW (2003) Open innovation: the new imperative for creating and profiting from technology. Harvard Business School Press, Boston

Chesbrough HW (2006) Open business models. How to thrive in the new innovation landscape. Harvard Business School Press, Boston

Chesbrough HW, Vanhaverbeke W, West J (2006) Open innovation: researching a new paradigm. Oxford University Press, Oxford

Cleland-Huang J, Settimi R, BenKhadra O, Berezhan E, Christina S (2005) Goal centric traceability for managing non-functional requirements. In: International conference on software engineering, St Louis, pp 362–371

Csikszentmihalyi M (1990) Flow: the problem of optimal experience. Harper Collins, New York

Csikszentmihalyi M (1996) Creativity: flow and the discovery of invention. Harper Collins, New York

Deming WE (1986) Out of the crisis: quality, productivity, and competitive position. Cambridge University Press, Cambridge

Gotel O, Finkelstein, AW (1994) An analysis of the requirements traceability problem. In: Proceedings of the international conference requirements engineering, IEEE Computer Society Press, Colorado Springs, pp 94–102

Henttonen K (2011) Open source as an innovation enabler: case study of an Indian SME. Dissertation, University of Manchester

Ideathlon. http://www.sinnobok.org/innovation-solutions/ideathlon. Accessed Mar 2011

iGoogle. http://www.google.com/ig. Accessed Mar 2011

Innovation Competition in Wikipedia. http://en.wikipedia.org/wiki/Innovation_competition. Accessed Mar 2011

Järvilehto M, Similä J, Liukkunen K, Kangas T (2010) Active innovation – case study in smart exercise environments: comparing traditional and experimental innovation methods. In: Proceedings of the 2nd ISPIM innovation symposium – stimulating recovery – the role of innovation management, New York City, 6–9 Dec 2009 (Nominee for the best student paper award)

Juran JM, Godfrey AB (1998) Juran's quality handbook, 5th edn. McGraw-Hill, New York (1st edition, 1951)

Khabbazi MR, Ismail N, Ismail MY (2009) Data modeling of traceability information for manufacturing control system. In: Proceedings of the international conference on information management and engineering, Kuala Lumpur, pp 633–637

Koskela K, Näkki P, Pikkarainen M (2009) Towards a framework for lead user driven innovation in software intensive companies. In: Proceedings of the XX ISPIM conference, Vienna, 21–24 June 2009. Wiley

Larman C, Basili VR (2003a) Iterative and incremental development: a brief history. IEEE Comput 36(6):47–56

Larman C, Basili VR (2003b) Iterative and incremental development: a brief history. Computer 36:47–56

Lilien GL, Morrison PD, Searls K, Sonnack M, von Hippel E (2002) Performance assessment of the lead user idea-generation process for the new product development. Manage Sci 48(8):1042–1059

OSQA. http://www.osqa.net/. Accessed Mar 2011

Pikkarainen M, Koivumäki T, Codenie W, Boucart N, Biot, O, Kuvaja, P, Heredia, J (2010a) Impacts of product development strategy on innovation activities in software intensive corporations. In: Proceedings of ISPIM conference 2010, Wiley, Bilbao

Pikkarainen M, Korkala M, Kääriäinen J, Välimäki A (2010b) Practices for efficient customer collaboration for innovation in pulp systems. In: 3rd ISPIM innovation symposium – managing the art of innovation: turning concepts into reality, Quebec City, 12–15 Dec 2010. Wiley

Piller F, Ihl C (2009) Open innovation with customers – foundations, competences and international trends. RWTH ZLW-IMA 2009, Aachen (Published as part of the project 'International Monitoring')

Piller FT, Walcher D (2006) Toolkits for idea competitions: a novel method to integrate users in new product development. R&D Manage 36(3):307–318

Sawyer K (2008) Group genius: the creative power of collaboration. Basic Books, New York

Seyff N, Graf F, Maiden N, Grünbacher P (2009) Scenarios in the wild: experiences with a contextual requirements discovery method. In: Glinz M, Heymans P (eds) Requirements engineering: foundation for software quality. Lecture notes in computer science, vol 5512. Springer, Berlin/Heidelberg, pp 147–161, doi = http://dx.doi.org/10.1007/978-3-642-02050-6_13

Skarzynski P, Gibson R (2008) Innovation to the core. Harvard Business School Press, Boston

Terwiesch C, Ulrich KT (2009) Innovation tournaments – creating and selecting exceptional opportunities. Harvard Business Press, Boston

Välimäki A, Kääriäinen J (2007) Product managers' requirement management practices as patterns in distributed development. In: 8th international PROFES (product focused software development and process improvement) conference, Riga, Latvia, 2–4 July 2007, http://www.liis.lv/profes2007/www.lu.lv. Accessed Mar 2011

von Hippel E (1986) Lead users: a source of novel product concepts. Manag Sci 32(8):691–705

von Hippel E (2005) Democratizing innovation. The MIT Press, Cambridge

Whyte WF (1991) Participatory action research. Sage, Newbury Park

Williams L, Cockburn A (2003) Agile software development it is about feedback and change. Computer 36(6):39–42

Yin RK (2009) Case study research, design and methods, vol 5, 4th edn, Applied social research methods series. Sage, Thousand Oaks

Chapter 4
Conclusions

Minna Pikkarainen, Wim Codenie, and Nick Boucart

As the authors of this book, we hope you have enjoyed this journey and found it useful to you and your company.

In the past decades, we have witnessed major advances in the field of software engineering. Agile development has become a commodity, and many software companies have successfully deployed agile methods (e.g., Scrum) and lean approaches to make their software development more continuous, faster and more efficient.

In the current market environment, however, being good at delivering software on time and within budget is no longer enough to be competitive. Being more agile is not a guarantee of growth.

Software companies are shifting their focus. Instead of being engineering-driven organizations, they are trying to become more innovation-driven. This is new to many software companies and can affect them in different ways, even up to the business model.

During the 3 years we worked on this book, we realized that innovation has different faces, depending on the type of software company and the strategy used. Project-based companies, for example, focus on process innovations, whereas for out-of-the-box product companies, product innovations seem more important.

The goal of this book is to demystify software innovation. We are proud of the outcome: 8 practice areas and 47 activities that software companies can adopt to master the art of software innovation in their contexts.

We hope we have inspired you with these practice areas and that the software innovation canvas has somehow triggered you to think about innovation in your software company: *Do we perform these activities today? Should we perform them at all? How could we perform them in the future to create new opportunities?*

Besides the theory, this book also includes 21 industrial case studies that address different aspects of innovation with software. The Steria case, for example, illustrated how a large software project company defined its innovation targets. The Mobideas case introduced novel innovative ways to include lead users in idea harvesting and valuation. The Answare case introduced a practical framework to

M. Pikkarainen et al. (eds.), *The Art of Software Innovation*,
DOI 10.1007/978-3-642-21049-5_4, © Springer-Verlag Berlin Heidelberg 2011

harvest ideas using brainstorming techniques. InnoCoop stimulated and improved innovation with innovation tournaments.

This book does not lead to an end point. There is still a long road ahead and many things remain to be learned with respect to innovation with software.

We have therefore launched an online community (sinnobok.org) that contains articles, solutions, techniques and a forum in which to share your experiences of innovation with software. The purpose of the sinnobok.org community is threefold: first, to support software companies to share their experiences of innovation with software; second, to help researchers find industrially related research topics; and third, to connect with companies in this area.

We invite you to participate and join the SinnoBok.org community and to share your ideas, experiences, challenges and solutions concerning software innovation.

See you on sinnobok.org

Index

M. Pikkarainen et al. (eds.), *The Art of Software Innovation*,
DOI 10.1007/978-3-642-21049-5, © Springer-Verlag Berlin Heidelberg 2011